W9-CTG-549

By Degrees

The First 90 Years

of the Canadian
Federation of University
Women Edmonton

Edmonton

Copyright © 2002 Canadian Federation of University Women
Edmonton (CFUW Edmonton)

By Degrees

Includes bibliographical references.
ISBN No. 0–9689871–0–9

1. Canadian Federation of University Women. Edmonton--History. 2.
Women college graduates--Alberta--Edmonton--Societies, etc. I. Mellon,
Win. II. Canadian Federation of University Women. Edmonton.
HQ1910.E3B92 2002   367'.97123'34   C2002-910705-9

All rights reserved. No part of this book may be transmitted or reproduced in any form or by any means, electronic or mechanical, including photocopying, recording or by any information storage and
retrieval system, without the permission in writing from the publisher,
except by a reviewer or academic who may quote brief passages in a
review or critical study.

Editor: Heather Marshall
Cover design: Jackie Boyko
Interior design: Michael Slager
Printed and bound in Canada by Priority Printing Ltd.

The publishers gratefully acknowledge assistance
provided by the Canadian Millennium Partnership
Program, The Alberta Historical Resources Foundation and
members of CFUW Edmonton.

By Degrees

The First 90 Years of the Canadian Federation of University
Women Edmonton

Table of Contents

Acknowledgements

The authors, members of the CFUW Edmonton History Group, are indebted to many people whose work preceded ours. When we began our work, *As It Happened–The First 60 Years* provided a starting point. That book, compiled and edited by Marjorie Buckley, was put together by members to celebrate the Club's 60th anniversary in 1969. In 1985, Joan Wensel conducted interviews and did other research on the 1960s. In 1966, sociologist Frances Puffer's M.A. thesis was about our Club and its members. To all these women, and to those executive members who wrote and maintained minutes and other records, and to the archivists who made sure they were preserved, we are grateful.

We acknowledge the contributions of the many Club members who provided us with files, photos, and documents. We owe a special debt to those members who participated in the oral history project and willingly shared their memories of the Club's activities. Several present or former members provided invaluable information and insights. Among them are Rita Calhoun, Sheila Campbell, and Jean Monckton. Would that we could name all those whose collective contributions have gone into the making of the Club history, but it is obviously not possible.

We appreciate the cooperation of the Provincial Archives of Alberta, the University of Alberta Archives, the City of Edmonton Archives, the Alberta Teachers' Association, the Edmonton Art Gallery, and the Edmonton Public Schools Archives and Museum. Non-member Rhona Bilsland was of great help with the initial research in the University of Alberta Archives. We thank Priority Printing who did the design for this book. We are especially indebted to Heather Marshall of ParseNip Press, who so patiently and skillfully guided us on our way.

Finally, the authors gratefully acknowledge the financial support and encouragement of the Canadian Federation of University Women Edmonton, its members and friends. We also thank the Government of Canada's Millennium Partnership Program and the Alberta Historical Resources Foundation.

CFUW Edmonton History Group

Preface

This book is about the Canadian Federation of University Women Edmonton, a women's club in Edmonton, Alberta, which began in 1909 soon after the province was formed. It is about women working together to remedy social inequities and to further women's education, and about how they participated in the shaping of history. It is also about life within the group—the activities and events of the association.

The authors of this book worked together in the same spirit of co-operation. This is a collaborative effort of nine CFUW Edmonton members, none of who are historians or professional writers. But among us we have a variety of skills, talents and experience. We have bachelor degrees from four provinces, in arts, science and education; there are three master's degrees and one doctorate; length of membership in the Club varies from eighteen to fifty years; four have been Club president; three have chaired CFUW national committees and all have been active within the Club. This collective variety mirrors the variety within the Club itself and gives us authority to write about it.

The bias of written history has been toward political and economic events and has, to a large extent, left women's lives out of the record. There are accounts of women's organizations, but no comprehensive account of our 93-year-old organization. Our purpose is to put CFUW in the historical record. We have tried therefore to provide not only the hard facts about the Club and its accomplishments, but also glimpses into why women have belonged and continue to belong to it.

It will perhaps be said that insiders cannot be objective, are too close to the subject to evaluate it. However we think that the writing of this book is one time when insiders are needed. Materials used are varied: minutes and other formal Club records, newspaper accounts, archival records, submissions from other Club members (oral interviews, written reports of special projects and particular interest groups). The sources of data are primary sources, uneven in quality and reliability, often requiring the informed judgment of an insider to interpret.

We have written out of affection and pride. The book is not a history, but it is about historical matters. The intention is to put the Club on display, to exhibit its workings and its actions, to explain what it has been 'up to' over the years, and to show why women want to belong to it.

Indirectly the book is also about the national organization, the federation of which CFUW Edmonton is a part. The Club of course helps set policies and works to carry out national and international programs. Although the focus of the book is on local affairs, on its own specific milieu, these activities manifest agreed-upon values held by all clubs in the federation. In that sense the story of CFUW Edmonton is also a part of the story of the whole Canadian Federation of University Women.

History Group Members

The authors look over an early draft!
L to R: Mary Kostash, Peggy Rootes, Robin Robinson, Alberta Boytzun, Dr. Murina Bauer, Barbara Blackley, Win Mellon, Georgie Scafe (missing, Fran Reynolds)

Joined

Murina Bauer, BA, MA, U. of Manitoba, PhD, U. of Alberta *1943*

Barbara Blackley, BA, U. of Toronto *1951*

Alberta Boytzun, BEd, U. of Alberta; MEd, U. of Toronto *1961*

Mary Kostash, BEd, U. of Alberta *1971*

Win Mellon, BSc, MSc, U. of Alberta *1978*

Fran Reynolds, BSc, U. of Alberta *1948*

Robin Robinson, BA, U. of British Columbia *1966*

Peggy Rootes, BEd, U. of Alberta . . . . . *First joined in 1952 for 2 years, then 1962*

Georgie Scafe, BA, U. of Western Ontario *1983*

Introduction

When the University of Alberta was founded in 1908, it was unusual for women to be among the student body. There were so few women that the first Canadian Federation of University Women Edmonton (CFUW Edmonton) Scholarship Fund had to make a provision for what to do with monies raised for scholarships should there be no female students. The founding members of CFUW Edmonton were committed to providing scholarships for female students in the early years of the university. The vision and audacity of these women remains a vital part of the club today. Times have changed over the century. Women's presence in academic life is no longer questioned–though often underrepresented), and women's access to knowledge is now a given. CFUW Edmonton still provides access to funding to make women's education possible.

In community affairs, even before it was legal for women to vote, CFUW Edmonton encouraged women to stand for public office of various kinds, and organized numerous opportunities for the debate of political issues. Today, women take on lobbying in a variety of forms: letter writing public challenges to government policy, conversations with political representatives, and getting elected to various public offices.

Despite the improvements in conditions for women in society, vigilance is still necessary over women's access to channels of social control and to opportunities for serving the cause of social justice. This is not limited to local activities, but includes those causes that are global in nature. International understanding, global peace, exploitation and abuse of women–all are of equal importance in the struggle for positive social change. Our solidarity with women worldwide is greater than ever before.

The several waves of feminism over the last century have accomplished a great deal. Women have learned to claim their voice, to speak up and be heard–to become audible and therefore visible. Claiming our collective voice is another way to improve the status of women, which was implicit in the Club's activities from its inception. It is incumbent upon members to speak up and provide an account of themselves.

It is challenging to incorporate women's activities into the historical record because it is not a simple matter of insertion of facts and anecdotes into existing accounts of politics and social crises. Nor can we simply add heroic women to the list of heroic men in an attempt to redress the imbalance. Instead, new forms of telling our stories must be sought to encapsulate the significant records of women's pasts. Historians, in particular feminist historians, are seeking such forms, responding to the need to "shift our stance" in order to accommodate information that is relevant to the lives of women. This allows writers to take a more "qualitative" approach to the telling of our stories, giving room for personal accounts, oral interviews, anecdotal records, photographs, artifacts, archived club records and submissions from members as source material.

By Degrees begins where all stories must–at the beginning. How was CFUW Edmonton formed, what were its objectives, who were the members in those first years, and what were the issues that were close to their hearts? What did they accomplish? What challenges did they face as an organization? And finally, how did those early beginnings of the club set the stage for the decades to come?

We then move in for a closer look at the Purposes of the CFUW, and it is around these that the core of our story is organized. What kinds of things were done over the past 90 plus years to meet the Club's goals? How were these purposes acted upon, who was involved, and what accomplishments need to be celebrated?

A group's history is more than the sum of its activities. The social dimensions of any organization provide insights into the importance of the organization for its members, their families and friends. CFUW Edmonton has provided opportunities for its members to grow and develop in their intellectual, emotional, physical and spiritual lives. In the final section of the book, the smorgasbord of social activities that were planned and carried out over the past nine decades is explored. We have tried to reflect the deep sense of community, friendship and commitment that developed as a result of these "just for fun" activities.

CFUW Edmonton is an organization that has been plugging away for almost a century on social issues. The work of CFUW Edmonton is of interest to some people only in a general way. For others, such as feminists, educators and social scientists, the history of the Club will offer insights into the individuals and the social context of the group through nearly a century of work.

Telling the story of CFUW Edmonton allows a closer look at the possibilities for the future. Are the goals still relevant in today's world of rapid change and new social contexts and issues for women? Do the strategies from the past help shape social action in the present? How can members "keep with tradition," yet respond to the questions of the new century in fresh and engaging ways? This look back over 90 plus years of CFUW Edmonton life provides a roadmap into an exciting new century of social activism.

Section 1
Small Beginnings

Key to picture on facing page:

Top Row, L to R: Barbara Hinton, Fran Reynolds, Shirley Gifford, Tammy Irwin, Jean Tucker, Donna Dahlmer

Second Row, L to R: Margery Petruk, Ruth Culham

Third Row, L to R: Audrey Keen, Alka Kembhavi, Anne Valentine, Jan McMillan, Margaret Reine, Jennifer Kouri, Joan Dame, Bonnie Bell, June Edwards, Peggy Giffen

Fourth Row, L to R: Jean Pare, Joan Cowling, Peggy Rootes, Myrtle Seguin, Suzanne Connell, Jean Robson, Jessica Hanna

Fifth Row, L to R: Aldis Hunt, Joyce MacDonald, Bev Cormack, Willa Woods, Hiske Gerding, Dr. Lila Fahlman, Olga Shklanka, Donna Reddecopp

Small Beginnings

Edmonton was becoming a major urban centre in the early 1900s. With its own Legislature Building under construction, a university on the way, and electricity gracing homes, offices and stores, it was rapidly becoming the destination of choice for many middle-class and educated North Americans and Europeans.

Divided by the North Saskatchewan River, the two communities of Edmonton and Strathcona boasted a combined population of 23,000 in 1910; 18,000 lived in Edmonton and 5,000 resided on the south side in Strathcona. Streetcars joined the two communities over the one Low Level Bridge, while ferries in summer or ice roads in the winter were the only other way to get from one side to the other. Cars were a rarity, while horse-and-buggy still provided the primary means of travel. The telephone was still a novelty for most people.

The University of Alberta had no building of its own. Beginning in September 1908, classes for the initial 38 students, including seven women, were held on the top story of the Duggan Street School (later called Queen Alexandra School) in Strathcona. The University moved to the top floor of Strathcona Collegiate Institute in January 1909.

In this environment a small group of women saw the need for an education club that would encourage female students by enhancing the quality of their cultural life and by providing financial support. This founding group of like-minded women

Agnes (Wilson) Teviotdale, a long term active Club member was interviewed in 1969 by the Women's Editor of the Edmonton Journal, Ruth Bowen, and gave her thoughts on what it was like to be one of the first students at the University of Alberta (1908 to 1912) as well as an early member of the then Alberta Women's Association. As she said, "I was in at the beginning of both, the University and the Club and saw each grow through the decades from their 'small beginnings'–the Club's objective in 1910 was communication among women interested in matters of education, and at the new university, to provide certain social amenities to the women students until a residence should be complete and a Dean appointed."

sparked enough energy among themselves to have a fully functioning organization within two months (November 1909 to January 1910), complete with an executive, a constitution, a set of purposes, and a names committee. One can speculate that for those women to simply get together was probably as important to them as were the services they provided to female students. Historians have noted the energy and enterprise of Edmonton women in those early years, and advocacy for women was more a part of the western scene than in some other parts of Canada. In a nation where women did not vote, where higher education for women was new, where gender inequities in the law were common—here was an opportunity to push for a brave new world.

The first meeting of the Club was held at the home of Mrs. Howard Riley at three o'clock, Tuesday, November 30th, 1909, at which time a motion was passed to organize a women's education club, followed by the election of Mrs. E. K. Broadus as President Pro Tem and Mrs. E. T. Bishop as Secretary. The meeting was then adjourned until further notice. Behind the scenes much activity ensued, including a meeting at the home of Mrs. W. D. Ferris on Christmas Day, so that by January 8, 1910 a proposed Executive and Constitution were presented and approved at the first general meeting of the group.

The order of business at the next regular meeting on February 12th, which was held at the Strathcona Collegiate Institute, included plans to invite the female students of the university to three small teas where they could meet the members. In addition, a letter was to be sent to the Senate of the University, Strathcona, Alberta to inform them of the expectations of the new Club. It read as follows:

February 18, 1910

Gentlemen:

Recently a group of women of Edmonton and Strathcona, mainly college women and wives of officers of the University of Alberta, have formed an association to promote educational interests especially those of women in the province of Alberta. The Association hopes during the remainder of the Academic year to do two things:

First, to assist in giving to the women students of the University, a social life that will be both cultural and wholesome.

Second, to offer a scholarship of $50.00 to the woman of the freshman class whose record of scholarship for the year shall be highest.

It is also the hope of the Association that similar groups of women in other parts of the province may be brought into association with us in order that we may co-operate in promoting educational work.

We await the judgment of the Senate as to the desirability of the scholarship which we propose to offer and we ask the interest of the Senate in this Association to the extent of their calling to our attention any work relating to the University which such an organization as ours can assist.

Yours sincerely,

Thyrza Bishop, Secretary

A reply was received from the University of Alberta President, Dr. H. M. Tory, kindly accepting the offer of the Association to found a scholarship for women students.

By March 8, 1910 the Names Committee had proposed seven names, including such suggestions as Twentieth Century, Woman's Association for Educational Service, Univalta Woman's Organization, Alberta Sorority, Causa Alliarium and Alberta Women's Association. The latter name was chosen. Although variously referred to as Alberta Woman's or Women's Association in the early Club Minutes, it is generally accepted that the plural case was the preferred one.

The women who gathered together to form the new education club were either university graduates or belonged by virtue of their husband's position. Those eligible to join were listed in Article 3 of the Club's first Constitution under the following categories:

- The wife of the Official Visitor of the University of Alberta–the Lieutenant-Governor of the Province

- Wives of the Minister and the Deputy Minister of Education

- Wives of Officers of the Senate and the faculty of the University of Alberta

- Women members of the Founding Convocation of the University of Alberta

- Alumnae of colleges of recognized standing in Canada, Great Britain and the United States

• Women graduates of medical and legal schools of recognized standing.

The fact that the Club's membership was made up of graduate and non-graduate women was to become a matter of great debate by the end of the decade, when the suggestion to form an organization solely composed of graduate women was brought before the Club. Because the non-graduate women, many with connections to the U of A and a strong interest in education, were highly valued members of the Club, any proposals that excluded them were unacceptable at the time. The ensuing debate on this issue and its repercussions are related in *National and International Affairs: CFUW and IFUW.*

First Executive and Charter Members

The first Executive included the Honorary President, Mrs. G. H. V. Bulyea, wife of the Lieutenant-Governor, and two Honorary Vice-Presidents, Mrs. Tory, wife of the first President of the U of A, and Mrs. A. C. Rutherford, wife of the first Premier of the Province. These women fulfilled honorary roles for many other organizations on campus and in the city. They were gracious hostesses and lent not only their prestige but often their homes, and many a Club Reception or Tea was held at their residences.

President Eleanor Broadus, a graduate of Radcliffe College, married to the U of A's first English professor, Dr. E. K. Broadus. Little is known about Mrs. Broadus, but she is often recalled by older members of the Club as the person who got their mothers or friends involved in the organization. No doubt it was her enthusiasm and commitment that drew others to it.

First Vice-President Mrs. W. D. Ferris, a graduate of the University of Toronto, wife of an early Edmonton doctor who was a member of the University Senate.

Second Vice-President Evelyn Muir Edwards, a non-graduate, married to the first professor of mathematics and engineering. Mr. William Muir Edwards was the son of Henrietta Muir Edwards, well known as one of Alberta's Famous Five Women. The younger Mrs. Muir Edwards was President of the Club (1916-18), but tragically her young husband died in the influenza epidemic of 1918 at age 33 and she subsequently moved to eastern Canada.

Secretary Thryza Bishop, a graduate of the University of Toronto whose husband was on the University Senate. A vital and active member of the Community, Mrs. Bishop was also on the Executive of the Local Council of Women (President, 1910s). With the encouragement of the Club and other women's groups, she successfully ran for the Edmonton Public School Board in 1921 and was named the first woman Chair of the Board in 1923.

Corresponding Secretary Mrs. R. B. Wells, a graduate of University of Toronto (1895), was an active and long-time member of the Club. It has been noted that her home was often the centre of Club teas where many distinguished visitors were welcomed.

Treasurer Mrs. H. Riley, who served pro tem until February 1910 when she moved to Calgary. Not long afterward her name appeared as a member of the executive of a newly established university women's club there. Annie Race followed as Treasurer.

These officers were chosen by acclamation. Three councilors were also elected from a choice of seven names and included Mrs. Knight, a University of Toronto graduate, Dr. Synge and Louisa Beck. A non-graduate, Mrs. Beck was married to Senate member Justice N. D. Beck and served as second President from 1912 to 1913.

The Founding Convocation of the U of A (Category 4) was called together for the purposes of forming a University Senate and electing a Chancellor. The University Act provided that the first Convocation should be made up of graduates of universities in Canada and Great Britain who had registered at a specific date and who had paid a fee of $2.00 to the Provincial Secretary. Their credentials were then duly approved. Upwards of 354 graduates registered at the time and became potential first members of the Founding Convocation, which was held on March 18, 1908. Members of the Founding Convocation of the University of Alberta included at least four charter members, four of whom were present at the 1948 reunion of the First Convocation. They were Mrs. Bishop, Mrs. Ferris, Mrs. Wells and Mrs. Race. The first formal Convocation of the University was held in October 1908.

Other Charter members included Mrs. James McCaig and Mrs. D. S. MacKenzie. Mrs. James McCaig was wife of the first full-time Superintendent of Schools in Edmonton and Strathcona. Mrs. MacKenzie, a BA graduate from Ontario, came west in 1900. She taught for a number of years in the Edmonton area where she met and married the principal

Mrs. K. (Eleanor) Broadus
President

Mrs. W. (Evelyn) Muir Edwards
2nd Vice-President

Mrs. H.M. Tory
Honorary
Vice-President

Mrs. E.T. (Thryza) Bishop
Secretary

Mrs. C.E. (Annie) Race
Treasurer

of Strathcona High School, D. S. MacKenzie, who was later to become the Deputy Minister of Education. A very community-minded woman, Mrs. MacKenzie was also a charter member of the Women's Canadian Club, and served as President of several organizations, including the Local Council of Women, the YWCA Board and the Club.

Early Members (1910 to 1914)

Mrs. E. L. Hill (Jenny S.) was an active member of the Club during this period and initiated many of the early actions regarding education and the status of women. In the Fall of 1910 she chaired a committee that presented several motions asking the Club to "further the matter of the election of a woman to the Senate of the University of Alberta" (a matter which was taken up by a committee of the 'members of the Convocation') and to "further the election of women on school boards in the province and to be particularly concerned with the election in Edmonton and Strathcona." Mrs. Hill was to become a successful candidate herself for the Edmonton Public School Board in 1913 in one of the city's most controversial elections. (see *Education*).

At the time of the University's founding in 1908, university women graduates could be part of the first Convocation to elect members to the U of A Senate, but were not allowed to be members of the Senate themselves. Though they were able to vote in the local civic elections of 1912, women were not eligible to hold office. Such was the situation women faced in Edmonton in the early part of the twentieth century.

Mrs. E. W. (Helen) Sheldon, wife of the first mathematics professor at the U of A and first Advisor to Women Students (1911-1912), was invited to join the Club in 1911. She had come to Edmonton as a young bride from New York in 1910. Although not a graduate, Mrs. Sheldon was involved with activities at the University and Club until her husband's retirement. She remained in Alberta until her death in the 1980s. Among the members who joined in 1911 were future Club Presidents Mrs. S. Dickson and Mrs. John Gillespie.

According to a 1913 Report of the Membership Committee, there were 14 new members. Included in this list were two women who played important roles in the history of the Club, Dr. Geneva Misener, Professor of Classics, and Agnes Wilson. Dr. Misener, a graduate of Queen's University with a PhD from the University of Chicago (1905), was the first woman appointed to the staff of the University of Alberta in

U of A Archives: 69.132.2

L: Kathleen Lavell (Mrs. I. F. Morrison)
R: Agnes Wilson (Mrs. D. J. Teviotdale)

Two of the women students entertained by the Club in the early years. Agnes Wilson was one of seven women enrolled in the first class at U of A (1908-1912). Kathleen Lavell was in the second class. Both women joined the club soon after graduating and were active and life-long members.

1912. Agnes Wilson (Mrs. D. J. Teviotdale) was one of the original seven women students at the University (1908–1912). Other new members were Mrs. A. E. Ottewell and Decima Robinson (Mitchell) who was the first woman to receive a BA (1911) and an MSc (1912) from the University of Alberta.

By 1914 there was a total membership of 64. Thirty-eight were holders of degrees from the Universities of Alberta, Toronto, Dalhousie, Queen's, Manitoba, Chicago, Radcliffe, New York, Wisconsin, Nebraska, Illinois, Pennsylvania and London, England. The remaining members were admitted under Section 3 of Article 3 of the Club's Constitution, wives of Senate Officers and Faculty members.

Elizabeth Cogswell, a graduate with several degrees, and a recent arrival to Edmonton (1907) was typical of he members of the early years. Newly married to an up-and-coming Crown Prosecutor, Mrs. Cogswell was encouraged to join the Club by her neighbour and acquaintance, Mrs. Broadus. She was also a friend of Nellie McClung and knew Judge Emily Murphy. Edmonton was still a small community and many of those in the various professions were well acquainted with one another. In fact, it has been pointed out that a great deal got accomplished because members had such connections.

The story of Mrs. Cogswell was brought to light in an interview with her daughter, Libby Frost (President 1968–70). Here was a woman with not only a BA from Dalhousie University, but a Master's in English from Radcliffe University in the United States. She had been offered a scholarship for her doctorate, but opted instead to get married and move to Western Canada. Libby related that her mother's sister was a medical doctor and that both women had received a great deal of encouragement in their education by their Scottish parents of Nova Scotia. Women such as Mrs. Cogswell would have found an intellectual home in the organization.

The early members were for the most part conservative women of standing in the community. The official government overseer of city schools (the school inspector) described Miss Kay Teskey at the time as a "young lady of culture and refinement and possessing a strong personality." This is probably an apt description of many of the members. It was a period when women wore long skirts, white gloves and carried calling cards and the students wore black gowns to classes—all very traditional and a holdover from the 19th century. In a light-hearted historical sketch 'Salad Days' at the Club's 50th anniversary in September 1960, Agnes Teviotdale acknowledged this fact in verse (the yellowing pages referring to the hand-written Minutes of the first few years):

> The yellowing pages bear testimony
> To a definite tale of propriety
> The tone of the 19th century
> Carried on to the next quite definitely.

"These pioneers met together to encourage other women toward higher education, to perpetuate their own friendship and to do constructive work in citizenship," stated Mrs. A. S. Morton, CFUW National President, in acknowledging the early members at the Edmonton Club's 50th anniversary. Based on their own experience as some of the first women in Canada to receive a higher education, the early members were in a position to understand the problems women students might encounter. They not only staged social events such as teas and get-togethers for the girls to provide companionship and encouragement, but made efforts to meet other requests of a cultural nature that came their way, including pictures for the Wauneita Lounge at Assiniboia Hall and books to set up a library in the women's residence at Pembina Hall. They also met requests from outside the University from organizations such as the YWCA and the Edmonton Music Society.

By 1917, when the name was changed to *Women's University Club of Edmonton,* the Club was not confined to the aid and support of women at the U of A only, but had expanded its advocacy in a number of ways in the community. As it became better established the Club sought collaboration with similar groups at Canadian universities. By 1919, when Margaret McWilliams of Winnipeg organized a Canada-wide conference with the hope of establishing a Federation of University Women, the local membership was ready to commit to expanded horizons, though not to let go of its original goals. The Club's ten years of development prior to the inception of the Federation paved the way for more concerted action by the larger, organized group of women.

Canadian and International Federations Get off the Ground

University women's clubs and alumnae associations existed around the turn of the century on many campuses. The American Association of College Alumnae had been founded in 1882 and the British Federation of University Women in 1907. As early as 1901, the Convenor of Victoria College in Toronto had written to all the associations of Canadian alumnae urging them to unite or join the American Association, which a few individuals did. By 1915 there was talk of forming an association of international women alumnae. However, it wasn't until after the turmoil of World War I that deliberate action was taken to found an international association of university women, propelled by the deeply felt need for women to work together for peace.

In the Fall of 1918, the Chair of International Relations of the American Association of College Alumnae, Dr. Virginia Gildersleeve, met with two visiting members of the British Federation of University Women who were in the United States as part of a British Government Universities Mission. The germ of an international organization of university women was spawned between these women one evening when Professor Caroline Spurgeon from Britain (who became the first President of the IFUW) said "we should have an international federation of university women, so that we at least shall have done all we can to prevent another such catastrophe." With that the women agreed to rally their respective organizations, and by July 1919 they met in London to lay the groundwork for such an association.

The groups were anxious to have Canada join them and great pressure was brought to bear on the existing university women's clubs to organize into a federation so that they could be represented at the first official meeting of IFUW called for July 1920. It was largely owing to the energetic pressure of Margaret McWilliams that the founding meeting of the Canadian Federation was held on the 26th and 27th of August 1919 in Winnipeg (not only a central location, but the home of

PAA, CFUW Edmonton: 69.22/120

Organizational Meeting of Canadian Federation of University Women,
Winnipeg, Manitoba, 1919
Back row, L to R: Mrs. C. Wiley, Ottawa; Mrs. E. Smith, Victoria; Mrs. Sadler,
Winnipeg; Miss Jessie Dykes, Toronto; Miss Kathleen Teskey, Edmonton
Front row, L to R: Miss Lexa Denne, Victoria; Miss M. H. Skinner, Toronto;
Dr. Margaret McWilliams, Winnipeg; Mrs. G. L. Lennox, Winnipeg;
Dr. Geneva Misener, Edmonton

Mrs. McWilliams). The Canadian Federation of University Women
was born.

Currently CFUW is made up of 123 member clubs with an enrollment of
over 10,000 members; IFUW has a membership of approximately 70
countries with an enrollment of 170,000 members and has special
consultative status with the United Nations Economic and Social Council
and other allied UN agencies and commissions.

Identity of Club and Relationship with the National Federation

The fact that the Club has regularly held meetings on the U of A campus has led people to believe that it is part of the University rather than an independent Club of university women graduates belonging to a larger national and international association. From its inception, the Club relied on the staff and facilities of the University, and later maintained a close association with the Faculty Women's Club. These connections were immensely beneficial to the Club, however through the years it became more and more difficult to define a separate image. The Club was often referred to as the U of A Women's Club or just a women's university club, the connection to U of A being understood. The confusion was understandable and was to continue when the name was changed in 1941 to the *University Women's Club* and later to the *University Women's Club of Edmonton (1968)*. To avoid further confusion and to more properly identify with the national federation, the Club's name was changed in 1989 to the *Canadian Federation of University Women Edmonton (CFUW Edmonton)*.

The nature of an organization is not always plain from its name. Some people may think the name suggests that the Club includes all the women on Canadian campuses; in fact it is only those women university graduates who seek membership and support Federation goals that belong. Further ambiguity comes from a belief that CFUW Edmonton's goals themselves are generated by the need to promote university women per se, on their own account. Rather, CFUW Edmonton's perspective is the more general one of how university women graduates can best benefit society. The University has nothing to say about CFUW Edmonton's doings except through ordinary public channels. Many Federation clubs exist, in fact, in cities with no university. Despite ambiguities such as these, CFUW Edmonton has come to designate a particular Edmonton women's club with a long track record.

As one of the clubs in the Canadian Federation, CFUW Edmonton shares in Federation accomplishments although it has its own individuality. After all, as a founding member, CFUW Edmonton was one of the earliest and strongest of such groups and brought the energy of a frontier outlook to the early activities of the Federation. Among women's organizations, the Club shares the Federation's pride in being a contributor to several waves of effort on behalf of improving the status of women. CFUW Edmonton has an unusually long span of actively promoting women's rights. But that is not its whole story. One should not overlook its contributions to public education in general, its concern for community welfare or its promotion of debate over public issues. CFUW Edmonton is far from being a one-dimensional organization.

$\mathscr{A}$ Framework for Action

A Framework For Action

The 1919 Winnipeg meeting at which the assembled university women's clubs decided to join together in a federation articulated four main purposes. Briefly these purposes had to do with the importance of *education* in general but especially for women, improving the *status of women* in society, encouraging women to serve in the community and to be active in *public affairs* and support for *national and international efforts* on behalf of women. These purposes provided a mandate and some machinery for action on their behalf, all of which continue as centrally relevant to each club in the Federation.

"Through community of action CFUW offers the university woman a medium by which her work may be made to count as no isolated effort ever can."

– *Mrs. Margaret McWilliams, Founder and First President of CFUW*

The 1920 conference in London, England assembled similar federations from around the world, and put in place the International Federation of University Women (IFUW). The conference reaffirmed and expanded the implications of CFUW's fourth purpose, that of fostering international understanding and friendship. Thus by 1921 there existed a layered set of imperatives for the Edmonton Club that have provided parameters of action through the years.

Pre-dating the Federation by almost a decade, CFUW Edmonton already had an elected executive that carried out the day-to-day duties of the Club, as well as Standing Committees and Study Groups through which much of the research was carried out. It was ready to join the community of action offered by the national organization.

The four purposes cited above are in the CFUW Edmonton constitution. They parallel those of the national federation but in a more abbreviated form. CFUW Edmonton assumes the CFUW mandate and is entitled to the expanded version as well as its own. The more complete CFUW version is the one used as reference in *By Degrees*.

Structure of the CFUW and Local Clubs

Whereas the four purposes focus concerns, the organizational structure channels action. How CFUW determines its policies and action initiatives is enlarged upon in the section on National and International Affairs, but it is important to note that the Federation defines its policies through a grassroots generation of resolutions that are presented for nationwide review and amendment at the Annual General Meetings. The adopted resolutions then become policy.

The work at the local level provides impetus to the activities of CFUW as well as serving the community through its own particular actions. Members are kept informed and challenged through regular monthly programs that offer speakers, or by coming together in study groups or workshops. Ideas raised at the local level through these avenues, plus ideas raised at the national meetings, often provide the basis for resolutions that go on to define CFUW policy.

The research of the issues is carried out mainly through the Club's Standing Committees, Special Committees or Study Groups. These groups vary from formal ones that customarily meet on a regular basis and submit annual reports (such as the Standing Committees) to more loosely organized groups created to study a particular cause and subsequently prepare a situation paper or brief.

The realms of action of CFUW are education, public affairs, the status of women and human rights, and national and international affairs. As a category each assumes the other and sometimes they overlap since an action may serve several purposes. The following four sections show the varied fronts of Club activities as well as their interdependencies.

Chapter 1

$\mathcal{E}$ducation

Purpose One: to assist in developing a sound concept of educational values and in maintaining high standards of public education in Canada; to encourage advanced study and research by women university graduates.

"The object of this organization shall be to promote educational interests, especially those of women in the Province of Alberta." Article 2 of the Club's first Constitution of 1909/10 stated these ideals, and they have remained central to the organization ever since. The ways in which the Club's educational interests have manifested themselves within its history are outlined below.

The word 'education' invokes a range of understandings from personal growth to the fostering of institutions such as libraries, museums and archives that provide social benefits through their educational function. CFUW Edmonton's activities have encompassed this range. It has been an agency of education for its own members through the study groups and through inviting speakers to Club meetings.

It is in the area of public education, however, that the Club's activities are most clearly identifiable. The Club's interests in education are reviewed from the initial concern for the welfare of young women in the community to broader issues of public education.

The interest in women's education initially took two forms. One, to assist in giving women students of the University a social life that would be both cultural and wholesome, and second, to offer a scholarship of $50.00 to the woman in the freshman class whose record of scholarship was highest. Over time, efforts of the Club concentrated on financial initiatives to aid women students through the scholarship and bursary programs. The history of the early scholarships and the development of the Club's current Academic Awards Program are discussed in Chapter 2.

Education Standing Committee (ESC)

The Education Standing Committee (ESC) was the premier committee of the Club for the first five decades of the life of CFUW Edmonton. Many meetings revolved around issues brought forward by this committee. To describe all the subjects that the ESC addressed through the years would be impossible, therefore only those that resulted in a Brief or Recommendation are summarized here. This synopsis will give some idea of the wide range of research that the ESC members undertook through the years and emphasizes the Club's commitment to the betterment of public education. This includes improved curriculum, early childhood studies, concern for better teaching conditions and better use of federal and provincial educational dollars.

Early Days

The Convenors of the ESC during the Club's first decade, Dr. Geneva Misener, Kathleen Teskey and Jessie Montgomery figure prominently in the early history of the Canadian Federation. Each was involved in the founding meeting of the CFUW in 1919, and Dr. Misener and Miss Montgomery were named Convenors of the first National Standing Committees on Education and Libraries, respectively. Kathleen Teskey was the Club's Federation representative. Through their efforts and through the Club's ESC, they helped shape the direction of the Edmonton Club.

One of the first actions of the fledgling Education Standing Committee in 1910 was to promote the election of women as public school trustees. Under the Chairmanship of Mrs. E. L. Hill, an active member of the Club during its formative years, the committee not only furthered the election of a woman to the School Board, but also was to see Mrs. Hill herself elected to the Board in 1914.

This came about following a resolution from the Local Council of Women (LCW) in October 1913. The resolution, which went to all

Council affiliates, including the Club, suggested that in the event of the retirement from office of Miss Bessie Nichols (the first woman elected as an Edmonton Public School Board Trustee in 1912), the Council nominate a woman candidate to the School Board. It also called for Mrs. E. L. Hill to be the nominee of the Executive Committee of the Council. Although the Club approved the first part of the resolution, they vetoed the second part, hoping instead to advance Mrs. Hill's name as nominee of the Club and not the LCW. Perhaps wisely, Mrs. Hill chose the backing of the LCW and the 35 women's groups that it represented at the time.

It was during Jenny Hill's term on the Edmonton Public School Board (EPSB) that the Club embarked in 1915 on its first major involvement with the EPSB. The event was a special public meeting held under the Club's auspices at McKay Avenue School to oppose the School Board's proposal to curtail the positions of Supervisors of Music and Arts. As a follow-up, the Club President and Committee members attended a School Board meeting; it was noted that their influence was effective in having the Supervisors retained. The Club saw the role of Supervisor as a necessary resource person to encourage and develop programs.

A Most Controversial Election

In 1913 Mrs. E. L. (Jenny S.) Hill ran successfully for the Edmonton Public School Board election for the 1914 to 1916 term. She had the unanimous support of the women's societies in Edmonton and an endorsement by Emily Murphy who signed her nomination papers. By running a well-organized campaign and by being a persuasive orator she was able to overcome her male opposition's skullduggery in what has been called one of the most controversial elections in the school board's history. Among several maneuvers, her opposition coerced a Mrs. Alice Hill to run in the election to confuse voters. The ruse didn't work and Jenny Hill won decisively.

The first Supervisor of Music was Kate Chegwin, a pioneer teacher with the Edmonton Public School Board since 1899. In 1914 she was appointed as Edmonton's first female principal of a large permanent school (McDougall School). Recognizing and supporting her work in education and that of her sister, also a teacher, the Club wrote to the School Board in 1928, suggesting the names of the Chegwin sisters for

U of A Archives: 2315-2

EPS Archives and Museum: p85.20.22

Dr. Geneva Misener

Kathleen Teskey

Three Remarkable Women: Misener, Teskey and Montgomery

In those first heady years of the University Women's Club, the names of Dr. Geneva Misener, Kathleen Teskey and Jessie Montgomery would have come easily to the tongues of many of the Club members. These three were active on many levels in the group, and their contributions were considerable.

Dr. Misener had a remarkable academic record, which included being the first woman professor at the University of Alberta, post-graduate studies at the University of Berlin and the School of Archeology in Athens. She was awarded numerous prizes and scholarships, and had worked in a variety of institutions before coming to Edmonton (see also *Status of Women*).

Kathleen Teskey is another woman of considerable academic talent. With a Master's degree in Arts from Queen's University, Teskey continued her studies in Quebec and Toronto, as well as at the Sorbonne in France. Teskey came to Edmonton in 1911 to teach French at Victoria High School where she remained until

U of A Archives: 81-117-1

Jessie Montgomery

her retirement in 1947. Kathleen Teskey is first mentioned in the Club records in 1913, when the Club was only four years old. She later became President in 1918. Her contribution to the community included the initiating of a group to help French teachers in the public schools speak French. Teskey's name comes up again and again in regard to the efforts of the Club to make changes in the education system of Alberta.

Jessie Montgomery is certainly another of the larger than life figures whose participation in the Club made it what it is today. Before the advent of the Library Committee, Montgomery served on the Education Committee where she provided leadership in getting the Club to examine library facilities in the public school system. She was influential in pressing the government for changes. Born in Ontario, but educated in Scotland, Montgomery returned to Canada in 1904 and taught for a number of years in rural Alberta. This experience gave her invaluable insight into what an extension library service could mean to people in remote settlements.

At the time of CFUW's establishment, Jessie Montgomery was just beginning her career and was a fairly recent graduate (BA, U of A, 1914). She had joined the Department of Extension part-time in 1913 and assumed the responsibility for organizing the Department's first traveling libraries. After obtaining her BLS (Bachelor of Library Studies, University of Wisconsin, 1915), she took up full-time duties with the Department of Extension Library Services. Here she established the traveling library system. On her retirement after 32 years it was written: "Hundreds of communities will treasure pleasant memories of happy hours spent in the realm of books and will remember with affection the friendly white-haired lady who to them was Alberta's first Librarian to the Hinterland." (New Trail, 1945)

a new school being built in Edmonton. Although the Board replied that it had already chosen the name Spruce Avenue, recognition came to Kate Chegwin in 1991, 63 years later, when a junior high school was named in her honour.

In 1916 the Club sponsored a special meeting at McKay Avenue School where eight school board candidates spoke. Seventy years later (1986) the Club, still true to its interest and support of education, co-hosted two widely attended forums for the very large slate of candidates running for the Edmonton Public and Separate School Boards. This time there were 59 candidates for the Public School Board.

Welfare of Young Women

As World War I came to an end there was concern among women's groups regarding the welfare of young, single women in the cities. In 1917 Dr. Geneva Misener was asked to head a Provincial Committee to determine the needs of these girls in relation to available recreation and training. Her committee came to the conclusion that the situation would best be met by a series of conferences held in conjunction with other concerned groups such as church Sunday Schools, the YWCA and the United Farm Women of Alberta (UFWA).

In a 1918 article in the *South Side Diary,* a column in one of Edmonton's newspapers, it was reported that "a very successful Girls' Conference had its inception in the Education Committee of the University Women's Club–chief organizers were members of the Club–it was a very successful year considering the fact that many of its members are among the most active in war work."

In its fall agenda of 1918 the ESC included plans to provide "fitting recreation" for those young women not reached by churches or the YWCA. "There are many plans for a winter of practical work among girls in the City and the committee hoped to begin work with a small group and endeavor to offer them amusement and instruction which would brighten and enlarge their outlook on life." (ESC Report, 1918) Unfortunately the influenza epidemic of 1918 put an end to these initial plans. However, by January of the following year it was reported that they had resumed their efforts with a survey of 'public places of amusement open to the girls.'

Concern was not only for girls. Following World War I, there was a zealous movement afoot to find morally uplifting and instructive activities for the whole adolescent population in order to counteract the growing "perils" that face young people–tobacco, alcohol, dancing and moving pictures. Finding ways to counteract these problems became a major preoccupation of churches and volunteer groups.

"On learning that the School Board was being asked to allow dancing at Grade 12 class parties, the Edmonton Superintendent of Schools opposed the move by saying that "a wave of immorality involving young people was sweeping the country and that dancing was precisely the type of amusement that demonstrated the problem." (From 1922 minutes of the EPSB, found in *"Patrolling the Passions of Youth"* from: **Edmonton: The Life of A City**) This was no doubt the view held by many adults at the time.

The ESC's approach to the problem appears to have been consistent with their belief that education, vocational guidance and training, and recreation were important to the well-being of young people. The ESC not only played a leadership role in the organization of the Girls' Conferences that included these girls' activities, but also provided assistance to the YWCA in expanding their programs and in volunteer teaching.

Volunteer Teaching

Members were involved in volunteer teaching in one form or another throughout the Club's history. As early as 1914 records indicate that ESC members were recruited to teach "English to foreign girls" through the YMCA Educational Committee. These efforts continued for many years. By 1919 the ESC's attention turned to the problems connected with the education of new immigrants in general. In order to alleviate the demands placed on community volunteer teachers by the great influx of immigrants in the post-war period, the Committee organized a petition to the EPSB to re-open classes for 'foreigners.' This would not be the only time the Club would ask the government or the School Board to take on the task of teaching English as a Second Language.

In 1925, the Club received a request for volunteer teachers for the shut-in children at the Royal Alexandra and University Hospitals. Again members of the ESC offered to assist, but only with the full support of the Club, which they received. Although they read and instructed the children at both hospitals for a number of years, it was eventually the University Hospital that became the centre of their focus throughout the 1920s and early 1930s.

Several names are noted for their commitment to volunteer teaching, including Mrs. R. K. Gordon who conducted a kindergarten in the University Hospital three afternoons a week, and Mrs. A. E. Ottewell who donated her time on behalf of the Club's Library Standing Committee (LSC), teaching the handicapped children in the Red Cross Hut.

This was obviously a major commitment on the part of members. In 1927 the Club, in cooperation with the Junior Red Cross Committee (Junior Hospital League), made the first of several submissions to the Minister of Education regarding the need for a regular teacher at the hospital. After much urging a commitment was finally received from the EPSB in 1932. One full-time teacher and a vocational teacher one day a week were assigned to the children in the University Hospital, including the Red Cross Hut.

During this same period, members of the Library Standing Committee regularly read to children in the hospitals, again mainly at the University Hospital. Librarian Jessie Montgomery had books sent over from the University Extension Department and arranged a story hour once a week. According to the 1927 Library Standing Committee Report, the eight readers of the committee also provided book handling twice a week in three wards of the University Hospital. It was through these latter efforts that a long time association was developed with the University Hospital. It led to the Club taking over the library services of the public wards under the banner of the Women's University Club Hospital Library. This major project between 1935 and 1967 is detailed under the Library Standing Committee in *Public Affairs.*

The 1920s

The growth in the population of Edmonton and Alberta between 1910 and 1940 affected the work of the ESC. The social expectations and constrictions placed upon women also influenced their work. Very few university women graduates were to be found in the workplace, which meant there was a pool of women's knowledge, expertise and energy that found its outlet in the study and actions undertaken by the Club's ESC. Customarily the Committee's work was done in depth and the projects were long-term ones. The effect was dual; women found a place in the Club to exercise their knowledge and skills, and the Club and community benefited from their many talents.

Curriculum Studies

By the 1920s, the ESC interests were directed to various aspects of the public school curriculum, including the content of textbooks, relevance of courses and exam standards. In 1920, when there was concern about the introduction of American literature and history texts into the province, the ESC wrote to the Deputy Minister of Education requesting that British or Canadian texts be used instead of those from the United States (despite the lower tariff of the latter). The Committee received a very congenial reply from the Deputy Minister, Dr. Ross, stating that "if at any time your organization desires to make an inquiry into the question of text books, course of study, or any question relating to education in the province, the Department will be pleased to meet with a committee which you appoint and give them all the information needed." It was noted that the U. S. history text was not ordered.

In 1922 the Club was asked to have representation at all meetings of a lay committee called by the Department of Education to make a first draft of the revised course of study for secondary schools. The special committee was made up of senior educational officials, superintendents, inspectors and representatives of ten provincial groups with an interest in education. In the 1922 Annual Report of the Department of Education, the Deputy Minister stated that "the task was a formidable one and the committee members gave unsparingly in their efforts." The work of this particular Committee was completed at the end of 1923, but the Club continued to have representation on various curriculum advisory committees both with the government and the EPSB through to the 1970s.

The year 1922 appears to have been a banner year for the Club. Having recently become part of a larger national and international federation, members were enthusiastic to promote their education policies. In August of that year, Kathleen Teskey was an official Canadian representative at the first major IFUW Conference held in Paris, which gave her an opportunity to make contact with other women in the educational field. One of the first priorities set out by the IFUW was the advancement of educational standards at the secondary level, and Kathleen Teskey would have returned from the meeting with renewed enthusiasm to forward these policies locally.

The IFUW experience may have provided the impetus for the ESC's next project. Starting in 1922 the Committee, under convenor Mary Crawford, embarked on an ambitious two-fold program of study that involved a survey of the educational systems of European countries and the United States. This was to provide a basis of comparison to the systems in use in the different provinces of Canada. For statistics in North America, the Committee wrote to the Departments of Education of the Canadian provinces and to Washington, D. C. For studies of the European educational system they may have relied in part on their counterparts in the IFUW, since they had set up a Committee on the Exchange of Information regarding Secondary Education to encourage interaction among secondary school teachers.

Using the information gathered through the surveys, the ESC put together an extensive questionnaire that was sent out to the school authorities in Alberta. The results led to one of the first major resolutions of the Club that called for the raising of exam standards in the province. This was forwarded to the EPSB in 1924. Research continued through the 1920s and a further questionnaire dealing with secondary school curriculum was sent out by the Committee in 1931 and 1932. The ESC must have felt some reward when it was reported in a 1924 Department of Education Report that the standard of scholarship demanded from high school students had been raised slightly. Students had to have an average of 40% in each subject (30% previously) and an average of 50% overall to be granted a diploma. By 1925 the standards were raised again, requiring 50% in each subject.

The impetus for the studies may have come from another direction as well, and that is the teaching community itself. It has been noted in a history of the Alberta Teachers' Association (**Teachers of the Foothills Province,** p. 47), research in education was one area that the ATA was unable to pursue, much as they wished to in the early years. "Although it never lost sight of its 'professional objectives' [school curriculum, teacher training and education research], or wholly neglected them, it [the ATA] and the leaders had only a limited amount of time, money and energy." First priority was given to improvement of the teachers' economic position and security. Thus the comparative studies and resulting questionnaires provided valuable information to the local educational community.

Despite all the enthusiasm for improving the standards of education in the 1920s, economic conditions in Alberta precluded any real substantive changes. In the 1922 Department of Education Report it was noted the harvest had failed that year and that the government had had to cut back in all departments. This also meant that the Normal School in Edmonton was to be closed, leaving only schools in Camrose and Calgary. Except for a period from 1925 to 1929, during which time a new Normal School was started on the U of A campus (1928), the economic fortunes of the province didn't improve measurably until the end of the 1930s.

Pre-School Child Studies

In 1929, a new Study Group was organized within the ESC to study theories of children's education and learning problems. Much of the concern at the time was with providing the proper learning environment for the pre-schooler as a preventative measure against juvenile delinquency. There appears to have been great interest in the subject. In the following year, a group of fifteen women met twice a month to discuss and present papers on fundamentals of child psychology and their applications to the behavioural problems of children. Other topics included proper literature for children and teaching childcare in high school. Spirited discussions often followed.

The 1930s

In 1932 and 1933 the subject under discussion was the preparation of the child for school. Between 1921 and 1968 kindergarten was not included in the public school system in Edmonton, which meant that many children attended co-operative kindergartens in church basements and community halls in Edmonton. By 1933 the Study Group was investigating children's educational films, radio programs and plays. Interest in pre-school education during this period led CFUW to petition for

U of A Archives: 82-155-75

Minerva–Goddess of Wisdom
Education was the theme when members donned cap and gown for the 1920 parade commemorating the 250th Anniversary of the Hudson's Bay Company. Miss Norrington as Minerva was a commanding figure complete with helmet and draperies over a coat of mail.

children's programming on public radio. In 1936 the Club negotiated with CKUA to have a children's program. Established in 1927 as a public broadcasting station, CKUA was the first educational radio station in Canada. It operated out of the University of Alberta Extension Department, which provided convenient access for such a program. It allowed the Club to expand its influence to CKUA listeners.

Teacher Training

Until Alberta became a province in 1905, education came under federal jurisdiction. At the time of the Club's founding in 1909, the Provincial Department of Education was still relatively new and teaching was in its early stages of being recognized as a profession on the prairies. There were many rural one-room schools staffed by teachers with minimum qualifications who also received minimum pay.

In 1918 an Alberta Teachers' Alliance (ATA), later called the Alberta Teachers' Association, was established for the purposes of improving the educational and financial position of teachers in the province. Improvements were slow in coming. Through the years that the United Farmers Association (UFA) was in power, from 1921 to 1935, the ATA met with a modicum of acceptance. The UFA represented a largely rural constituency whose fortunes were not much different from the teachers, and although they recognized many of the teachers' needs, they chose mainly to ignore them rather than raise the tax base of their constituents.

The 1922 Department of Education Annual Report also stated "the most difficult administrative problem that the School Boards face, and in the presence of which all others seem insignificant, is that of procuring properly qualified and trained teachers. The time has come when our higher education institutions, the university and Normal School should take the necessary steps for the adequate preparation of teachers for secondary school work." The ESC was to turn its attention to a study of standards of teacher training by the end of the decade, and to revisit the issue again and again, as the pendulum swung from a teacher surplus to a teacher shortage through the decades.

Because of an over supply of teachers in Alberta in the early 1930s, the Club felt it was an opportune time to bring up the question of raising the standard of entrance to the Normal School of Alberta. As a result of their research and discussions, the ESC put forward the following resolution, which was passed by the Club and forwarded to the Minister of Education in 1930:

> WHEREAS there is an over supply of certified teachers and
>
> WHEREAS the increased age resulting from such raising of standards would tend to produce new teachers, who being more mature and experienced would have a greater sense of responsibility and therefore be of greater influence in their school and communities, and
>
> WHEREAS such a change would also tend to eliminate those who might be unsuccessful or only temporarily in the profession,
>
> THEREFORE be it resolved that the Women's University Club of Edmonton petition the Minister of Education to require the successful completion of the 12th grade for entrance into Normal School of the Province of Alberta.

The Minister replied that the government did not feel it was an opportune time to act on the resolution, but assured the Club that definite steps would be taken to limit the number of students enrolling in Normal School.

With the election of the Social Credit government in August 1935, the plight of the teachers was acknowledged and acted on. The newly elected Premier, William Aberhart, was a former Calgary school principal and teacher, and many of his cabinet ministers had a teaching background. This certainly set the stage for a conciliatory period.

A Teaching Profession Act was enacted in 1935, which made it legal to refer to teaching as a profession, and the ATA was officially changed to the Alberta Teachers' Association, retaining its acronym ATA. The Social Credit government then slowly moved to implement and improve on many of the educational issues that had languished with the former government, including teachers' pensions, tenure, and collective bargaining. It also instituted larger units of school administration, which led to the coming together of rural school districts and the end of one-room schools.

In the fall of 1935 the Club sponsored a public forum on education that received wide coverage in the Edmonton Journal (September 2, 1935). The article noted the broader aspects of curriculum that were discussed (uniformity of curriculum and textbooks throughout the province) and also the consolidation of rural schools. These were judged to be advantageous to the rural child. Later in the year, Dr. Donalda Dickie spoke further on the subject of curriculum changes at a meeting of the Club. As a leading educator in Alberta and Canada for over 30 years, her expertise was invaluable to the ESC.

Dr. Donalda Dickie, 1883–1972, was one of Canada's foremost educators. She promoted John Dewey's progressive education in Alberta and throughout Canada. She was educated at Queen's University, Ontario, Columbia University, New York, Oxford University, England and the University of Toronto, Ontario. Through teaching at Normal Schools, revising curricula and writing textbooks she attempted to shift the focus in education from being subject matter-centered to being problem-centered. She authored more than 40 books, including many childrens' history readers. As an expert of condensation, she was able to distill the essence of historical facts for childrens' readers. In

Glenbow: ND-3-6336I
Dr. Donalda Dickie

1950 Dr. Dickie won the Governor General's Literacy Award for Juveniles for her history of Canada, *The Great Adventure*; it was later condensed for elementary grade school children into *My First History of Canada*. Miss Dickie, a well-known Edmonton teacher and a valued member of the Club, transferred to the Calgary Normal School in 1923 but returned in the 1940s. She was a leading member of the ESC and on the Club Executive (VP twice) throughout the 1940s. Dr. Dickie was honoured with a life membership in the ATA.

Women in Education

By the late 1930s, the ESC's attention included status of women issues. The EPSB brought a resolution forward in 1937 stating, "elementary schools of more than five rooms should not have women as principals." The Club strongly opposed the motion. Such action presumably led the ESC to concentrate on women in administrative positions in education during the next few years. In 1937 they produced a report entitled "A Psychological Analysis of Differences which Might Hinder Women Applicants for Positions of Administration in Education" that provided a basis for discussion. Contributions by Club members to women in education issues are detailed in *Status of Women*.

Vocations Special Committee–Guidance and Training

Vocational training was an integral part of CFUW Education policy and one of the first five Standing Committees set up by the Federation in 1919 was Vocations. In the 1920s the Club worked in conjunction with the YWCA in setting up training programs in domestic science and recreation for young women, and devised various means to find employment for young women students in the 1930s. In 1936, during the Depression years and the period of wide unemployment, the Club undertook a survey for the CFUW Vocations Standing Committee. A Special Committee was established under the ESC, headed by Convenor Agnes MacLeod, Head of the U of A School of Nursing, which undertook a *Survey of Conditions of Vocations and Guidance in Edmonton*. Areas of concern included the quality and type of facilities available for training of young people and appropriateness of guidance instruction. Were women being provided with information regarding non-traditional jobs available to them? The results of the surveys conducted by Edmonton and other CFUW Clubs were compiled into a pamphlet distributed to educational institutions and businesses.

Educational Trends in the 1940s

Traditional versus Progressive Learning

Because of their university backgrounds, Club members were often on the vanguard of practical educational change. Club members were aware of many educational trends and issues, and were confident in their ability to take action when needed. However, the work of the ESC did not always result in a Brief or Resolution. In some cases a great deal of time was spent simply studying the ramifications of new educational trends. This was the case in the early 1940s.

One of the trends in education during that time was the re-defining of the traditional or subject-centred curricula of the past, and the subsequent move toward progressive or problem-centred learning. In the 1942/43 season, a special Curriculum Study Group, under ESC Convenor Mrs. H. E. (Ethel) Smith carried out an extensive study of the School Board's First Bulletin on the *Revision of the High School Programme*.

In 1944 the ESC looked at "current trends in the philosophy of secondary education and their relationship to the development of democratic citizenship," a study recommended by the National ESC. After examining the underlying philosophies of the old and new types of education, gleaned from a variety of sources, the Committee came to the conclusion that "the needs of youth would probably be well served by incorporating the best procedures of both systems into the secondary school." (ESC report, 1944)

Ethel Smith was one of the leading members of the ESC during the 1930s and 1940s. Her husband was one of the first staff members of the U of A Education Department (1930–1955) and was appointed Dean of the Faculty (1950). Her interest in educational matters ranged from pre-school child care to adult education. In 1943 she was named the Club's representative to the inaugural meeting of the Alberta Association for Adult Education.

Adult Education

Another educational development of the forties was the formalization of adult education in Canada. Courses were established to meet the demands of returning servicemen and women for their re-entry into the workforce.

In 1943 Dr. E. A. Corbett addressed the Club regarding adult education in a talk entitled "Education of the Soldier Citizen." As Director of the Canadian Association for Adult Education and former Director of the U of A Extension Department, he was recognized as a leading proponent of adult education and led Alberta educators in establishing a strong adult education program. The Club's connection with the U of A Extension Department and adult education dated back to the time of Jessie Montgomery, whose lifetime work with the Department is profiled in *Public Affairs*.

The first meeting of the Alberta Association for Adult Education was held in Edmonton in October 1943. Operating with a grant from the Department of Education, the Association (changed in 1945 to Alberta Education Association) provided information to all Albertans regarding adult education, assisted in the development of community action programs and coordinated conferences. Following Mrs. Smith as Club representative was Chrissie Wootton who served on the Executive Committee of the Association in the late forties.

Teacher Shortages

Some concerned groups realized that there would be great pressure on the school system at the end of the war because many qualified to teach had left the profession for better paying positions. Schools were crowded and the remaining teachers were over-worked and underpaid. The Club strongly supported a CFUW Calgary Resolution that asked the Provincial Government to recognize the probable shortage of teachers after the war, secure gifted students for teacher training, and give financial support for such a program. The Resolution also urged the Federal Government to give grants-in-aid to the province for recruiting and training of such personnel (1944).

The national war effort had done much to awaken Canadians to the inequality in education across the country. Education authorities sought an ideal balance between federal and provincial grants for education (ESC report 1945). Although the average amount spent on education per child varied from province to province (this is still the case in Canada today) and the need for a uniform educational system was shown to be a national responsibility, it was agreed by all concerned that there should not be any grant or gifts that would relieve the local authorities of their responsibility. There was much debate nationwide on finding this ideal funding balance.

Teaching Opportunities

Peggy Rootes, who taught at several two-teacher high schools in rural Alberta in the 1940s, was asked how she got the job. "You just answered an ad in the paper," she replied. "There were always two to three, even four columns for high school teachers in the Edmonton Journal— there was no shortage of schools looking for teachers, and you were expected to teach the whole range of subjects." These situations only aided the cause of the ATA and supportive groups such as the ESC in their quest for improved teaching standards. The ESC continued to be involved over the next decade with issues related to teacher training and certification.

Not everyone anticipated the continued shortage of teachers after the war. The Alberta Boards of Education and others had hoped that former teachers who had left during the war would return to the classroom. Instead, many veterans returned to university for up-grading or to prepare for entirely different and better paying positions. This made the situation even worse for the Alberta education system.

In some cases the reaction of the Department of Education to the teacher shortage was to authorize unqualified personnel to take charge of classrooms, particularly in the rural areas. In other cases, whole school populations were registered as correspondence pupils so that their work could then be classified as being handled by certified teachers in the government's Correspondence Branch. This was known as the "sitter system"–such classes lasted from 1946 to 1960.

Alberta Education Council (AEC)

To arouse the public's interest in the issue of the teacher shortage and teacher recruitment, a new version of the earlier Alberta Education Association was formed in 1946, the Alberta Education Council (AEC). It invited public representation of 21 groups with an interest in education to come together to form a Council. Its primary purpose was to arouse public interest and to work together to promote and improve legislation relating to all phases of elementary and secondary education in Alberta. The AEC also took on the sponsorship of Education Week to publicize educational activities. Many members were involved in the activities of the AEC during this period. In 1952, Club member Chrissie Wootton assumed Chair of the Education Week Committee and detailed a host of activities the job entailed–it was a full agenda.

The Club had representation on the AEC from the time of its inception and several members served on the Executive, including Mary Butterworth and Helen Sinclair. Mary Butterworth was Secretary of the first Council in 1948 while she was an EPSB Trustee (see also Status of Women). Helen Sinclair, who represented the Club for many years, was elected President of AEC for a three-year term in 1965. Upon her retirement, Helen Sinclair was the recipient of many accolades for her leadership in promoting the work of the Council.

The 1950s

Similar conditions that prevailed in the post-war period of the 1940s were to confront the Alberta School Board authorities in the 1950s. Edmonton in particular faced a further problem with the great influx of people to Alberta following the oil strike at Leduc in 1947, which meant a renewed demand for qualified teachers and school facilities. To meet these new challenges various proposals were put forward to both levels of government, stressing the need for additional government grants for facilities and to secure gifted students for teaching.

Dr. M. E. Lazerte, retired Dean of the Faculty of Education, headed a commission that looked at some of these issues. The Committee recommended that students receive greater federal aid for education in order to promote an equalization of opportunity for all students and to attract some of the best to enter education. The report of the Lazerte Commission provided a basis of study for the ESC in the early 1950s.

Teacher Training and Certification

Background to Teacher Training in Alberta

A two-year program leading to a B Ed was offered by U of A Graduate Studies from 1921-1939. Through to 1945 teacher training was also available variously at Normal Schools in Camrose, Calgary or Edmonton under the aegis of the Alberta Department of Education. In 1929 a new Normal School was built on campus for the Department. Known today as E. A. Corbett Hall, the facility then housed the U of A's new School of Education. In 1935 the School's status was raised to College of Education and integration of the existing B Ed program followed by 1939. In 1942 full Faculty status was attained. In December 1944, the Board of Governors at U of A approved a memorandum of agreement between the University and the Government of Alberta by which all teacher education in the province of Alberta was taken over by the University. Under the agreement, the Minister of Education still retained control of policy for the training of teachers, but the University undertook to provide "the programs and courses of instruction for certification of teachers in the elementary, intermediate and high-school grades of Alberta Schools." All staff of the Edmonton and Calgary Normal Schools, including library and office staffs, were to become members of the staff of the Faculty of Education, and the physical assets of the Normal Schools were to be placed at the disposal of the University of Alberta.

This was the first instance in Canada of a provincial university offering integrated programs of academic and professional subjects for teacher education. Though received with mixed feelings, it proved to be a genuine pioneering step and was later copied in other provinces. (*A History of the University of Alberta 1908-1969*, Walter H. Johns, pp. 192, 193)

In November, 1951, **Hilda Neatby,** the only woman on the Massey Commission, was entertained at the home of Club President Winnifred Long. She later addressed the Club in 1953. Miss Neatby was recognized as one of Canada's leading educationalists. She had followed up her work on the Commission with a personal critique of the school system, called So Little for the Mind. She felt that society was regressing in its quality of education and that the tendency was to skirt unequal abilities in students in order to give a child what he can do, not what he ought to try to do. One member related that when she joined the Club in 1957 the book had just been published and inspired much debate, for Miss Neatby was a noted traditionalist in the field of education.

The ESC feared that the standards of teacher training might be relaxed because of the teacher shortages. Always alert to such problems, they took it upon themselves in the 1950s to make regular detailed studies of the standards of teacher training at the U of A. In 1954 a Resolution was sent to the Provincial Government to the effect that the ESC opposed any action of the Provincial Government which would lower entrance requirements for the Faculty of Education at the U of A, and shorten the training period required for certification of teachers. A meeting followed the Resolution with appropriate government officials and letters were sent to members of parliament.

The ESC submitted a detailed summary report to the Club dealing with teacher certification. It included recommendations for entrance requirements and required courses for all teacher training in the Faculty of Education. The committee outlined what they felt were minimum acceptable standards for each level of the teaching from grade school through high school. Copies were sent to the Department of Education, the Edmonton Public School Board and school superintendents.

By the late 1950s the school system was to face many new challenges. With the advent of TV and space age technology, there was an opening up of educational thought in different directions.

In Alberta the 1950s had begun with an education debate spawned in part by the Massey Commission on the Development of Arts, Letters and Sciences, which outlined among other issues the place of humanities in secondary school education.

It emphasized the role of humanities versus the new curriculum, which was felt to be too utilitarian. The decade ended with debate surrounding the findings of the Alberta Cameron Royal Commission on Education.

The Alberta Cameron Royal Commission on Education

The Cameron Royal Commission was established on December 31, 1957 to conduct a comprehensive survey of the various phases of the elementary and secondary school systems of the province. It was to pay particular attention to programs of study and pupil achievement. The terms of reference included seven areas: curricular programs, age of entrance to school and related requirements, special services (including guidance counseling, health services), physical facilities, quality and supply of teachers and the relationship of schools to the community and industry. The Club responded with a Brief and personal presentation to the Commission in 1958 that focused on curriculum and standards of education.

In all, 280 recommendations were made to the Commission from the public. Some of the key issues were the upgrading of teacher qualifications to a university degree, community colleges, revamping of school programs with greater emphasis on language, math and sciences and reinstitution of grade 10 and 11 departmental exams. Many of the concerns the ESC had regarding standards of teacher training and curriculum were addressed by the Commission, but implementation was not always immediate and the ESC maintained its watchdog role throughout the 1960s.

English as a Second Language

In 1953 the Club was asked to assist with teaching English to a group of displaced women from Central Europe who were working as kitchen help at the Aberhart Hospital. Because of their working hours, they had been unable to attend the English classes offered at Victoria Composite High School. Lucile Kane, who was Convenor of a Displaced Persons Committee at the time, remembers asking Lillian Munroe and Kathleen Teskey to assist with the project. She remembers that the women, with the assistance of Mary Crawford a gifted linguist, gathered up books from the Alberta Government and EPSB. The hospital gave them a room to teach in. The dozen or so women were very eager students and hoped to get better jobs after learning English. Lillian Munroe and Kathleen Teskey taught the women for four years, resulting in a lifelong association between the teachers and their pupils.

The 1960s

Guidance Counseling

One area that the ESC continued to watch was that of guidance counseling. Although the matter had been addressed by the Commission, there appeared to be no follow-up. In November 1962 the ESC Convenor, Mrs. Fullerton, reported that they had embarked on an extensive fact-finding study of vocational guidance as it was practiced in Edmonton and surrounding areas. The results of their studies were reported in the Edmonton Journal, April 16, 1963 under the heading "Varsity Women's Group Raps School Guidance Program." The Committee claimed that there were no guidelines or stated objectives at the high school level and the "special services staff" carrying out the guidance counseling appeared to be understaffed, overworked and lacking the necessary facilities.

Education Study Group

When the Club rewrote its Constitution in the mid 1960s, the Education Standing Committee, which had been a basic component of the Club since its inception, was renamed a Study Group. Whereas the Standing Committee had made regular reports at each April meeting, the Study Group operated on a more informal schedule. It continued to monitor issues relating to school curriculum and attended meetings of the EPSB into the 1970s.

As a wrap-up to all their studies carried out through the previous years on curriculum and teacher training, the Education Study Group put together a comprehensive guide to Edmonton's public school system (1970). It incorporated in one place every facet of public education, from the various school acts to details on administration, teacher qualifications and salaries, school financing including federal-provincial agreements, school facilities (number of schools, type, required dimensions of playground space), teacher/pupil ratios, textbooks and finally library services. The 37-page guide was made available to the public through Hurtig's Book Store for $.25. Even today this major review of the public education system remains of value for comparative studies.

Continuing Education for Women

By the mid 1960s there was growing public interest in continuing education for adults and the efforts of many groups came together to further the cause. From CFUW's standpoint, the interest was particularly centred on women. Under the guidance of National President Laura Sabia, a Resolution was passed at the CFUW Triennial in Winnipeg in 1964 resolving that:

CFUW provide active and immediate leadership in the field of continuing education. And further that CFUW support and assist any programs undertaken by the government to promote the retraining of professional women whose careers had been interrupted by marriage.

That same year, the Edmonton Club's Education Chair attended a conference on *Continuing Education for Women*. Two Club members were appointed to a Consulting Committee for "Women in Continuing Education" with the U of A Extension Department. By fall of 1964, a new Study Group called Continuing Education for Women was formed.

In October 1965, Laura Sabia attended a regional conference in Calgary of the Alberta CFUW Clubs. The theme of the conference was continuing education for women "Your Future is Present, is your Education Past?" Following the meeting, Mrs. Sabia was invited to Edmonton and was guest speaker at a special tea in her honour. She was interviewed by the Edmonton Journal and had this to say about women and education:

CFUW is taking a survey of women graduates which will try to ascertain how many women graduates want to go back to get a further degree. When the survey comes out, it is the responsibility of every club to do something with the answers. We need to shed the 'feminine mystique' and assume responsibility as intellectual equals–society needs to draw leaders from the best brains available. (Edmonton Journal, October 26, 1965)

In addition to individual member participation in the survey, the newly formed Continuing Education for Women Study Group conducted a preliminary investigation into the existing opportunities for continuing education at various institutions of higher learning in both the United States and Canada. Under the direction of Helen Dawson, a political economist, a more complete national survey of universities across Canada was drawn up to determine how many would allow part-time study. It was discovered that there was only one–Concordia in Montreal. The results were combined with the work of other CFUW Clubs and a compilation, known as the *CFUW Continuing Education Survey,* was published by the University of Toronto Press (1968). It was distributed to clubs, universities, major public libraries, women's organizations and other institutions across Canada for an initial fee of $5.

In 1966 the Study Group (which later evolved into the Status of Women Study Group) carried out a further needs assessment of mature women at university with regard to financial aid and daycare. They were encouraged by Laura Sabia as head of a coalition of women's groups, to submit their additional findings to the as yet unnamed commission on the status of women that was being proposed. Six recommendations were sent to the Royal Commission on the Status of Women in Canada after it was established in 1967, the results of which are discussed in _Status of Women._

The above questionnaires, surveys and submissions on _Continuing Education for Women_ helped form CFUW policy. The Federation and local Clubs began to look at new ways of supporting women in advanced education through the establishment of permanent endowment funds–the CFUW Charitable Trust Fund for national fellowships and the Academic Awards Fund for the Club's Mature Women's Bursaries. The latter became a major thrust of the Edmonton Club's energies in the 1970s and is discussed in the following chapter on _Academic Awards._

The 1970s

The Education Study Group continued to focus on various aspects of the school curriculum, including standards of literacy of high school students, social studies, second language programs and sex education (urging that it be taught). They also put forward several initiatives regarding the Status of Women in Administration (See _Submissions,_ 1975). However, the role of the Group was to change over the decade. Instead of being a general advocate on behalf of many aspects of education reform, separate groups with special interests emerged within the Club.

In November 1973, members of the Club toured Evelyn Unger School for Children with Learning Difficulties. From this experience a special interest group was formed to find out what pressure could and should be put on the government to provide better funding for specialized schooling. Letters were sent to the appropriate authorities.

In 1979, the International Year of the Child, a special interest group addressed the issue of speech therapy. It was later acknowledged that their lobbying had played an instrumental part in preventing dissolution of the Speech Therapy Program in the Edmonton public schools.

The 1980s and 1990s

The last full agenda proposed by the Education Study Group was in the 1979/80 term. In it the Convenor proposed to focus on "the child not best served by standard educational arrangements." Out of these studies came a number of Briefs, one of which was presented to the Task Force on Gifted and Talented Students (1982), another to the Task Force on Children with Learning Disabilities (1979), and yet another dealing with Mature Students (1982).

Many Club members who were parents became involved in issues relating to their children's education. They often served in key positions of community-based organizations, such as the popular parent-run co-operative pre-schools. They also served on the Parent/Teacher (PTA) Associations, which had found new relevance in the 1980s, as well as on Parent Advisory Committees for the new and varied bilingualism programs. It was through her work as Chair of the Edmonton Public School Parent Advisory Committee that Joan Cowling (Club President 1988–90) gained support for her successful bid for Public School Trustee. During a hiatus from Club involvement, she served on the EPSB from 1980 to 1992 and was Chair of the Board for three separate terms. Other parent members were involved with the Canadian Parents for French Association, and Associations for Gifted and Talented Students and Children with Learning Disabilities.

There were several attempts to revive the Education Study Group in the mid-eighties. A small group of concerned members were involved in the 1986 School Board elections by co-sponsoring two very successful forums for the large slate of candidates in both the public and separate school systems. In 1987, a fledgling education group organized a public forum in conjunction with a parent/teacher organization at a local school to discuss changes to the Provincial School Act, Bill 59. Through her concern for educational matters one of the members, Rose Rosenberger, ran for the EPSB and was elected in 1989 for two terms. She was subsequently elected to the Edmonton City Council in 1995. Club interest in education continues, and action is taken when issues present themselves.

Adult Literacy

1990 was declared International Literacy Year (ILY) and members again became involved in the role of tutoring, as they had in earlier years. CFUW made literacy a priority in co-operation with ILY and asked for members to volunteer as literacy tutors and to support community literacy programs. Several members began tutoring for Prospects for Learning, an Edmonton adult literacy project. Notable was Margaret Reine who as Coordinator of Volunteers with Prospects for Learning encouraged others to become involved.

Life-Long Learning

The term 'life-long learning' was used in the 1960s and was central to the theme of the Worth Report which looked at the future of education in Alberta from 1970 to 2000. By the end of the century its meaning had greater relevance.

The future of women in Canada lies in creative application of life experience and knowledge through life-long learning–this was the essence of a talk given by Dr. Martha Piper, Vice President of the U of A who gave the opening address to the Club in September 1996. Life-long learning was also the highlight of a provincial meeting of the CFUW in October of that year. Members were told that the criteria for success had previously been linked to education, responsibility, loyalty to employers and hard work. Now we must look for vision, creativity and connections–we have to work smarter–life-long learning is a requirement. This was not news to members of CFUW Edmonton, for it could be said that the Interest and Study Groups had provided such a learning experience from the Club's inception.

Members of Boards

CFUW Edmonton members have served on both sides of the educational table. They have served as School Board Trustees and as representatives in government, university and EPSB advisory committees. They have represented somewhat different perspectives by serving on the Alberta Teachers' Association Executive, as teachers in the public and separate school systems, and members of the U of A faculty. The combined experience of these members indicates the depth of talent that the Club was able to draw on for leadership in its quest for improved educational standards in Alberta. These members also set a role model, and their accomplishments reflected not only on educational matters but also on their involvement in public affairs and the status of women.

Members who served as EPSB Trustees include Jenny S. Hill (1914–1916); Mrs. E. T. Bishop, first woman Chair of the EPSB (1921–1930, Chair 1923), and Mrs. W. D. Ferris (1931–1934); Mary Butterworth, second woman Chair of the Board (1946–1957, Chair 1955–1956); Shirley Forbes (1961–1962, 1974–1983, Chair 1977–1978, 1981–1982); Helen Sinclair (1963–1964); Lois Campbell (1969–1974); Catherine Ford (1974–1980); Joan Cowling (1980–1992, Chair 1983–1985, 1986–1987, 1989–1990) and Canadian School Boards' President (1992); Dr. Lila Fahlman (1986–1989) and Rose Rosenberger (1989–1995).

Members who served on the Executive of the ATA include Mary Crawford; Marian Gimby, first woman President of the Association in 1951–1953; Jean Saville (1959–1961) and Fran Savage (President 1990–1993). Mary Crawford was a charter member of the Alberta Education Association and President (1922–1923). Helen Sinclair was President of the later Alberta Education Council from 1965 to 1968.

Many women were named to advisory boards throughout the Club's history, yet there is no accurate record of their names and positions. It is known that among the later appointments to advisory bodies on curriculum and education were Sheila Abercrombie, who was named to the Advanced Education Joint Committee of Government and High Schools (1960), Edith (Mickey) McCannel, member of an Advisory Committee on Further Education and Rita Calhoun, member of an Advisory Committee on University Affairs–named by the Honourable A. E. Hohol, Minister of Advanced Education and Manpower) in the 1970s.

Mickey McCannel was later nominated by the Club to the U of A Senate in 1972 and served for a four-year period. Club nominee Georgina Brooks followed her on the Senate in 1975. Although not a Club nominee, member Margaret Skelley served on the U of A Senate from 1994 to 2000. Dr. Geneva Misener, Lucile Kane and Mary Crawford were earlier Senate members.

$\mathcal{A}$cademic Awards

At its inception, one of the two aims of the Alberta Women's Association was to offer "a scholarship of $50 to the freshman woman whose record of scholarship shall be the highest." Since that time the Club has continuously supported and initiated awards to university students. These awards have taken various forms from gold medals to books to dollars–all of which reinforce the dedication of the membership to encouraging women in education.

In the early days there were three separate awards offered: The Alberta Women's Association Scholarship, a Matriculation Scholarship, and a Gold Medal. The initial scholarship of $50 was awarded in 1911 (the Alberta Women's Association Scholarship) leading to the eventual establishment in 1914 of an Endowment Fund for a scholarship for women with an "incentive to scholarly work and to intellectual idealism." The Fund consisted of $600 in cash plus a $200 mortgage assumed by Mrs. Rutherford and Maude Bowman. Unfortunately, the value of the mortgage declined considerably over the next few years and by 1917/18 there was not enough money in the fund to pay for the $50 scholarship. In 1920, $250 was added to the Fund to enable the Club to provide for this award.

In 1917 a $25 award was offered to a Grade XI matriculating female of Alberta with the highest standing in English, Latin, French and History and with marks not less than 75%. This was payable upon registration at the University of Alberta. In the 1920s the amount was raised to $100 for a Grade XII woman student even though there was some difficulty in awarding it as possible candidates were not being notified in time for them to make the decision to attend the University of Alberta. Monies continued to be set aside for this scholarship for the following four decades although it was not awarded on a regular basis.

In 1914 the first Gold Medal, valued at $30, was given upon graduation to a student obtaining the highest standing in eight senior courses required in the 3rd and 4th years in the Faculty of Arts and Sciences, providing an average mark of not less than 75% was obtained. Men as well as women were eligible. This continued to be awarded until 1942/43.

In 1914, The Student Aid Fund, later known as the Student Loan Fund, was established using money from Club initiation fees. University President Tory had been asked if any student was in need of financial support. His reply of "several cases, and $50 could be used to great advantage in one case" led to the establishment of this fund. It was advertised, as: "Small loans are available to women students who have completed two years of University work. Loans are interest free for one year after which interest at the rate of 3% per annum will be charged." Throughout the 1930s and 1940s the Loan Fund was maintained and actively used. By 1958 it was discontinued because other sources of financial aid were available and it was decided that the money would serve the cause of education better by putting it into the Bursary Award.

In the early 1930s, the Club established a Scholarship Fund which incorporated all awards being given by the Club to University of Alberta students. An appointed member assisted the University Bursar to administer these awards. Surplus Club funds (over $100) were to be put into this Fund from which a scholarship of $100 would go to a Grade XII student (Matriculation), one of $50 to a first year student (Endowment) and a gold medal to a graduating student, male or female.

In 1942/43, a special committee on scholarships, under the guidance of Mabel Patrick, was formed to review the awards being offered. They recommended discontinuing the Gold Medal and changing the Matriculation Scholarship to a bursary awarded on the basis of Grade XII record and financial need. The amount of the bursary was to be increased to $150 and was open to women students entering the University from Alberta high schools who completed grades X to XII in not more than four years.

By 1945/46, the Bursary Fund had $3100 invested and approximately $500 in interest. It was decided that special one-time awards would be given out using this interest. Four $25 awards were given to ex-service women on the basis of average standing for a full year's work. $325 was given to a graduate woman student of the class of 1946 under the following conditions: the winner was not to be contemplating marriage, it was preferable that graduate work would be done at some other university, financial need as well as academic excellence was to be indicated, and the preference would be for an ex-service woman. This was awarded in 1946.

Throughout the years, extra Club funds and various fundraising events sustained these awards, plus others given on a one-time basis. Monetary support was given to awards initiated by the University, especially during the war years, and regular contributions were made to the national CFUW scholarships.

Johanna (Magera) Michalenko, remembers her first introduction to CFUW Edmonton. When she graduated in 1936 from Home Economics, she still owed the University of Alberta $36.00, but she also had to get a wisdom tooth removed which would cost $5.00. The dentist, Dr. Bulyea, extracted the tooth for $3.00 since Johanna allowed some Australian students to watch. Mabel Patrick, a Club member and Home Economics Director, knew of the Club's Student Loan Fund. Johanna applied and was given a loan for $39.00 to cover the two expenses. (From a personal anecdote recounted on the 50th anniversary of her graduation.)

By the late 1960s, the Matriculation Scholarship was given over to the University to administer. It was by then self-sustaining and continues to be awarded every year in the name of the Club. The criteria remain: academic excellence, a graduating student (male or female) may receive it, and it is carried over for one year if the student maintains his or her grades in the first year of university.

During this time, a reassessment of the focus of Club support for education led to the establishment of a fund called "The Mature Women's Bursary Fund" which would be administered entirely by the Club. This development followed the Club's study and submission of a Brief in 1970 to the Royal Commission on the Status of Women that stated among other items, the need to encourage mature women to return to University. Also noteworthy was the suggestion that part-time studies should be allowed. Enid Crockett, Joan Wensel and Avery Fleming prepared and presented this Brief.

The Club offered its first mature (over age 25) woman's bursary of $250 in 1971, to be administered by a Bursary Committee composed of two Club members (Joan Wensel, Rita Calhoun) and the Dean of Women (Isabel Munroe). This was to be on a trial basis for one year and it was hoped that the offering would be helpful in determining the degree of need and the amount and type of assistance required, i.e. bursaries, loans and grants. The large number of applicants (50) with obvious financial need led to the following actions: an appeal to other groups for assistance and contact with the government indicating the

Celebrating 25 years of the Bursary Program

Members who helped establish the Mature Women's Bursary Program and led major funding-drive (1971–1976) were honored at AAF meeting in January, 1996

Seated, L to R: Jean Monckton, Jean Saville, Betty Gravett

Standing, L to R: Margaret Skelley, Carol (Carbyn) Bustin, Robin Robinson, Barbara Blackley, Tammy Irwin, Rita Calhoun

financial pressure being faced by female students, especially those on social allowance. Fourteen bursaries were awarded as a result of additional donations to the Club by the Kinette Club and Friends of the University. One of the beneficial side effects of the bursary activity led to an active, personal involvement by Club members with mature women students on campus. A former bursary recipient was eventually hired by the University to become the Mature Student Advisor on campus.

In 1972 the Academic Awards Fund was formally established with the goal of setting up a perpetuating fund to be used for bursaries for mature women in need attending the University of Alberta. The Constitution established the executive and defined recipients and distribution of funds. They also applied for and received charitable status from Revenue Canada. It was understood that this fund could not provide large dollar support for a student, but could help them with unexpected expenses. The process for evaluating applicants remains essentially the same today. Members of the Academic Awards Committee meet individually with the students who have submitted a detailed application. This personal approach not only allows an assessment of the student's needs, but also provides the opportunity to give moral support and guidance, which often are as necessary as the monetary support to struggling students.

Throughout the early 1970s, the Club met with various government ministers and departments to discuss their concerns regarding women students, particularly those on social allowance with family responsibilities. Discussions were also held with the University concerning student loans and their repayment requirements. In 1982, Club President Jean Lund presented a Brief to the University Senate's Task Force on the Mature Student. By now the Club was recognized as an organization with a knowledgeable interest in aiding mature students, with a particular focus on women and single parents.

Over the years, appeals to foundations and associations for funding allowed the Club to continue to distribute bursary funds to a growing number of students. The Winspear Foundation and Friends of the University were especially outstanding in their support. Fundraising activities by the Club involved garage sales, fashion shows, bridge parties, book sales, auctions, and special events. In 1976, a donation by the daughters of Elsie Mitchell Newland (Doris Tanner and Enid Tredger) provided the money for a bursary which continues to be named in her honour. In 1980/81, the largest bursary awarded each year was to be given in the name of Margaret Brine for her long-time support. In 1982, the Club received a $10,000 bequest from Frances Dorothy McConnell's estate. This was transferred to the Academic Awards Fund to be used at their discretion and with the understanding that an award be given out annually in her name. Thus the Fund has grown through diligence and dedication. As of 2000, 676 students have received $267,316 since its inception in 1971.

Elsie Mitchell Newland graduated from the University of Alberta after her marriage and the birth of her two daughters, something rarely done at the time. She was a Club member and President (1940–41) and active in the Scholarship Committee. The intent of her daughters' memorial donation was to "encourage older women to return to university."

Frances McConnell was born in Edmonton but lived most of her life in Red Deer. A keen music lover, she would drive up for symphony weekends and stay with friends who were members of the University Women's Club, thus learning about the Club's support for mature women students. The McConnell Bursary is named in honour of this generous and committed woman.

Margaret Brine
A well-known benefactor of the performing arts in Edmonton, Margaret Brine held two degrees in Classics from the University of Alberta. In the 1920s she went off to Paris to study at the Sorbonne and to climb the Alps. In fact, she climbed several mountains in her lifetime, including the Matterhorn. In later years both Sir Edmund Hillary, the first man to climb Everest, and Tenzing Norquay, his famous Sherpa guide, visited her in Edmonton. Margaret Brine was described as having dignity and class, but she was obviously a woman of action as well, as her vast range of activities would indicate. Her husband's financial success as a house builder in Edmonton enabled Margaret Brine to pursue her philanthropy, but she also enjoyed being involved with the various groups that she supported and was a Club member for many years. Mrs. Brine's initial support and generous contributions to the Club's Academic Awards Fund gave members a great lift and in appreciation for her efforts, the largest bursary each year and the graduate women's scholarships are given in her name.

In 1985 an additional $5000 from the McConnell estate enabled the Club to offer three graduate scholarships, which were the Jubilee Scholarships for $1000 each in honour of the Club's 75th Anniversary (one each in Humanities and Social Sciences, Natural Sciences or Engineering, and Fine Arts and Education). From this money, $500 was also given to the Red Deer Club to assist with the establishment of their scholarship program. The following year an anonymous donation by a Club member provided for a graduate scholarship for 1986. Then in 1987, the Fund received a large endowment from Margaret Brine's estate. This money provided the capital base required for establishment of a permanent scholarship fund for graduate women, to be called the Margaret Brine Scholarship(s). In 1996 two categories of scholarship were established, one for students at the Master's level and one for students at the PhD level. The application process and awarding of the scholarships are the responsibility of Club members. The current year winners are requested to make a presentation describing their research at the Academic Awards Fund annual general meeting. This provides the opportunity for Club members to focus on the activities of Academic Awards and meet with the scholarship winners. This fund has awarded $43,500 to 40 graduate females since 1985.

Credit for the success of the awards program over the years lies with the membership of CFUW Edmonton. Without their energy, time, devotion and donations this ongoing program would not be possible.

Why do women need the scholarships and bursaries offered by the Club? The following account speaks for itself.

> She comes in brightly, her nose pink from the cold November wind outside, and drops her heavy backpack on the floor. We begin with some small talk about the icy roads, the unusual amount of snow and the bitter weather. Her classes are going well she says eagerly. Her last paper was a challenge but she got a good mark and she's looking forward to her practicum experiences later on. Yes, her two children are still living with her, and no, there is still no maintenance or child support from her husband. The student loan appeal was sent in on time as requested but the backlog is such that she doesn't expect to hear anything until perhaps the last week in December.
>
> There have been a few changes since she applied. She has had to pay some fees she hadn't expected for certain computing services and practicum costs. Her son fell getting onto the school bus and chipped a front tooth, and her daughter has grown out of last year's winter

boots. We tell her about the dental services she can get at the Faculty of Dentistry for herself and her children. While we're at it, we mention the cheaper prescriptions available at the Health Sciences Clinic, but she already knew about that. She says it's hard to concentrate on her studies when she doesn't know whether she'll have enough money to carry on after Christmas, and though she hates to use credit cards she has lately begun to in order to cover some of the essentials. The campus Food Bank has been a godsend on more than one occasion.

We explain who we are, that we are all volunteers, women with university degrees who believe in the value of women's education. Many of us went through difficult times when we were at university, and we want to give something back and support those currently struggling. We tell her our club has been raising and investing money for 25 years and giving out the interest in bursaries each December. We point out the fact that interest rates have more than halved in the last two years and that our available money is therefore limited. That we wish we could help everyone who applies, but that we can't. That it's really hard to decide who gets a bursary and who doesn't. Gently we say, 'We do understand how very hard it is for you to have to ask for money. But we need you to tell us why we should support *you*'.

And the tears begin. She apologizes and reaches for a Kleenex from the box we have ready on the table. 'I'm so sorry,' she says huskily. 'All I can say is that I'm desperate. I have used up all my savings and spent two and a half years towards my university goals. I can't give up now. I need that degree because more than ever I will need a good job to support myself and my children now we are on our own. I must finish. All my life I've prided myself on my independence. It really hurts to have to ask for money. I planned so carefully but the higher tuition costs and the 'little extras' we now get charged for have changed things. I've been doing really well. I'm good at what I do and I really want to use it on the job. And I'm trying still to be there for my kids. But some days it's so hard. I need help.'

By Pam Laing, CFUWE Newsletter, 1996

Many recipients of CFUW Edmonton scholarships, awards and bursaries have expressed their thanks in the numerous notes the Academic Awards Committee receives. "I can't thank you enough," says one. "Just knowing that such a marvelous group as yours exists has somehow given me renewed vigour at a time when I was beginning to wonder if what I had set out to achieve was a selfish day-dream."

A recipient of the Mature Women's Bursary says: "I am impressed by the Club's sensitivity to the unique needs and circumstances of the mature student. Having faced adversity which ultimately led to academic failure, I am gratified by this positive acknowledgement of my capability. The committee's support and my successful mid-term results have strengthened my resolve to persevere."

The importance of the academic awards is perhaps best expressed in the following from a thank you note from a bursary recipient: "I cannot express here how much of a help this will be to me. Your Federation probably thinks it is just handing out bursaries. What you are actually handing out is [sic] lifelines."

Chapter 3

*P*ublic Affairs

Purpose Two: to arouse and sustain among members an intelligent interest in all aspects of public affairs in the political, social, cultural and scientific fields; to encourage an active participation in such affairs by qualified women; and to promote an opportunity for effectual, concerted action.

Throughout its history the CFUW Edmonton has worked diligently to foster "intelligent interest" and to encourage leadership among women, especially when there were opportunities for social action. Though flying no particular flag of reform, the Club was proactive on many local issues, especially those affecting women. Members quickly learned that women did not need to be major political actors to participate in public affairs. They also learned that one learns by doing.

The Club was involved in community affairs almost from its inception–projects both large and small were undertaken, from major provincial projects to the giving of books, pictures and awards. Study groups were often created to look into particular issues that arose, such as Family and Child Welfare or Penal Reform, or concerns such as library services, heritage preservation and environmental pollution. Not every issue can be detailed here, but some of those that represent the Club's wide interest in public and community affairs are summarized.

In the early days there was considerable interchange between the provincial government and community groups, and the advice of the Club was sought on various issues; on rare occasions members met with the Provincial Cabinet. This rapport continued through the 1960s,

Mrs. Sam Dickson
(Joined in 1911)

Mrs. I. F. (Kathleen) Morrison
(1910s)

Mabel Patrick
(1920)

Mrs. E. K. (Lucile Barker) Kane
(1927)

Maimie Simpson
(1922)

Mrs. W. (Inez) Calhoun
(1920s)

Grace Studholme
(1928)

but gradually changed as the complexity of issues and size of the government grew.

Association with other Women's Groups

From the beginning there was a close working relationship with both the Edmonton YWCA (the Y) and the Local Council of Women (LCW). These relationships continued throughout the Club's history in one form or another. The Club contributed books and magazines to the young women of the YWCA as early as 1910 to 1912 and cooperated with the Y's Education Committee in teaching English to newcomers to Canada.

A close affiliation with the LCW began about 1910. The LCW acted to unify the work of the various women's organizations. Through this central body affiliated societies could express matters of common concern. Minutes of the early days are filled with the agenda of the LCW, for the Club not only discussed and voted on LCW Resolutions, but also proposed their own to the Council. A few of these resolutions are highlighted here as they provide a context in which women worked for social change.

In March 1912 the Club sought support from LCW for a resolution "calling on the problems of cleanliness, ventilation, overcrowded conditions and expectoration on the Strathcona street-cars to be brought before the City Council." Later, the Club supported an LCW resolution asking City Council to construct and maintain public lavatories for women, with entrances as inconspicuous as possible, and to be open at all times, particularly Sunday, when most stores were closed.

There were many important issues, such as women's enfranchisement, the prevention of "Traffic in Women" in Edmonton, equal property rights and venereal diseases (1910s), on which the Club and LCW worked together. In the 1920s and 1930s the Club was concerned about the eyesight of children in the schools, unemployment and re-training of women, and the establishment of a pre-natal clinic. They also addressed the matter of a birth control clinic, believing that it was appropriate when deemed advisable by the doctor for the health and welfare of the patient. Many of these ideas were very progressive for the time.

The Club was an active supporter of fledgling cultural institutions in Edmonton. In 1929 the Club presented a $50 painting to the Edmonton Art Museum (forerunner of the Edmonton Art Gallery) entitled "Splash of Sunlight" (oil on board) by Mary Wrinch (1877–1969) which was significant in a number of ways. It represented the second painting of the Museum's collection (the first one having been given by the Local Council of Women) and had been carefully chosen because it was done by a woman, an established and well-known artist of her day who exhibited with the Group of Seven. This painting remains in the Edmonton Art Gallery's collection.

During the 1930s, a LCW resolution came to the Club regarding *Liberty* Magazine, which was deemed "to be not conducive to the best morals of Canadians and should be excluded from the mails." The moral perspective tended to be emphasized in talks presented during this period, so resolutions of this nature were in keeping with the times. However, the Club was never comfortable with the issue of censorship, and took an equivocal position. General censorship was never part of CFUW's mandate. They did in later years take a strong stand against visual depiction of blatant sexual exploitation in print and other media.

Initially the affiliation with LCW had been considered beneficial both to the Club and to the Council. However, with the increasing amount of business the LCW expected the Club to address, and the growing number of resolutions coming from the CFUW organization itself, the Club reluctantly ended the long-standing affiliation in 1946. In its place an informal association has continued.

Arts and Culture

One of the Club's initial purposes was to enrich the cultural life of the women students at the U of A. In addition to social gatherings and teas, members attempted to enlarge the students' university experiences through art, music, drama and literature. The Club sponsored lectures and plays at Convocation Hall in the Arts building to which they invited female university students. The role the Club played in providing this enrichment revealed much about the lifestyle and interests of its members.

An example of this commitment is found in a 1911 hand written report by Club President Eleanor Broadus, making the suggestion "that the

Club should consider giving to the women students of the university one or more photographs of famous paintings." As Convenor of a Committee on Pictures, she was charged with looking into the cost of such pictures. With the generous assistance of Mr. John A. McDougall, a prominent Edmonton businessman who offered to fund the purchases, Mrs. Broadus was able to make a selection of three prints. She chose from personal visits to print shops and studios in London and Paris. The pictures were presented to the women students on May 1, 1912 and were hung in the rooms of the Wauneita Society in Assiniboia Hall. The whereabouts of these pictures remains unknown.

During this period the Club gave numerous books of an uplifting nature to the girls of the YWCA–works of the English masters, including 15 volumes of Thackery; biographies of Browning, Tennyson and Mathew Arnold and a collection of Victorian poets. By 1912, the YMCA said that they had received a donation of Dickens' works and that their bookshelves were now full. They suggested members provide magazine subscriptions for the Y's Clubroom.

War Efforts

Efforts of the Club during the First World War were mainly directed toward U of A students serving in the military and the Red Cross. "Although we never set out to be a money-raising club in the First World War, we got involved, not for ourselves, but for various causes," stated Mrs. Teviotdale in an early publication.

In 1914, as part of a public relations venture, the Club arranged with the U of A History Department for six lectures on the European War. The graduating girls of Edmonton's two high schools were invited. The lectures

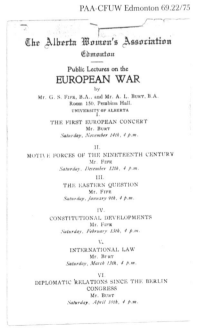

PAA-CFUW Edmonton 69.22/75

The Alberta Women's Association
Edmonton

Public Lectures on the
EUROPEAN WAR
by
Mr. G. S. Fife, B.A., and Mr. A. L. Burt, B.A.
Room 150, Pembina Hall.
UNIVERSITY OF ALBERTA
I.
THE FIRST EUROPEAN CONCERT
Mr. Burt
Saturday, November 14th, 4 p.m.

II.
MOTIVE FORCES OF THE NINETEENTH CENTURY
Mr. Fife
Saturday, December 12th, 4 p.m.

III.
THE EASTERN QUESTION
Mr. Fife
Saturday, January 9th, 4 p.m.

IV.
CONSTITUTIONAL DEVELOPMENTS
Mr. Fife
Saturday, February 13th, 4 p.m.

V.
INTERNATIONAL LAW
Mr. Burt
Saturday, March 13th, 4 p.m.

VI.
DIPLOMATIC RELATIONS SINCE THE BERLIN CONGRESS
Mr. Burt
Saturday, April 10th, 4 p.m.

Program for Series of History Lectures
(1914–1915)

were evidently popular, and on one occasion it was reported that there was a large turnout, including girls from Standard's XI and XII of Edmonton High School, Strathcona Collegiate Institute and Alberta College. For several years the Club also gave an annual gift of $25 to the History Department for books (1914–17).

The student publication, The Gateway, reported in 1918 that the "Women's University Club, whose members have always taken an active knitting interest in the Club, did more this year [knitted socks were a mainstay of the comforts packages]. With Mr. Adam's assistance they presented two plays 'The Troth' and 'Thompson' and devoted the proceeds to the Soldiers' Comforts Club."

By 1919 the Club had entered a new phase. In becoming part of CFUW and in turn part of IFUW, the Club's mandate was considerably enlarged. Although education and the well-being of female students remained constant, their efforts regarding Public Affairs were broadened to include national and international interests.

Library Standing Committee

One of the first Standing Committees named by the national organization (1919) was that of Libraries, and its first convenor was Edmonton member Jessie Montgomery. Under her leadership the charter members initiated comprehensive surveys of library facilities across the country and urged all CFUW clubs to press for action to improve both the facilities and the conditions of the library profession. The Edmonton Club became one of the Federation's leading advocates for improved library services under Miss Montgomery's leadership, and a Library Standing Committee (LSC) was established locally in 1923.

The early activities of the LSC included a preliminary investigation into Edmonton's school libraries and a study of the Library Acts of British Columbia and Ontario, with reference to re-drafting the Library Act of Alberta. Subsequently, members declared Alberta's Act obsolete and provided input on its re-writing (1923/4). By 1927 it was announced that they planned an extensive survey of school libraries in the province and also a general survey for comparative purposes of library grants and regulations in other provinces. It was acknowledged that they had taken on a formidable task. The members were able to complete a survey of the western provinces and a submission was made to the provincial government calling for an increase in grants.

Pembina Hall Library

The Club had not forgotten the students at the University, and set up a library in the Pembina Hall Women's Residence in 1927 at the request of the students. Members of the LSC who were professional librarians helped set up the system and catalogued the books. They filled the shelves by holding periodic book showers at the Club's general meetings and by making small outlays of funds for books. By 1930 it was reported that the library was well used with a student librarian in charge who kept a record of all books used.

University Women's Club Hospital Library

LSC members were also concerned with the education and well being of 'shut-in' children at the hospitals, the U of A Hospital in particular. In 1925 members volunteered to read and instruct the children in an attempt to keep them caught up with their schoolwork. The Club arranged for books to be sent weekly to the hospital from the Department of Extension and Jessie Montgomery arranged story hours once a week. As a special treat the members arranged Halloween and Valentine's Day parties for the young patients.

Twelfth Street Beat, University Hospital Newsletter, Vol. 4, No. 2, Feb., 1965

Although the Club arranged for schoolbooks to be sent to the patients, the hospital itself operated a fledgling library to which the Club also contributed books and volunteers. As the Club's commitment grew through the years and the donation of books increased, the Director of the library suggested that the library be turned over to the Club as the Women's University Club Library in 1935. Thus began a thirty-year commitment.

Library Committee member Mrs. Oestrich and Inga Gelhad choose books for cart that Club members wheeled around the wards (1966).

Volunteer staffing of the Library became the responsibility of the Library Standing Committee and required a great commitment from those involved. By 1940 there were 12 members who regularly volunteered on Friday evenings. Members would go in pairs, wheeling the book trolley around.

By 1949/50 the demands became even greater when the Well's Pavilion (long-term care) was added to the visits. A few years later it was increased again with the addition of polio patients. "In the last 2–3 years we've had a great number of polio patients to deal with. Many are young and restless, so that there is a need for a variety of reading matter—magazines, comics, science fiction to match their interest," stated the LSC Chair in a 1953 report. By this time, members were taking books around twice a week, necessitating an even larger committee. Many friends, Faculty Women's Club members and even students were recruited as volunteers to meet the demands.

By 1960, volunteers were going to the hospital three times a week and needed a regular committee of 20 members. Although their efforts were greatly appreciated—members were told that simply walking through the wards and chatting with the patients justified their expenditure of time and money—it was becoming very time consuming. Furthermore, for about twenty years the books had been housed in any available space; corridors, sun rooms, the basement of the hospital and finally in the Women's Auxiliary Office where volunteers and books fought for space. The library had begun to reach its limit of efficiency, and changes were needed.

An Advisory Committee of Librarians was formed in 1961 to study the incorporation of the existing hospital libraries, including the medical and children's libraries, under the services of a salaried librarian. After a study of library facilities in hospitals across Canada, this committee led by Margaret Greenhill, came to the conclusion that to be of use the library should cease to be an amateur affair. It needed the services of a professional librarian to run it, and a separate room of decent size to house the books.

After much negotiation, the Superintendent of the hospital, Dr. Snell, obtained a room for the library, as well as equipment and shelving. Members of the Club who were professional librarians, including Convenor Olga Shklanka, Norma Friefield, Aleta Vikse, Mary Dodds and Alma Webster, did an inventory of the holdings and catalogued the books. This was much needed, since many of the books were worn, out-of-date and of little interest to the patients. A Dewey Decimal system was instituted. A call went out to the membership for more up-to-date books or monetary gifts to buy new books and magazine subscriptions.

Funding for the books came from several sources. Members donated books and money, book showers were held and some funds were earned through a Magazine Subscription Program. After 1950, $150 was budgeted annually for purchase of books and materials; prior to that it had been $20 annually. The Club also received funding and books from the Ukrainian Women's Benevolent Association for several years, and from the Consulates of Great Britain and the Federal Republic of Germany.

According to LSC Chair, Barbara Blackley in a 1965 report, "We managed in 1962 to set up the Hospital Library on a professional basis offering week-day service to the 1,000 bed hospital. The library is in a large, bright room with good library equipment and has 1700 hard-covered books and 600 pocket books."

Centennial Project

In January of 1964 one of the Club's honorary members, Dr. Allison Proctor, passed away (1880–1964) and left an open bequest to the Club. Because she had been responsible to a considerable degree for getting a teacher for hospitalized children in the 1930s and was instrumental in the Club's involvement in the Hospital Library project, it was hoped to honour the Proctor family, as well as celebrate Canada's Centennial by establishing an improved library facility at the University Hospital.

The LSC suggested the Hospital Library become the Club's Centennial Project. In May, 1965, the Club passed the following motion:

"that the UWC of Edmonton authorize the Executive Committee to make up a committee under the direction of the President to attempt to establish the Proctor Centennial Library as a branch of the Edmonton Public Library in the University Hospital; the financial commitment of the UWC to consist of not more than the $1,000 bequest from Dr. Allison Proctor without further approval of the organization."

Dr. Allison Proctor was one of Alberta's most distinguished social workers, and was particularly well known for her wartime work with the Red Cross Society, for which she received an honorary life membership in 1945. Among her other achievements, she became Commissioner of the Girl Guides of Northern Alberta in 1923 and organized the movement on a provincial scale. She was also President and executive member of the Royal Victorian Order of Nurses (VON) and Honorary President of the Junior Hospital League for five years.

In 1946, Mrs. Proctor became the first woman in Alberta to be awarded the Order of the British Empire (OBE) and the second woman to receive an Honorary Doctorate of Laws degree from the U of A. Tragically both her sons were killed in active duty in World War II. The war work and other achievements of this courageous and vital woman must have been a great influence on the women of the Club, and it was unfortunate that the library did not become a reality.

After a prolonged series of negotiations with the Edmonton Public Library, no agreement could be reached on the name of the library or on funds for the project, and with much regret the project was abandoned. In 1967 the Club handed over the inventory to the Hospital Auxiliary and the $1,000 bequest was donated to the Rare Book Collection of the Peel Library at the U of A.

Public Libraries

The Club had several professional librarians among its membership. Their knowledge was of immense value and prompted many of the recommendations put forward. One of these women was Norma Freifield, who chaired the committee in the 1940s, was involved with the Hospital Library and under whose guidance the recommendations for a National Library were drafted.

Norma Freifield worked as a Librarian at the U of A from 1941–1980. After graduating from U of A with a BA, she took her BLS at the University of Toronto and returned to Edmonton in 1941. She recalled that there were not many openings for librarians and she was taken on as a substitute while the regular librarian was in the Armed Services. Fortunately, she was kept on at the University even after the regular librarian returned. She went on to provide a great deal of expertise to the Club and to the University. In 1980 the University of Alberta honoured her when the Reserve Room in the Cameron Library was named for her.

By the end of the Second World War, there were renewed calls for increased funding for educational institutions, including libraries. CFUW played a leading role in promoting the accessibility of books for public use. They were particularly interested in the area of children's libraries and school libraries. In 1946, the CFUW Library Standing Committee set up a fund to establish Reading Stimulation Grants to assist small, isolated community libraries in Canada. The purpose was to provide hard cover books to stimulate children's reading habits (see *National and International Affairs*).

In 1946 the Club supported action taken by the Post-War Reconstruction Education Sub-Committee calling for the establishment of a Public Library Commission to study the library needs of the province. Under the LSC Convenor, Ruth Hyndman, a letter was drafted to the provincial government recommending the appointment of a Library Commissioner, the establishment of a system of regional libraries in the province and the need for a library building at the U of A.

Although the Public Library Act of 1948 empowered the government to appoint a Provincial Library Supervisor and to provide grants for the establishment of regional libraries, there appeared to be little action taken. In 1949 the Club received a letter from the Alberta Library Association "urging the Club as an organization interested in the promotion of library service, to do all in its power to persuade the provincial government to restore its former grants." Eventually the Library Act of 1956 set the parameters for a series of regional library centres serving a population base of 60,000. The ultimate success of these proposals would depend upon how well the municipalities took advantage of them. It required raising mill rates to qualify for government grants.

Women's groups such as the Alberta Women's Institute, who had worked so diligently through the years to provide library facilities in isolated areas, were encouraged to continue their efforts so that regional library integration programs would become a reality. Alberta had lagged behind other provinces in providing library services and expansion of these services was slow in coming.

In a report to the Club in April 1963, President Margaret Greenhill, on behalf of the LSC, expressed concern about the situation.

A Supervisor of (Public) Libraries has been appointed, but is without a budget or staff and the lack of finances and trained personnel are

The need for improved libraries was illustrated by Sheila Abercrombie, a Club member who was an elementary teacher in the late 1950s. She found very little resource material in the school for her students, especially in the area of Canadian history and literature, and she championed the cause of better school libraries. "When I started teaching Grade 5, there was the most inadequate text, the most boring text, so I spent most of my pay cheque buying stuff—educational materials, books and things for the kids to stimulate interest in history, especially Canadian History. There was not a single book in the school library on the subject. The best source was Maclean's magazine –it was preparing for the upcoming Centennial so did several series on Canadian History. The resources they have now, and the books are marvelous, but there really weren't any at the time."

drawbacks for rural library services in particular-although the U of A Extension Library carries out programs for Central [Provincial] Library Services, the LSC believes that the concept of regional library development involves 'larger units of library service' than that offered by the Extension Department.

Regarding the question of school-public library co-operation, we recommend that they not be combined–it is not a question of good school library service or good public library service, but of the development of both.

Although the Club lobbied for improved public libraries, their main interest was with children's and school libraries.

School Libraries

Between 1958 and 1964 six separate Briefs were prepared by the LSC regarding libraries. The first, and most inclusive, *A Brief Concerning School Library Services,* was presented to the Cameron Royal Commission on Education in 1958. In it, the Club made 11 recommendations regarding school libraries that received wide publicity in the local newspaper. Some of the recommendations were a call for central school libraries with trained librarians, a provincial supervisor of libraries with a recognized library science degree, a compulsory course for all teachers-in-training in the use of library facilities, adequate space for school libraries and better service and lower prices from the School Book Board.

In 1961 another Brief concerning school library development was sent to the Edmonton Public School Board reiterating many of these recommendations. Although the Committee started the Brief by congratulating the EPSB on the appointment of a Library Specialist and for increasing the annual book budget, they felt that the actions taken by the Board fell short of the needed requirements. They recommended that the specialist be upgraded to a Supervisor of School Libraries with adequate staff to carry out citywide programs.

Mrs. Greenhill's 1963 report to the Club (mentioned above) concluded that despite the fact that the government had appointed two groups to study and make recommendations concerning school libraries in the late 1950s and early 1960s, concerned groups were not aware that any of the recommendations had been implemented by 1963. The Club felt that there was a desire to improve service but overall co-operation and leadership was needed. Two further Briefs were sent to the provincial government concerning the need for a Provincial Supervisor of School Libraries and improved public library services.

In an interview in August 1999, Margaret Greenhill recalled her work with the LSC. She said that she became involved because, "To my astonishment I discovered that they [her children] had no school library and trying to get the Parent Teacher Association to do something was not easy because they were generally happy with the Bookmobile in those days. So that was one thing that I was really keen to see [school libraries], and I did quite a lot of work with libraries while I was active with the Club. I was on the Library Committee, doing reports and studies and such."

The Club continued to press for improved school library services through the 1960s, in conjunction with other groups including member CFUW Clubs in Alberta and the Alberta Federation of Home and School Associations. There is no doubt that these combined efforts played a major role in the establishment of school libraries in the province.

The LSC, like the ESC, was dropped as a Standing Committee with the re-writing of the Club Constitution in the mid 1960s. As increased funding became available for libraries within the province after the 1960s, the Club relaxed its lobbying efforts, but has continued its watchdog role.

Peace Initiatives

After World War I, CFUW spent a great deal of effort promoting world peace and disarmament. The IFUW, to which it belonged, was established after the First World War in the belief that by fostering peace and understanding among people of different cultures, the women would have done their best to prevent another such catastrophe as World War I. Clubs were urged to become involved in the "World Peace Activity" from the National Office and to speak out on peace issues. To this end various guest speakers were brought in to address the Club.

Notable among the speakers was Irene Parlby, who was one of the first Canadian women appointed official representative to the League of Nations. She spoke at a dinner meeting in the early 1930s and was subsequently made an honorary member of the Club. In 1934 the Club entertained Winifred Kydd, the young President of the National Council of Women, and one of three Canadian delegates to the League of Nations Disarmament Conference in Geneva.

Several members of the Club, such as Dr. Geneva Misener and Cora Casselman, also had an active interest in international affairs and made an effort to encourage others to become actively involved. It was said of Dr. Misener that international peace and understanding were her abiding passions and in this regard she was very involved with the Women's Committee of the Pan Pacific Conferences, which hoped to further international peace by bringing women together from countries bordering the Pacific. Dr. Misener was appointed a delegate to the 3rd Annual Conference in Honolulu in 1934.

Cora Casselman's interests and concerns were manifested in several ways—through her long-time association with the League of Nations Society, her involvement with the CFUW International Relations Committee on Refugees and through representation as Federal MP at several international conferences in the early 1940s. Between 1942 and 1945, Cora Casselman served as Liberal Member of Parliament for Edmonton East, the first woman elected from Alberta to the House of Commons (See *Status of Women*). In recognition of her long-standing involvement in international affairs, she was chosen as a member of the delegation from Canada to take part in the organizational meeting of the United Nations in San Francisco in 1945, a highlight in a career dedicated to international peace and understanding.

Numerous peace groups appeared on the scene soliciting support in the 1930s. The Club deplored the dissipation of efforts among so many groups and decided to join only the League of Nations. For many years a delegate was sent to meetings and a yearly fee paid to the League of Nations Society.

World War II

By the Second World War, the Club's activities had broadened to include the community at large and members were involved in entertaining servicemen at the Garrison Hostess Club or attending social evenings (dances) at the YMCA United Services Club, all under the auspices of the Club. They also volunteered for the Red Cross, donated to the Spitfire Fund (a City of Edmonton project) and to the War Savings Campaign and made many personal donations of time and money. After the war the Club held "Vanishing Teas" and raised over $1300 for a U of A Memorial Fund (1947). Parcels were also sent to several of the members of the Club serving overseas, including Agnes MacLeod, former Head of Nursing at the U of A. In a letter sent to Club President Lucile Kane in March 1944, Agnes told of her experiences in the Italian campaign of 1943 and of serving in Sicily and on the Adriatic Coast. She had only recently returned to England to find the parcels waiting for her. She expressed her surprise and gratitude to the Club members for remembering her so kindly, especially when members were so busy on the home front with war work.

Like so many other women of the period, members were busy knitting socks and other items for the servicemen. Some senior members have recollections of the clicking of knitting needles during meetings. Sometimes they felt it was a distraction to their guest speakers. By the early 1940s the Club discussed whether to have a War Work Group but decided that the Red Cross Work Room at St. Stephen's College on campus was fulfilling the needed role and members could go there to help.

Emergency Fund For Exiled Women

The Club established an emergency fund for exiled university women in Europe called the Refugee Fund. Through the auspices of the IFUW, the Club adopted Madame Weill, a refugee resident in Britain, and sent clothing to her and her daughter from 1941 through to the end of the war. Additional funds were raised to purchase new clothing for Polish refugee women in 1945.

Although the Refugee Fund was officially closed in January 1946, CFUW clubs were asked to continue donating food and clothing to university refugee women in Europe. Thus, in December 1946 the Club gathered up and sent 13 food parcels to England and 15 clothing parcels to women in Belgium and Holland. This was followed by a special clothing drive the following December. Club members Margaret Brine, Mrs. G. G. Reynolds, Mrs. A. Lang and Inez Calhoun packaged up another 28 parcels. Postage for these clothing parcels came out of the Club's social funds and a magazine subscription fund that was started on a trial basis in 1947.

Post-War Planning and Reconstruction

Even as they worked for the war effort, Canadians were making preparations for the war's end. Recognizing that there would be some major issues to be addressed at war's end, two new study groups were formed within the Club to coincide with National CFUW Committees of the same name—Reconstruction and Post-War Problems of Women. In Edmonton the government's Post-War Reconstruction Committee and its various sub-committees worked with city agencies to aid men and women returning from the service. Among their concerns were housing, adult education, job training and consumer affairs. The Club had representation on several organizations formed during the 1940s: the Consumers' League (1941), the Citizen's Volunteer Bureau (1943), and the Alberta Association for Adult Education (1943).

In 1941, women's organizations across the country were asked by the federal government to help maintain price ceilings on consumer goods as part of the war effort. From the early 1940s, the Club had a representative on the federal "Price Ceiling Records" under the Wartime Prices and Trade Board. In the Club's 1944/45 Annual Report it was noted that the Modern Trends Study Group was to make an impartial study of certain retail food prices each month and report the information to the Trade Board. They joined thousands of other volunteer groups across the country to carry out similar monitoring studies. These co-operative efforts provided a basis for a permanent consumer organization. After the war, 16 major women's organizations met in September 1947 to organize the Canadian Association of

Consumers, a voluntary, independent and non-profit organization. In the fall of that same year, Cora Casselman and Mrs. Roy Anderson represented the Club in the formation of an Edmonton branch of the Association, now known as the Consumers' Association of Canada.

One of the sub-committees of the Reconstruction Committee was Post-War Problems of Women, a name both CFUW and CFUW Edmonton adopted for study groups. This group studied several government sponsored reports including the McWilliams Report, which dealt with the re-training of women and the appointment of women to advisory positions after the war. Details of the report and of its author, Margaret McWilliams, founder and first president of the CFUW and a leading feminist of the period, are given further acknowledgement in *Status of Women.*

The group also studied two major reports on social welfare. One was the Marsh Report of 1943, which was a series of recommendations by two leading scholars of social welfare regarding the establishment of a comprehensive social security system for Canada. The second was a report on social security by Charlotte Whitton, a leading child welfare advocate in Ottawa. Whitton was well known in Edmonton as a fellow CFUW member and the Club welcomed opportunities to meet with her in the 1940s to discuss the war effort and current welfare issues.

Child Welfare

Miss Whitton had worked in social service from the time of her graduation from Queen's University in 1917 and had gained renown for building up the Canadian Council on Child Welfare in Ottawa, which she oversaw for 21 years. After leaving the Council in 1941, she undertook several speaking tours in the United States and Canada which brought her to Edmonton in 1942 and 1944. She compiled two major reports on social welfare, including the one mentioned above and a more controversial one regarding Alberta child welfare (1947).

With an increase of married women in Canada's workforce during and after World War II, there was a need for more day care facilities. To help meet this need, particularly in eastern Canada where women were required for factories and war plants, the federal government passed legislation to provide cost-sharing with the provinces to establish day nurseries. Day nurseries were quickly established in Ontario, but Alberta did not take advantage of the federal offer. Although both

Calgary and Edmonton had agreed to come under the agreement, they were blocked by the action of a provincially appointed advisory committee who declared that there was no evidence of need.

It was in this environment that the Club joined with many other organizations in a concerted call for improved child care in Alberta. A special committee called the Committee to Investigate Child Welfare in the Province of Alberta was formed in 1943 under the Ministry of Health and Welfare (Dr. Cross was the Minister at the time). A Recommendation was sent by the Club to this Committee calling for the securing of "an independent investigator or social worker well recommended by the Canadian Welfare Council; the assurance of efficiency of the foster home placement by the addition of more trained and experienced inspectors and probation officers; and the compilation of complete records and statistics so that they can be compared with those of other provinces and that they may measure up to the Canadian Welfare Council." These recommendations were followed in 1944 by a letter to Premier Manning expressing concern for adequate nursery facilities in the province in view of the increasing number of working women. These actions have since come to represent the Club's first foray into the day care issue, one that the Club would take up again in the late 1950s.

Although the Alberta Government set up this Committee in 1943 to investigate child welfare, there was virtually no progress or change by 1946 and the province was receiving a poor reputation for its inaction. Concerned about this and the discontent among social workers in the province, the Edmonton Chapter of the Imperial Order of Daughters of the Empire (IODE) approached Miss Whitton in 1945 to advise them about the possibilities of a survey. Miss Whitton, reluctant to become involved without government approval, approached Premier Manning in September 1946 hoping to get his support. Although it was not given, she knew such a study was needed and decided to go ahead with it anyway in January 1947. She also knew the study would receive national publicity and would more than likely force Manning's Social Credit Government into making reforms.

When the final IODE Report "Welfare in Alberta" was released it included a scathing condemnation of ill-qualified staff and revealed that delinquent children were being ill-treated in detention homes or indentured as cheap labour to farmers. There was inadequate foster care, under-funded and under-staffed children's institutions, and too

Charlotte Whitton met with the Club while she was in Alberta in 1947. The significance of this early networking among CFUW members should be more fully recognized. Long-time member Libby Frost remembers the time Miss Whitton came to a meeting of one of the Study Groups (probably International Affairs) convened by Chrissie Wootton, who had been at Queen's with Charlotte. The conversation must have been animated, for Libby vividly recalls Miss Whitton saying (light-heartedly, we presume), "You people make me cross–if Chrissie tells you something, you're sure she's right. If I tell you something, you all have to argue with me." If Club members didn't fully subscribe to all of Charlotte Whitton's philosophies, in the area of child welfare they appear to have been largely in agreement.

Although she later became renowned as the Mayor of Ottawa (in the 1950s and 1960s), Miss Whitton devoted her many energies and talents to building up a social service framework for the country and her influence was far-reaching.

few trained social workers in the province and none in the Child Welfare Branch. Placement of adoptive children outside Canada, known as "bootlegging of babies," was common. The adverse press coverage as a result of this report, forced the Alberta Government to authorize a Royal Commission into Child Welfare in August 1947.

Club Minutes indicate that in 1947 a new Social Welfare Study Group, under Lucile Kane, was formed to look at child welfare and to study the IODE Report and the findings of the Royal Commission. Many of the issues the Club had addressed in the 1943 Brief were reinforced in their 1947 Recommendations.

Juvenile Delinquency and Penal Reform

As early as 1937, a local Penal Reform Study Group had addressed the issue of juvenile delinquency and put out a four-part report that included studies on young offenders and facts about probation. By the 1940s, the Club was concerned with juvenile delinquency and had a very active study group organized by Lucile Kane. This group arranged to have several distinguished people in the field of delinquency speak to the Club. In terms of the day, young offenders and juvenile delinquents often included children at risk–orphaned, homeless and unemployed. Recommendations by the Club included better educational programs for young offenders and better follow-up of probation.

There was obviously some overlap between the work of this group and that of the Child Welfare Study Group. Studies at the time suggested a correlation between good childcare and prevention of juvenile delinquency. When the Club was addressing the one issue, it was also often speaking for the other.

In the post-war period, there was a renewed emphasis on penal reform in Canada and such issues as training schools for juveniles, new training programs for prisoners and improved training for prison staff were addressed. It was in this environment that a special CFUW Committee on Penal Reform was established in 1947. Soon it was realized that such a Committee could be best served by having its convenor appointed from a different province each year in order to arouse interest in local problems as well as national ones. This arrangement lasted two years but the committee existed for a number of years. Because of her earlier leadership on juvenile delinquency, Lucile Kane was chosen as the second Convenor of this national Committee in 1948.

Under the Committee's direction, Clubs were encouraged to study relevant reports on prison reform, including the 1938 Archambault Report, whose recommendations had been gathering dust during the war years. They were also encouraged to pressure the government to ensure that the best of the proposed reforms were instituted. They were asked to work with local associations concerned with prison reform and to give special study to the treatment of women prisoners in penal institutions and the problems of their reestablishment when released from prison. Through the leadership of women such as Mrs. Kane, various recommendations were forwarded to appropriate authorities.

Public Policy

In 1944, the Club wrote letters in support of a CFUW Resolution asking the Parliament of Canada to take immediate steps to give CBC authority to direct all broadcasting in the Dominion. They further asked Parliament to empower the Prime Minister to make a public declaration that the independence and integrity of the CBC would be assured and a high standard maintained.

Norma Freifield
Libraries

Mrs. R. Anderson
Education and
Public Affairs

Vera Campbell
Archivist

Lucile Kane
Public Affairs

Chrissie Wootton
International
Affairs

Avery Fleming
Status of
Women

Barbara Blackley
By-Laws and
Constitution

Kay Farnham
Author–Editor

Sheila Campbell
Day Care

Libby Frost
Public Affairs

Under the guidance of Norma Freifield, the Edmonton Club suggested the need for a central national library to be set up in Ottawa in 1944. With strong support of the member Clubs across the country, a Resolution was adopted by the National Federation "urging the parliament of Canada to make provision for the establishment of a National Library as one of its more important post-war projects."

The same year the Club gave strong support to a Resolution put forward by the Calgary Club, for CFUW's endorsement, calling for a competent Commission on Indian Affairs with Indian representation, to be appointed by the Federal Government. Through the lobbying efforts of groups such as the CFUW, a Commission was in fact established under the Council of Canadian Unity in 1945, to investigate Indian Affairs, and the Club was asked to send a representative on behalf of CFUW.

An Indian Affairs Study Group was formed in 1951, at the request of Friends of the Indians to look into the welfare of the Indian and Metis population in the Edmonton area. As a result of their preliminary investigation a letter was sent to the Federal Minister of Citizenship and Immigration and local MPs citing two areas of concern—health and education. In the area of education, they recommended hiring qualified teachers on the reserves, equality in standards of education and that aboriginal ways be taught.

New Initiatives

The 1950s were a time of transition. The population of Edmonton grew rapidly, following the Leduc oil discovery of 1947, and the membership in the Club grew accordingly, reaching its peak in 1959/60. The Club had representation on a number of organizations including the Edmonton Citizenship Council, Edmonton Council of Community Services, Adult Education Association, United Nations Association, the YWCA, and the Unitarian Service Committee. President Norma Freifield noted in her Annual Report in 1959 that public relations among the various organizations with similar objectives ensured benefits to all concerned and hoped the Club would continue with such relations.

Throughout the 1950s the Club continued to look at a wide variety of concerns in the public domain. For example, after a serious poliomyelitis epidemic in 1953, the Club urged the provincial government to fly 12 physiotherapists to Edmonton from England, establish an out-patient clinic and therapy school, build a crippled children's hospital and set up mobile units equipped for transporting rural polio cases to Calgary and Edmonton.

One of the more interesting projects of the Club was with the Government's Advisory Board on Objectionable Publications. This came about when the Attorney General's Department sent a letter to the Club in 1954 soliciting their opinion on the controversial issue of crime comics and obscene literature. Given the Club's involvement with improving library facilities, this was a natural area of concern for them.

In response to the government's request, a special committee was set up by the Club to address the issue—an issue not unique to Alberta. The committee members set about collecting and reading some of the objectionable material in question. In an interview in 1999, one of the members, Muriel Affleck said that she remembered when they had to read all those comic books—she still had a strong memory of the numerous books they went through. This was typical of the Club's approach to a subject, be it critiquing comics in the 1950s or TV shows in later years, their recommendations were based on solid fact-finding procedures.

From their findings, the Club's committee was able to make several recommendations calling for improved library facilities, more trained librarians and increased parental awareness. They called for the setting up of a joint committee to bring all partners together—the Attorney General's Department, concerned parents, educators and the distributors of the obscene material. The proposed committee became the Advisory Board on Objectionable Publications. Mrs. A. J. Maure, a librarian, became its first Chairman. A well-known librarian in the community, having served five times on the Library Board, Mrs. Maure (though not a Club member) was nominated by the Alberta Library Association as well as the Club. A pamphlet put out by the Advisory Board included the following comments:

> The "comic" book problem is of world-wide concern. It has assumed such serious proportions that many governments, including those of Canada, the United Kingdom, the United States and the United Nations, have appointed committees to study this matter. In response to a growing outcry from parents, educators, religious leaders and others, the Government of the Province of Alberta issued an Order

in Council in 1954 which states: it is deemed advisable and in the public interest to establish a Board to be known as the ADVISORY BOARD ON OBJECTIONABLE PUBLICATIONS to study and investigate magazines and to recommend effective action to prevent their sale and distribution in the Province.

It was felt that crime comics were a contributing factor to juvenile delinquency, encouraged the commission of crime and contempt for lawful authority, and were detrimental to good reading skills. The latter was of particular concern to Club members.

Day Care

Through the 1950s, as the number of married women in the work force increased, so did the demand for day care. Unfortunately the pressure for available spaces often led to some very suspect conditions of care. The City Welfare Council began petitioning the provincial government for stricter guidelines on the operation of day care homes and nurseries. In early 1959 Saretta Sparling, one of the Club's two representatives on the Council, spoke to members regarding this situation. She reported that a committee had been set up within the Welfare Council to investigate services for the protection of children in the city and province, but for over a year their petition for stricter guidelines had met with little success. They consequently turned to the Club for assistance with their lobbying actions.

At the same time a group of young members were looking for a worthwhile project to undertake and volunteered to follow up on the Welfare Council's proposal. Many of the group had joined the Club in the early 1950s as Recent Grads and were just starting their families. As young parents, they were more aware of and concerned about the problems of adequate childcare. In February 1959 the group announced to the general membership that they were looking into the issue of child welfare and had already had several qualified speakers in to address them. They were then going to embark on a survey of day homes.

In cooperation with an informal group of about 15 women (which had evolved from a Church Women's Study Group and whose leader was an experienced social worker, Margaret Norquay), the newly formed Family Welfare Study Group (FWSG) set out to visit all the day homes and nurseries advertised in the Edmonton Journal for the month of April. The fact that one or more of the Club members was pregnant lent an air of authenticity to the project. They were to appear as genuine applicants, not just a group of women taking a survey. Of the homes investigated, some were deplorable, some they didn't even get into. Their survey of Edmonton and Jasper Place found 22% day homes that were good, 28% bad and 50% suitable only after change.

By May the Study Group had completed the survey and been asked by the Child Welfare Department officials to prepare a Brief on the subject. With the Club's backing, they presented their Brief to the Child Welfare Commission of the Provincial Department in June 1959. It outlined the following recommendations:

• A need for a new definition of day nurseries,
• that the responsibilities and powers of the licensing authority be clearly defined,
• that the responsibilities and rights of the licensee be spelled out,
• that no proprietor of nurseries should be allowed to advertise unless the nursery was licensed and approved,
• and that an annual inspection and renewal of the license be required.

The Club received favourable reviews in the Edmonton Journal (May 24/60). An editorial commended the work of the "University Women's Club Study" and stated that the public would be gratified to know that the government's proposed amendments to the Child Welfare Act would permit closer scrutiny of conduct in foster homes and nurseries. It would also enlarge the definition of nurseries, so that day homes could be better regulated.

In December of 1960, the Family Welfare Study Group joined other interested local groups in attending a meeting of the City By-Laws Committee. It was decided that since the province was definitely going ahead with new regulations, the City would not step in. Provincial regulations came into effect in 1961.

Fran Savage, Chair of the Study Group, reported the results of this City of Edmonton meeting to the Club on February 20, 1961 during a panel discussion on Welfare in Alberta. She related that a representative of the provincial department had been at the meeting and had suggested that interested study groups might meet to draw up a list of possible standards for day care centres to which the department could refer when they drew up their new regulations. She particularly stressed that the province was for the first time welcoming ideas from interested outsiders. The Club was to take on this proposed initiative, but it would take until 1966 for two Briefs regarding day care standards to be actually put forward.

Kindergartens

The group's investigation into nurseries also led to a better understanding of kindergartens in Edmonton. This was reiterated by Mrs. R. Brower in the second part of the panel discussion of February 20. The Family Welfare Study Group found in their survey that many so-called kindergartens were actually glorified baby-sitting agencies and were often inadequate. There were two types of kindergartens operating in the city; the privately owned ones, and those run by the Recreation Commission of the City of Edmonton. Both charged for the care and teaching of the pupil, although the private kindergartens were considerably more expensive.

Through the FWSG day care investigation and subsequent lobbying efforts of other concerned groups, changes were also made in kindergartens. Under the regulations set up in January 1961, the term kindergarten could only refer to an institution for children eligible for entry into first grade school classes in the next school year. Standards were set that required licensing and inspection for kindergartens by the Department of Welfare, but other issues still needed to be addressed. For instance, many of the teachers were unqualified and although Section 396 of the School Act stated that "no person should be engaged or employed to teach and train the children in such classes unless he holds qualifications approved by the Minister," the section was not enforced. As a result, there was no standardization for teaching methods. In their investigation, the Group had found that some kindergartens taught a reading readiness course, while others were no more than nurseries serving milk and cookies.

The Study Group, therefore, recommended that kindergarten programs come under the authority of the Department of Education, whereby they would then be offered to every child throughout the school system. Only qualified teachers would be employed and they would be trained for kindergarten teaching. They outlined what a good pre-school program should offer—it should teach independence, reasoning, observation and memory appropriate to the child's stage of mental development. Kindergartens were introduced into the public school system in 1968.

Times Of Major Accomplishments

In retrospect, the 1960s represented an epic period in the Club's history and its relationship to the community. CFUW Edmonton membership had peaked early in the decade and there was great enthusiasm and vitality among the members. The country was preparing to celebrate the Centennial in 1967, the second wave of the women's movement was galvanized into a Royal Commission (1967–70), and women were making advances in business and education. Members who were prominent in the Club at this time don't recall this period as anything but business as usual, but with the luxury of time and distance they themselves look back with a great deal of pride on their accomplishments.

Archives–Centennial Project

In October 1961, the Club chose the establishment of a Provincial Archives as its 1967 Centennial project. The subject was taken on by the Club's existing Edmonton History Study Group after examining what other provinces were doing regarding archives. They discovered that Alberta did not come up to standards in safeguarding archival material. The Club then decided that a provincial archives was a worthwhile project to pursue.

In April 1962, the Study Group had put together an initial brief and sent it to the Provincial Secretary, the Honorable A. R. Patrick, who subsequently offered to meet with a delegation. With his assistance and advice, the Group put together several well-researched recommendations calling for a fully qualified government archivist and legislation for safeguarding public documents. The recommendations were officially adopted by the Club as the Centennial project in October 1962.

By now renamed the Centennial Committee, the group proceeded to garner support for the project from other organizations in the province and with the strong backing of all these groups, submitted their recommendations to the Provincial Cabinet. In November 1962, a delegation of CFUW Edmonton members, including President Margaret Greenhill, was invited to meet with the Cabinet. She reported that this was a most successful meeting, and that the government had already decided to build an Archives. The Committee was asked to outline the status and powers that they felt should be involved in the archivist's duties. A qualified Provincial Archivist, Hugh Taylor, was appointed in 1966.

It had been a long process, but the members were finally rewarded for their efforts. The provincial government undertook to build a museum and archives as one of their centennial projects, and in 1967 the Provincial Archives, attached to the Provincial Museum was opened. The Provincial Archives project has become one of the most enduring examples of the CFUW Edmonton's contribution to the community.

In the summer of 1998, the Alberta Government proposed moving the Provincial Archives to a site at Stony Plain west of Edmonton. This was thought to be a solution to the crowded conditions at its current site adjoining the Provincial Museum of Alberta in central Edmonton. There was strong opposition to the move among the stakeholders–the historical/heritage groups in the province–who stressed the need for the Archives to remain in the provincial capital. Because of the Club's earlier advocacy role regarding the establishment of the Provincial Archives, members joined in the protest.

The Club voted in September 1998 to send a representative, Cynthia Boodram, to the first meeting of the stakeholders. They soon formed an *Alberta Heritage Alliance*–a collaborative organization of groups dedicated to preserving, interpreting and promoting the province's heritage resources, of which CFUW Edmonton became a part.

Education for Citizenship

At that earlier meeting with the Cabinet in 1962, the group not only presented their views on the archives project, but also on "several other issues that the Club had addressed over the past year and that the government had been dragging their feet on," noted Margaret Greenhill. This included such things as education for citizenship.

The Club was one of several organizations involved with the Edmonton Citizenship Council in the 1950s and 1960s. Once a year they were asked to participate in the New Citizen's Tea and to provide refreshments after the court ceremonies. Two members also served on the New Citizen's Library Committee that organized lectures for new Canadians. Through this involvement with the Library Committee, and because of its history of teaching English as a Second Language, the Club was asked to be responsible for a course for people who had been turned down for citizenship.

The proposal was put to the Club as an experimental program, but it was decided that there was no one qualified to do this sort of teaching.

A letter was sent to the Honorable Ellen Fairclough, Minister of Immigration, recommending that the Department of Citizenship and Immigration organize classes with a paid teacher and should "stop depending on volunteers."

Day Care

DAY CARE RULES URGED

Strict standards for day care centres have been recommended to the provincial government by the University Women's Club of Edmonton.

In a brief presented to Welfare Minister L. C. Halmrast today, the club urged establishment of a day care branch within the provincial welfare department to co-ordinate day care standards and training.

Edmonton Journal, June 10, 1966

In January 1966 a new Day Care Study Group (DCSG) was formed under Convenor Sheila Campbell. The purpose of the group was to submit recommendations to the Family Service Association, which had set up a Day Care Committee to investigate conditions in the City of Edmonton.

To gain public input, a series of meetings was held through February 1966. The DCSG was an active participant in these meetings, along with the Edmonton Welfare Council, the Family Service Association and other concerned groups. At the first meeting on February 2, Sheila Campbell indicated that the DCSG would focus on standards and training of day care custodians. In a letter to the Chairman of the Committee dated February 4, 1966, Mrs. Campbell outlined the order of priority for steps to be taken in day care in the City of Edmonton as envisioned by the Study Group:

- Public education to develop an understanding of the need for differing types of day care and their valuable long term dividends to the community.

- The establishing of child care courses for training in the care of well children at several levels: e.g. post-graduate University level, 3-year post-high school level and short course level (extension, continuing education, in-service training).

- The establishing of staff standards detailing required courses and minimum wages and proper ratios for public and private day care.

- The expansion of day care services to care for all the children needing day care by establishing community centres, foster home finding and homemaker services.

After establishing their guidelines, members of the DCSG worked diligently to refine the set of standards for day care outlined above. After a lengthy debate and several revisions, a draft was accepted by the membership in May 1966. It was divided into two parts. One part dealt with Standards for Training for Custodial and Supervisory Personnel in Day Care Services, and the second part with the training courses themselves.

In June 1966 Briefs were submitted to the Minister of Welfare and to the Board of Governors of the U of A respectively. The Brief to the Provincial Welfare Minister urged the establishment of a day care branch within the provincial welfare department to coordinate day care standards and training, and to establish certification for day care workers who had completed a program of training in child care at a recognized institution. The Brief to the U of A outlined the requirements for certification. The Study Group stressed the need for action in setting standards for certification by the government so that there would be a corresponding request for courses to meet the requirements. Without the one, there wouldn't be a need for the other. Again, the Study Group stressed that adequate day care services for children "were not only a social and economic necessity, but preventative welfare of a most essential kind."

At a public meeting on February 23rd, the Club presented a motion calling for an increase in day care facilities by a minimum of 500 spaces. Betty Mullen, one of the Club's representatives on the City Welfare Council, presented the motion.

The debate on day care and the increase in facilities was not without controversy within the Club. Some members were opposed; they did not believe there should be more spaces and that mothers should be home with young children. Sheila Campbell remembers some great arguments. "Although the majority obviously supported us, there was certainly a group that didn't feel that it was an appropriate thing."

As a consequence of being Chair of the Study Group, Sheila Campbell was asked to go on the Board of the Community Day Nursery and ended up as President of the Board. Subsequent to her work on the Nursery Board, Sheila was asked to develop curriculum for the Child

Care Section at W. P. Wagner High School. She then did a Masters' in Education (U of A), and was asked to set up an Early Childhood Development Program at Grant MacEwan Community College. She became Day Care Director for the City of Edmonton for a short period and was then persuaded to join the early childhood program of the U of A Department of Education, which led to a tenured position. She received her PhD in Early Childhood Education in 1980.

The Club's Briefs on day care established CFUW Edmonton as a group concerned with the care and welfare of children. Groups sought their support on the issue for many years thereafter. This was a controversial subject at the time and to advocate for more and better day care indicated the Club's awareness and commitment to the issue.

By the 1990s day care had become acceptable public policy and those companies that recognized the value of female employees offered "in-house" day care or drop-in facilities for children. Many of the changes that have been implemented to assist working women are due to the determination and vision of women's groups such as CFUW Edmonton who challenged the status quo and pressed governments and industry on the need for quality day care.

Rutherford House

Save Rutherford House, said the bumper stickers that the Club made up and distributed to the public as a show of determination to save the stately home of Alberta's first Premier and founder of the University of Alberta, Dr. A. C. Rutherford. Together with other concerned groups, the Club mounted a campaign in the late 1960s to preserve and restore Rutherford House. For their particular efforts, CFUW Edmonton was awarded a City of Edmonton Historical Board Award in 1987.

The story of Rutherford House goes back to 1911 when it was built by the Premier and occupied by his family until 1938. Two years later it was sold to the Delta Upsilon (DU) Fraternity, who owned it until 1968, at which time the University bought the house as part of a major campus expansion. As Rutherford House stood in direct competition with the site needs for a new Humanities Complex, the University wished to have the house either moved or demolished.

To give the University their due, a letter had been sent to Premier Manning in 1966 regarding the possibility of financing the restoration of the House, but the government did not feel it was a practical

Edmonton Journal Dec. 3, 1969

Must come down?

The fate of Rutherford House may hinge on the University Women's Club's plea to the U of A Board of Governors Friday. The club wants to save the home of Alberta's first premier to preserve a link with Alberta's past. The university says the house must come down to make way for a new humanities complex on the campus. So far the women have raised more than $12,000 to restore the mansion at 11153 Saskatchewan Drive.

Centennial project. The Mayor of Edmonton was contacted, who replied that Rutherford House would be a worthy project for a group of citizens. The consensus was that there was no political will to save the home.

Several heritage groups however, expressed an interest when they got wind of the University's plans. Lila Fahlman, who lived in the area slated for expansion, created the Society for the Preservation of Historical Homes in 1966 and petitioned the University and Provincial Government against demolition. Other groups became involved, including the Historical Society of Alberta, the Northern Alberta Pioneers and Old Timers Association and the DU Fraternity itself.

The U of A Board of Governors had the ultimate say in matters concerning construction and planning at the University, and they were anxious to have something done with the building, especially given its

Rita Calhoun, Convenor of Rutherford
House Study Group.

Christmas Party, 1991
Pictured in study of Rutherford House are:
L to R: Dorothy Buschkiel-Kozak,
Suzanne Connell,
Edith Miller, Pam Laing

City of Edmonton Archives #34 A87-170

Edmonton Historical Board Award
Presentation of award to President Marion
Gee by Mayor Terry Cavanagh, Sept. 10,
1987, in recognition of Club's leadership
role in the preservation and restoration of
Rutherford House.

Members Hazel (Rutherford) McCuaig
and Jean Lund (right) at Christmas
Party 1980.

run-down condition. In October 1969 representatives of the various interested organizations attended a meeting of the Building Committee of the Board. Included in the group were Libby Frost, Club President (1969–70) and Rita Calhoun, Convenor of the newly formed Preservation of Rutherford House Study Group. Rita Calhoun recounted the background of that meeting, and the subsequent drive to involve the community in restoring the home, at the Club's Christmas Meeting held at Rutherford House in 1986. A portion of her account is excerpted here.

I am so pleased to be invited to tell you of Rutherford House and the University Women's Club adventures of 17 years ago. I would like to introduce the members of our Rutherford House Study Group: Libby Frost, who was president of our Club in 1969, Peggy Rootes, Janet Tegart and Winnifred Long. Two members are not here tonight, Ruth Bondar, who was unable to come, and Marjorie Buckley. Marjorie died three years ago. She was a true spark for this committee as she had great imagination and great drive.

All members of the UWC were aware of the 1967 decision of the University and government to demolish Rutherford House when tenders were called for the new Humanities Complex. At a call from President Libby Frost, we six interested members gathered to discuss the possibilities of a club house, and in particular, of Rutherford House. We hoped that by offering to use the House as a club house it could be saved from demolition. The Study Group drafted a letter to Dr. Jack Bradley, then chairman of the Board of Governors of the U of A. Copies of the letter were sent to the Edmonton Journal, which reported the University Women's Club, as well as other organizations, were interested in saving Rutherford House.

Public Interest was sparked!

One of the associations contacted by the Study Group was the Historical Society of Alberta, Edmonton Branch–this society had long been interested, and had worked hard, for preservation of Rutherford House. The Historical Society called a meeting in June, 1969, of interested groups. Nineteen people attended, representing various interested organizations. From this meeting a decision was reached: "to request permission to appear before the Board of Governors so that our petition could be presented." A resolution was passed unanimously: "that a delegation go from this meeting to petition the University of Alberta to preserve Rutherford House."

On Friday, October 10, 1969, permission was granted and representatives of various organizations attended a meeting of the Building Committee of the Board of Governors. Libby Frost and I attended this meeting in University Hall as representatives of our Club. Libby and I reached a long way—we were imaginative! We said the Club could maintain the House through fees and donations! Libby frankly stated we were asking for the house as a gift; that we could handle the house as a club house if we were given time; that we would restore it and use it.

We were told by the Chairman of the Board that it would be cheaper to build a new club house! A representative of the Arts Building Committee, which opposed retention of the house on the present site, stated that the proposed Humanities Building would be a symbol of aspirations and hopes (of new architecture on the Campus); a member of the University's Campus Developments Committee stated that keeping the house on the present site placed an intolerable constraint on planning!

To counteract these comments, the Chairman of the Historical Board of Edmonton stated that the University had a responsibility to its beginnings. He summed up the situation very nicely, when he told the members of the Building Committee. "Its your building, but its our heritage."

I remember having a distinct hostile reaction at this meeting of October 10th, due to a put-down by a male member of the Board. This gentleman said "the house is a wreck, Mrs. Calhoun, just wait 'til you see the kitchen." I knew he thought women were interested only in kitchens! I was insulted and I felt our Club was challenged.

After the meeting, members trampled through the nearby Rutherford House with the Building Committee. It was in poor condition, but even in that condition you could sense the grandeur of the house we are in tonight. I can't even remember the kitchen! Libby and I came away very determined to meet with Club members. We were determined to carry through to preserve Rutherford House.

Our Study Group called a meeting of Club members on a Saturday morning in October. We toured an unheated house. The day was cold and bleak. Despite the very sad condition of Rutherford House, our Club members agreed to continue to support the Study Group's efforts. Alta Wood, one of our members had interested her architect husband, Bernie Wood, to attend the meeting. He spoke to the group encouragingly, but wisely told the members that it wasn't possible to fight this fight simply on an economic basis: our hearts and emotions had to be part of our efforts.

A well-known lawyer phoned and offered to have an estimate prepared of 'band-aid' repair to the house. Because of this offer we met with a contractor who looked over the house, pronouncing, for one thing, that it was made of durable 'double-faced brick.' The University had reported that the brick construction was of single brick and that the mortar was deteriorating. Upon hearing of the double-faced brick, Libby and I felt as if we'd discovered the pot of gold at the end of the rainbow!

The estimate for the band-aid repair amounted to $36,750.00. One of the sub-contractors offered to donate labor of $1,120.00, so that the UWC was faced with finding $35,630.00. Because of all the publicity about our efforts, we began to receive voluntary pledges to support our cause. Eventually a total of over $30,000.00 in unsolicited pledges was received.

We had started support for saving Rutherford House!

Meanwhile, Marjorie Buckley organized a petition and members sat in shopping malls as people signed it and expressed their interest in saving Rutherford House. Marjorie had 'Save Rutherford House' bumper stickers printed. Proudly, and with determination, Club members mounted the stickers on our cars. As well, Henry Ward, president of the Edmonton Historical Board, was also principal of Bonnie Doon High School and he interested the students in saving the House. One young woman wrote a song about saving our heritage and saving Rutherford House. The group that performed the song received much helpful television coverage.

Then we had a set-back. The Board of Governors had scheduled its final decision for November 7, 1969, just one month after our tour of Rutherford House. The UWC requested a postponement, to give time to prepare a 'detailed financial analysis' of our plans for restoration of the House. Our request was denied.

In desperation, on November 28, 1969, a letter was sent from the Study Group to Premier Harry Strom, selected members of the legislature and to the leader of the opposition, Peter Lougheed. A copy of the letter was submitted to the Edmonton Journal as well. Ross Munroe, then publisher of the Journal, agreed to meet with me to review the letter. He kindly agreed to have the paper cover the story of our latest effort to save Rutherford House. I'd like to read you a paragraph from the letter:

The members of the University Women's Club, as well as many interested people in this city, are very anxious to have this house remain. We have so little left that is tangible from this time in our history. The house, on its present site, represents much of the beginning of a province, a city, a university. To demolish this house is to knowingly destroy part of our provincial heritage.

Because of the resulting publicity generated by our letter, the Study Group was asked to meet with the Board of Governors on December 5, 1969. We asked the Board to reconsider its decision to 'remove Rutherford House' and to our relief, they said they would reconsider their decision at their January 9th meeting.

The groundswell of public interest convinced both the Board of Governors and the government to rethink their earlier positions. The Club's November 28 letter to the Board detailing spontaneous pledges and public interest proved instrumental in the reversal of the Board's decision. In March 1970, the Honorable Albert Ludwig, Minister of Public Works wrote to Rita Calhoun, praising the efforts of the Rutherford House Study Group. He felt that they "deserved all the credit for having prevailed over all opposition to the restoration of Rutherford House." In September 1970 an agreement was reached between the Board of Governors of the U of A and the Minister of Public Works. In November 1970 the Board of Governors agreed to lease the house, plus a surrounding perimeter of land to the Department of Public Works for 40 years at $1 a year. The lease stipulated that the exterior of the building be renovated by June 1, 1973 and that the House was to be used only as a museum or place of historical interest.

Rutherford House sat empty until August 1971, at which time the newly-elected Progressive Conservative Government proceeded with restoration. It was completed in 1973, and the official opening took place on May 11, 1974. At the opening, Mrs. Hazel McCuaig unveiled a portrait of her father, Dr. A. C. Rutherford. Hazel was a long-time member of the Club and she and her husband had been steadfast supporters of its efforts to save Rutherford House.

Study Group on Aging

In late 1966 when the University initiated plans to expand and take over the north Garneau area of Edmonton, it became evident that the government wasn't offering the residents of the area, many elderly, nearly enough money to re-locate. Elna Clark, whose mother was one of these residents, was interested to find out how many seniors were involved. With the assistance of Garneau United Church, she started a survey of the area. She sought support from the Club, and in March 1967 a Study Group on Aging was formed under her direction. Among the several members of the Club who became involved were Enid Crockett (President 1966–68) and Libby Frost (President 1968–70).

In her President's report of April 1969, Libby Frost reported that the Study Group on Aging had continued to work with the Garneau Community Group and were assisting in their attempts to obtain a home for the elderly in southwest Edmonton. "When we started out, we really didn't know what we were doing," she said. "We first met with the Deputy Ministers, but eventually ended up with the Cabinet Ministers and the Premier. I can remember I counted for one year we made 94 calls on people." It would appear that the Club's Group had become completely integrated with the Garneau Group and members had taken on leading roles in the campaign.

Initially, the authorities were thinking in terms of a senior's drop-in centre, Libby related, but the Group fought for an expanded senior's residence. With the assistance of the architectural firm Rule, Wynn and Rule who gave their work for free, as well as the assistance of government architects and other government officials, Strathcona Place Senior's Residence eventually became a reality.

In an interview in the 1990s, Libby Frost related that "Elna was the real leader of the Garneau Survey Group. She was also the key person behind Meals-On Wheels [revived in the late 1960s] and the Association for the Retired and Semi-Retired, although she never allowed her name to be published."

Environmental Issues

Whereas educational and social issues had concerned an earlier generation of members, after the 1960s environmental issues became a major area of study and action. As one member who had been prominent in the Club's activities in the 1940s and 1950s said in an interview, "we weren't concerned with the environment then because we didn't have any problems—it wasn't an issue."

It took until the 1960s for the environmental effects of unrestrained growth and conspicuous consumption of the post-war period to be recognized as a problem. In the context of post-war times, the chemical products and technological "breakthroughs" were the pride of North American society and gave rise to great economic growth.

"As governments respond to public concern about environmental protection by providing for increased public involvement and consultation in decision-making processes, members of the public will need to develop expertise on a wide range of complex environmental issues to enable full and effective participation in the consultation processes..."

– Marilyn Kansky, environmental lawyer from Environment Network News Alberta, No. 8 March/ April, 1990

By 1970 there was a growing awareness that many of the new chemicals were harmful to the environment, and the increasing burden on landfill sites posed a further hazard. Groups everywhere were coming together to discuss the issues, and within the Club an Anti-Pollution Study/Action Group was formed. By 1971, the Group decided they needed a more palatable name, one which described what they were about, not what they were against. They became the Environmental Concerns Study/Action Group. It is a basic tenant of CFUW women to do research and then to proceed with action and education.

For the 1970 CFUW Triennial Meeting held in Toronto the new Group prepared a resolution with background material that urged the Canadian Government to co-operate in fighting pollution. The resolution passed and was then taken forward the next year to the IFUW Triennial Meeting in Philadelphia. There it was also passed and became international policy.

About the same time, the Environmental Concerns Group decided to join forces with another local group called the Edmonton Anti-Pollution Group. They had presented a Brief in June 1970 to the Edmonton City Council concerning the proper disposal of garbage and recommended that, where possible, trash should be recycled. This impressed the Group, and through their instigation a motion was passed by the Executive of the Club (December, 1970) supporting the Brief in principal. A letter was then sent from the Club to the Mayor of Edmonton stating this support, and expressing the Club's equal concern "about the waste of our natural resources and the pollution of air, land and water." It is interesting to look back and see that these concerns have changed very little over the past thirty years.

Recycling was a project in which the Environmental Concerns Group wanted to become involved and they began by writing letters to both the public and separate school boards to arrange for elementary schools to hold paper drives. This was so successful that the Edmonton Salvage Company, to whom the paper was sold, had to put in new equipment to cope with the increased paper it was forced to handle once the schools became involved.

RECYCLED SCRAP PAPER IS FIGHTING POLLUTION

The University Women's Club of Edmonton may have one answer to the dilemma of what to do with those tons of waste paper people accumulate–the solution is paper recycling, a project recently undertaken by the club's pollution study group. As well as combating pollution, the project, begun last fall, aids conservation–"every ton of paper that's recycled saves 17 trees from being cut down," Mrs. J. R. Culham, organizer of the project, pointed out. "Already children in more than 10 schools are busy as beavers collecting waste paper of all kinds," although she added that three schools had already been running drives on their own over the past two years.

Edmonton Journal, February 24, 1971

The paper drives taught the students about pollution problems and the need for conservation, and at the same time allowed them to raise funds for such things as science equipment and other supplementary materials. Each school that held a paper drive received $9 per ton of collected paper from the salvage company. A bin was placed on the school property for about five days and a notice was placed in the Edmonton Journal each week giving the location of paper bins for that week. The waste paper–newspaper, magazines, cardboard boxes, etc.– was sold to building products companies and paper mills in Edmonton, Washington State and Japan to be recycled into corrugated cardboard and wallboard.

Not only was the Club one of the major groups involved in the paper drives, but it also arranged for the first pick-up of telephone books in Edmonton. Under Convenor Ruth Culham, over eight tons of books were collected.

To promote interest in the recycling project, a twenty-minute slide presentation was produced, with projectors borrowed from the U of A. Three sets of slides were flashed simultaneously on three screens with an accompaniment of taped music. The theme, "Alberta–Land for Living, or Losing?" contrasted beautiful scenes of clear lakes and mountains with polluted scenes, and urged the children to take their part in fighting pollution. This unique presentation was shown by

Three Figures in the Environmental Concerns Study Group

THE EDMONTON JOURNAL, Wednesday, May 13, 1981

Slide presentation vividly illustrates contrast of pollution and cleanliness

Jean Lauber

Tammy Irwin

Small group does its part in fight against pollution

Pat Wishart

CLUB COLLECTING
OLD PHONE BOOKS

Ecology Caravan

It was about 1970. We were a small study group (about 10 on a good night), but we were single-minded. We wanted to do something about pollution. We settled on the idea of encouraging school groups, churches and service clubs to carry out paper drives. We made a study of the recycling process, and took pictures to show in schools. At one point, we even conducted our own city-wide paper collection drive, at the time of the new telephone book delivery. We arranged for collection bins to be put in shopping malls and we made posters urging householders to bring in their old phone books.

At one meeting, we were chatting about what other environmentalist groups had done, and somebody mentioned hearing about a multi-screen slide show, with "dirty pictures" contrasting with scenic ones. Something happened to our collective chemistry that night: with one voice, it seemed, we found ourselves saying 'Yes, we could do that' and we did.

Jean Lauber, CFUW Edmonton Newsletter, January 1988

group members to 10,000 school children over the year, and by spring, the group decided it should be presented to a wider audience.

Dr. Jean Lauber of the Department of Zoology at the U of A successfully applied to her department for a grant which would enable her to hire a university student to take the presentation to parks and campsites in Alberta during the summer. A smaller grant was obtained from the Provincial Department of the Environment, which paid the traveling expenses. The Ecology Caravan was born. A student and a small utility trailer, outfitted with three plywood screens painted white and sprinkled with glass beads, toured Alberta for four summers. The Study Group estimated that close to 50,000 people saw the slide presentation by the end of the project.

The slide show was taken to an IFUW Conference in Philadelphia in 1971, where Marjorie Buckley, Club President, and Dr. Jean Lauber, an official CFUW Delegate, presented a resolution (originating in Edmonton) calling for all Clubs to urge their governments to co-operate in fighting pollution at an international level.

What started with a small group of women putting their collective thoughts together to address the issue of pollution grew into one of the

Club's most visible projects. For their efforts one member was honoured with an "Alberta Achievement Award" in the field of Environmental Concerns (Dr. Jean Lauber), another was awarded a City of Edmonton "Certificate of Appreciation" for her part in the Ecology Caravan project (Tammy Irwin), and yet another was appointed the first member to represent the Club on the Public Advisory Committee of the Environment Conservation Authority (Pat Wishart).

Environmental Advisory Committees

From 1971 to the early 1990s the Club had a representative on the Public Advisory Committee of the Environment Conservation Authority, later renamed the Environment Council of Alberta (ECA). Throughout this period, the Environmental Concerns Study Group made use of the ECA as well as the Environmental Law Society for information and support in its endeavors. The government disbanded the Advisory Committee in early 1990. About the same time, members of the Group had become increasingly aware of the work of the Alberta Environmental Network (AEN) and in 1989 joined the more than 100 other environmental groups that formed the AEN. Whereas the Advisory Committees to the ECA had been the Club's method of participating in environmental issues at the provincial level in the early period, the AEN came to provide a method of similar interaction through its caucus groups. The association continues to benefit both the AEN and the Club.

For a period from the mid-1970s to mid-1980s, there was no on-going Environmental Study Group within the Club and issues were addressed through Ad Hoc Committees as the need arose or through the Club's representative on the Public Advisory Committee who brought information to Club members including resolutions for possible endorsement.

Water Quality

Under the leadership of Tammy Irwin the Environmental Concerns Study Group was re-activated in 1986 with the intent of formulating a Resolution on the environment for debate at the National CFUW Annual General Meeting in 1988. "When we looked at past CFUW Resolutions on the environment, it was obvious that there was a large gap in the area of water and water quality," stated Irwin (Club Newsletter, 1987). "We considered studying the proposed [Federal] Environment Protection Act which would control pollution going *into* a water supply; however the Bill was likely to be passed before the 1988

AGM, so we then turned our attention to another area of water quality– of water *coming out* of out taps and wells and the need for a guarantee of its safety."

The Group prepared a resolution entitled *Drinking Water Quality* with the assistance of the Environmental Law Centre, Edmonton and the Toxics Watch Project at the Edmonton Environmental Resource Centre. It was passed at the 1988 AGM and became CFUW policy. The resolution read:

> Resolved that CFUW urge the Government of Canada, Department of Health and Welfare to pass a Safe Drinking Water Act which would establish substantive and procedural laws in order to 1) set rigorous ground and surface water quality standards and 2) fund research into identification and removal from tap and well water, substances harmful to human health and 3) promote emergency Planning Schemes that would require immediate public notification of instances of water contamination and the provision of alternate sources of safe water.

In order to develop a working knowledge of the numerous and complex environmental issues confronting the public, the Environmental Concerns Study Group made great efforts to become informed on environmental issues–no easy task as the number and complexity of issues escalated. Numerous environmental government Acts were introduced at the national and provincial levels, which spawned task forces, reviews, and subsequent workshops and forums. A whole new lexicon of environmental "buzzwords" came into use in an attempt to define and clarify the process.

The monthly meetings of the Group often increased to bi-monthly and then weekly meetings as deadlines approached for various task force submissions. But through it all, the members remained committed.

For two years, the Club was involved in preparations for hosting the 1989 national AGM which took as its theme, Stewardship of our Earth: an Environmental Imperative. Pat Wishart and Dr. Jean Lauber of the Environmental Concerns Study Group assumed responsibility for the program, and arranged for leading environmental speakers from the three levels of government, industry and the university. Many of the issues brought forward at the conference provided impetus for Club members to carry out further environmental studies.

Northern Boreal Studies

In the fall of 1989, the Study Group attended forums and information seminars on forestry development in Alberta's northern boreal forests in preparation for making a submission to the Alberta-Pacific Environmental Impact Assessment Review Board in December 1989. This Review Board was the first time both the Federal and Alberta governments had held a review jointly.

Along with other environment groups, members were taken aback by the magnitude of the pulp and paper development proposed for Northern Alberta and in particular with the proposed Alberta Pacific Forest Industries (Al-Pac) Mill near Athabasca. The prospective ecological consequences, as well as the economic and social issues alarmed many concerned citizens. The effects of this development would be felt into the Northwest Territories and beyond. A Brief was presented by the Environment Group to the Review Board at its hearing held in Edmonton. In it they highlighted their concerns regarding the cumulative effect of effluents from mills into the river system and the need for effective monitoring procedures by governmental environmental agencies.

Following the 1989 government hearing that led to approval of the Al-Pac pulp mill, a study on the Northern River Basins (NRBS) was launched in 1991. It was a four-year study aimed at examining the cumulative effects of development on the Peace, Athabasca and Slave River basins. A 25 person Study Board was established that invited public involvement. Robin Robinson represented the Club on an advisory group that gave support to the government-appointed environmental representative on the Board.

Involvement with Provincial and Federal Environmental Legislation

In the early 1990s the Study Group participated in several environmental initiatives of the provincial and federal governments. In response to an invitational document called *Alberta's Environment: Toward the 21st Century,* members made a presentation in March 1990 to Alberta Environment. At the same time they issued a press release citing CFUW policy on the environment. At the federal level *A Framework for Discussion on the Environment,* known as the Green Plan, was announced on March 29, 1990. A series of consultations were held across the country and five members registered for a two day session in Edmonton in June.

By the fall of 1991 the Group decided to ask the Club for Special Committee status. The quantity of proposed legislation and projects that had environmental implications was rapidly growing, and full Committee status would allow the Group to be more effective. "Because the group has been involved in social action and is perceived by outside groups to represent the CFUW Edmonton, and not merely an interest group of the club, it has been decided the most effective way is to have a pro-active group functioning within the club by-laws and policies and to recommend to the club executive that we become a Special Committee instead of an Interest Group."

Proposed environmental legislation in the province included the Alberta Environment Protection and Enhancement Act (AEPEA), the Alberta Water Resources Act, and Special Places 2000. The AEPEA became law on June 26, 1992 (effective Sept. 1, 1993). It created a new framework in a single act that took an integrated approach to the protection of air, land and water. In 1992, four Committee members attended a series of information meetings regarding the new AEPEA policies.

The Club's Environmental Special Committee became a member of the Alberta Environment Network Water Caucus, a coalition of environmental groups formed in 1992 in response to the Alberta Government's request for input into developing Alberta water management for the future. A new Act was needed because the original 1905 Federal Water Act for Alberta, revised in 1930 as the Alberta Water Resources Act, had remained unchanged for 60 years.

A new Water Act, Bill 51, was introduced in the fall of 1995 and Albertans were given an opportunity to review and provide comments before it was re-introduced in the spring of 1996. The Committee wrote to Premier Ralph Klein in December 1995, commenting that they "had followed the Water Resources Act revision process from the 1991 invitation for public input through to tabling of the Bill, and as the Act was written, it still failed to address key environmental protection recommendations." Many other points conforming to CFUW policy on water were also addressed.

The Special Places 2000 initiative was launched in 1992 as Alberta's response to the World Wildlife Fund's Endangered Spaces Campaign. Alberta has six natural regions that include 20 sub-regions. The strategy was meant to complete a network of Special Places that represent the environmental diversity of these six natural regions. The Environment Committee addressed concerns surrounding the Alberta

Legislation on Special Places several times. In a letter (December 1994) to the Honorable Ty Lund, Minister of Environmental Protection, they stressed the continued lack of commitment from the government to set aside a network of special places by 2000 that would serve as a legacy for future generations. The Committee also cited a poll by the World Wildlife Fund showing that 93% of Albertans supported protecting a full range of provincial landscapes.

The initiative begun in 1992 is still without any firm government policy to restrict industrial development in protected areas. Environmental groups, including CFUW Edmonton, continue to call for stronger legislation to protect Alberta's Special Places.

Beginning in March 1993, members Marg Reine and Robin Robinson attended a series of meetings sponsored by the Alberta Round Table on Environment and Economy. This was a 24-member body established (May 1990) to provide leadership, policy advice and long-term strategies on sustainable development in Alberta. Another of the Club's members, City Councillor Pat Mackenzie (President 1986-87) served as a member of the Alberta Round Table, representing the Alberta Urban Municipalities Association. During her term on City Council Pat was involved in several environmental projects.

Water Export

With the advent of the North American Free Trade Agreement (NAFTA) in 1993, the Committee was concerned about water being declared a commodity under the terms of the NAFTA and its possible export across international boundaries. It therefore proposed a resolution dealing with the issue which was passed at the 1993 National AGM.

> Be it resolved that the CFUW urge the Government of Canada to pass and enforce a Canada Water Preservation Act, which will prohibit further diversion of water between drainage basins and which will ensure Canada's sovereignty over its domestic water resources; and that the CFUW urge the Government of Canada to resolve immediately the uncertainty surrounding the water-trade issue through the execution of a separate and binding joint diplomatic agreement, ratified by both the U.S. Congress and the Canadian Parliament, which ensures that nothing in the Canada-U.S. Free Trade Agreement shall apply to Canada's water resource in other than bottled form.

Edmonton's Natural History Areas

In 1998–99, the Environment Study Group (formerly the Environmental Special Committee) supported the Edmonton Natural History Club in its fight for "the acquisition and conservation of natural areas on Edmonton's tablelands (the area back from the North Saskatchewan River Valley)." The initial fight for the preservation of a 47-kilometre area called Little Mountain was not successful.

In a presentation to the City of Edmonton Community Services Committee in 1999, the Group called for protection of our natural heritage and said that it was up to the City Council to create by-laws which mandate that, on lands purchased for development where natural areas exist, sustainable portions must be allocated for preservation. The Group was heartened by the Council's creation of a Reserve Fund for Natural Areas in March 1999 and noted that momentum was building at the municipal and provincial level for new attitudes about the necessity of natural areas in City of Edmonton planning.

Revisiting Hazardous Waste Problems

The Club had addressed the issue of hazardous waste management on several occasions; their first Brief regarding the issue had been made in 1980, and at the 1989 AGM in Edmonton they featured a speaker from Alberta Special Waste Management. In the 1990s they monitored the Swan Hills Toxic Waste Site. When the issue arose regarding a low-grade hazardous waste site at Ryley near a world-renowned bird sanctuary, several members swung into action in September 1996. They spearheaded a group of Edmonton women, not all Club members, in protesting the granting of a license to an environmental services company that would allow the landfill of low-grade hazardous wastes at a site located only a few kilometres from Beaverhill Lake, a World Wildlife refuge.

Twelfth Street Beat, University Hospital Newsletter, Vol. 4, No. 2, Feb., 1965

Members of Environment Group visiting low grade hazardous waste site at Ryley, Alberta (1996).
L to R: Tammy Irwin, Plant Manager, Anna Guest, Robin Robinson, Olga Shklanka, Pat Wishart

Not all the local residents opposed the site, but sufficient numbers did and sought support from outside interveners. Alberta legislation allowed only those directly affected to make appeals against granting of the license to build the extension. Nevertheless, the Group wrote to the Alberta Environment Review Board stating, "Since the landfill site at Ryley accepts waste from Edmonton, so members of this Environment Group consider themselves "directly affected."" The members were only a small part of the active protestation of environmentalists and scientists who were present at the 1997 Ryley hearings of the Environmental Review Board. Their support was valuable and several letters of thanks were received from the residents. "Thanks to the ladies from Edmonton who offered support for the cause—your presence filled the room!" Though not a complete victory, further expansion of the site was restricted.

Toward a Cleaner River

The members of the Environment Study Group have taken on some interesting projects on behalf of the environment, including one in 1999 involving the City's combined sewer overflow. Edmonton's "Towards a Cleaner River" project was initiated to improve the quality of the North Saskatchewan River by reducing the impact of flows from the City's drainage system that enter the river untreated. Club member Pat Wishart traveled up and down the river, inspecting over 80 overflow sites.

Pat Wishart was well chosen as the Club's representative on the "Towards a Cleaner River" project, for she had been involved with environmental awareness and education since the early 1970s when she was part of the Club's Ecology Caravan. In the early 1970s she was appointed the Club's first representative to the Public Advisory Committee of the Environment Conservation Authority, later known as the Environmental Council of Alberta. Pat has had a long-standing interest in keeping the City of Edmonton river valley natural.

Throughout the 1990s Club members were encouraged by the Environment Group to write supportive letters or sign petitions supporting CFUW environmental policies on such matters as ozone-depleting substances legislation (1994), reducing greenhouse emissions (1995), proposed amendments to the Endangered Species Act–Bill C-65 (1997) and the preservation of Banff National Park.

Since the 1970s the women of CFUW Edmonton have recognized the issues related to environmental degradation and have acted positively and knowledgeably to lobby for change. Whether it was water quality, recycling, forests and sustainable development, hazardous waste, natural area protection—the Club not only made great efforts to educate themselves and others, but also put their knowledge into positive social and political action.

Community Service

From the 1970s onward many members of CFUW Edmonton were nominated by the Club and served on various City Boards, Councils, the U of A Senate, Grant MacEwan Community College Board of Governors, Public Advisory Committee of City Parks and Recreation and the Provincial Conservation Authority (Environment Council of Alberta). Others took leadership roles in major events such as the Commonwealth Games, Universidade and in art and music festivals. Others served on City Council and as Edmonton Public School Board Trustees.

In the early days of the CFUW Edmonton, women would have been involved in these activities on behalf of the Club, but by the 1970s involvement was often more personal and not necessarily as official representatives of the Club. The commitment of members to public affairs appears to have been maintained, but official recognition may have come from other places. Several members have received life-time achievement awards from the City of Edmonton and the Province of Alberta, and life memberships in the YWCA and the Alberta Teacher's Association. Several received honorary doctorates from the U of A for their outstanding contribution as volunteers. Through the years the women of the Club have made many contributions to society. It is not possible to mention each one, but collectively they have enhanced the reputation of the Club in the community.

Chapter 4

Status of Women

Purpose Three: To foster a sense of responsibility and encourage women university graduates to place their education and professional training at the service of the community in local, national and international fields; to be concerned with human rights and at the same time to safeguard and improve the economic, legal and professional status of Canadian women.

CFUW Edmonton has taken an active interest in status of women issues through practical educational support for women, through advocacy for legislation changes to enhance women's position in Canadian society and through cooperative efforts with other women's groups. While recognizing the inclusion of human rights in Purpose Three, discussion in this section has centred mainly on Status of Women issues.

Early Years: 1909 to 1939

The first few decades of the 1900s must have been an invigorating time for the women of CFUW Edmonton. From the Club's inception they had been making overtures regarding the importance of women's participation in the political process. Soon after its founding in 1910, the Club indicated that they planned to further the election of a woman to the U of A Senate and a woman to the School Board of Edmonton and Strathcona as a means of influencing educational policy at all levels.

Members also joined with other Alberta women in petitioning for "women's enfranchisement." By 1914, the Edmonton Local Council of Women (LCW) had formed a Standing Committee on the Franchise of Women and local women's groups were asked to sign a petition and

The first female trustee elected to the Edmonton Public School Board was Bessie Nichols in 1912. She was strongly supported by the Local Council of Women representing some 30 women's societies, but was barred by a City of Edmonton Charter which carried a provision for females to vote but did not indicate that females could be elected to civic office.

Thus, the first female candidate ever to be elected to hold civic office in Edmonton was legally barred from becoming a school board trustee. Immediate steps were taken to correct the discrimination through a petition to the provincial government which approved the right of women to be elected school board trustees.

From: A Century and Ten: The History of Edmonton Public Schools, by M. A. Kostek

become involved. Talks were presented leading up to the vote in Alberta and noted personalities were brought to town to speak on the matter. Though CFUW Edmonton records show little direct official involvement in the enfranchisement of women cause, there is no doubt that many of these socially active and well-educated women participated in advocating for the vote. It is probable that members felt that by combining their individual efforts with those of the LCW there would be more likelihood of success.

Women of Alberta received voting rights in 1916, the third province to do so; Manitoba and Saskatchewan women had received the vote earlier that year. In the City of Edmonton however, a provision had been made by 1912 to allow women to vote in civic elections. Women's groups rallied behind the election of a woman to the local public school board and Bessie Nichols was elected first woman trustee that year. The following year, women's groups further supported the election of Mrs. E. L. (Jenny) Hill, a Club member, in the widely publicized and controversial elections of 1913. (See *Education*)

Because there was no official Status of Women Study Group until the 1960s, much of the work on equality issues in the early days was done under the aegis of the Education Standing Committee (ESC). Of particular note is the direction provided by Jenny Hill, Dr. Geneva Misener, and later Mary Butterworth.

During the 1920s and 1930s many women shared Dr. Misener's interest in international peace and understanding.

Dr. Geneva Misener

Among the membership in the early days was a woman whose life work embodied the women's movement. Current Club members, aside from her involvement on the Club's Executive, knew little about Dr. Misener. By perusing the University of Alberta Archives a picture of this trend-setting woman emerges. Dr. Misener, with her remarkable academic record, was the first woman professor at the University of Alberta where she taught Classics for thirty-three years. She was one of Canada's earliest women graduates (Queen's University, 1899) and obtained a PhD (on scholarship) from the University of Chicago in 1903. She was Advisor to Women Students at the University of Alberta from 1913 to 1920 and was named a member of the University's Senate in 1926.

Dr. Misener was one of two Edmonton delegates to the founding meeting of CFUW and served as Education Chair on the first national Executive. She was also on the Executive of the National Council of Women and was a delegate to the Women's Committee of the Institute of Pacific Relations (Hawaii, 1934) that promoted international understanding, an abiding interest of hers.

Dr. Misener was a woman who early in her career successfully combined her family and professional commitments; she became a single parent by adopting two young nieces and raising them to adulthood.

These issues were considered women's issues—whatever led to a secure home life was of concern to women. Records show that during this period, the Club lobbied continuously on behalf of peace and disarmament. Many peace groups appeared on the scene and solicited Club support. One group was the Women's International League for Peace and Freedom, which asked the Club to sell 5¢ picture postcards to defray expenses of the organization. As more and more groups requested assistance, the Club eventually resolved to support only the League of Nations.

During the 1930s, CFUW had members who were leaders within the women's movement and who lobbied for such things as divorce reform and women's property rights. By 1937 a Legal and Economic Status of Women Committee had been established by the National organization. Although Clubs were encouraged to establish similar committees it does not appear that the issues were taken up locally. Concern at the time was on unemployment and retraining programs—issues that seemed more pertinent in the era of the depression.

The Club's Vocations Committee (a National Vocations Committee had been formed in 1919) looked at conditions under which women worked in factories, and had representation on an Advisory Committee for Training of Unemployed Women. The Club also put a great deal of effort into finding job placements for women students, in conjunction with a university project under the guidance of Dr. Misener.

War and Post War Years

By the 1940s attention was turned to the war effort, and the employment climate for women changed dramatically. As men left for the service women stepped into their jobs. The contribution of Canadian women to the war effort is well documented and is mentioned here as it relates to the post-war problems of job dislocation and retraining faced by women, and the Club's response to these problems.

Mrs. Cora Casselman

Cora Casselman

During and after the war a member of the Club was to play a unique part in the Status of Women story–Mrs. Frederick C. (Cora) Casselman. In 1942 Cora Casselman was elected Liberal Member of Parliament for Edmonton East following the death of her husband who had been the previous MP. Although her election was considered at the time "a widow's succession," Cora Casselman proved her mettle in Parliament. Her years on the Executive of CFUW at the local level (President 1926–27 and 1932–33) and at the national level (Vice-President 1934–37) would have provided valuable experience, but are not mentioned in published articles about her life. She achieved many firsts in her own right–first woman elected from Alberta to the House of Commons, first woman with a university education to become a Member of Parliament and first woman invited to sit in the Speaker's Chair in the House of Commons.

Continued on page 119

Continued from page 118

It was reported in the Edmonton Journal on May 15, 1942 that Mrs. Casselman made history in the Commons when she presided as Chairman of the Committee of the Whole in the absence of the Deputy Speaker, Thomas Vien. When she took the chair there was a burst of applause. Prime Minister Mackenzie King congratulated her on the fact there was a woman occupying the seat of chairman of the committee "for the first time in the history of this House."

Mrs. Casselman was an active member of the House Committee on Social Security, where she lobbied the government for mothers' allowances, better pensions and health insurance.

In 1943, she traveled to Washington and New York on behalf of the Canadian Women's Committee on International Relations and spoke on foreign policy at women's meetings. She also went to Philadelphia as part of Canada's delegation to the International Labour Organization, which had a mandate to draw up a new charter of international labor laws for the post-war market. After her successful representation at the Philadelphia meeting, Mrs. Casselman was sent as the only woman in Canada's delegation to the founding meeting of the United Nations in San Francisco in 1945. As a long-time supporter of the League of Nations (and an executive member of Canada's League of Nations Society) she considered this one of the highlights of her career.

Following her impressive career in politics and international affairs (she was defeated in her bid for re-election in 1945, as were most of her liberal colleagues in Alberta), Mrs. Casselman assumed the position of Executive Director of the YWCA in Edmonton from 1945–53. As a widowed, single mother, she was aware of the need for change in the post-war era and through her involvement in the 'Y' and many other organizations, she worked continuously for the rights of women. In 1947 the CFUW put forward her name for Senator to fill one of the positions vacant, but the nomination was not successful.

In 1953 Queen Elizabeth presented her with the Coronation Medal for her outstanding contributions to society.

Recognizing that major concerns would have to be addressed at war's end, two new Study Groups were formed within the Club: Reconstruction, and Post War Problems of Women. The former Group worked with other fledgling city agencies to aid men and women returning from the service. The Post War Problems Group concerned itself with the availability of information on re-training for women.

They recommended that material of the National Employment Bureau be given wide publicity in high, schools, universities, women's clubs and training centres. They were also concerned with housing for the lower income groups, calling for the appointment of women as members of Boards considering any housing schemes. The Club established a special committee that compiled a list of women to act on Boards. The names of 46 city women (including members of the Club) qualified to serve on Government Committees and Boards were forwarded to National CFUW in April 1945.

Mrs. McWilliams–An Interwar Feminist

Mrs. McWilliams, founder and first CFUW President, was a leader in civic, provincial (Manitoba), national and international affairs from the 1920s through to the 1940s. It was in recognition of her outstanding service of two decades that Mrs. McWilliams was appointed in 1943 to Chair the (Federal) Subcommittee on Post-War Problems of Women (of the Advisory Committee on Reconstruction) in 1943. She worked for international understanding and the advancement of women and was a delegate to the Pacific Relations Conference in 1931. Mrs. McWilliams was also advisor to the federal government's delegation to the labour conference of the League of Nations. Many of the concerns the Club addressed arose from a study of the McWilliams Report on Post War Problems.

Mrs. McWilliams has been described as an "interwar feminist," a title that could also describe several Club members, including Mrs. Cora Casselman and Dr. Geneva Misener. Canadian interwar feminist history is an important and fascinating period that is only now being explored and re-examined by historians. It is to the credit of CFUW and to Mrs. McWilliams that she focused so much of her energy through this organization.

Three Champions of Women's Rights in the 1940s

One of the 46 women included in the list of women qualified for public office was **Mary Butterworth** who, supported by the Club, ran for the EPSB in 1945. Not only was she successful in her bid (1945–1957), but she also became the second woman to serve as Chair of the Board. The first was an earlier member, Mrs. E. T. Bishop. Mrs. Butterworth was able to put the experience gained as a member of the Club's Executive to work in the wider arena of civic politics.

EPS Archives & Museum: P85.25.18

Mary Butterworth was a graduate from Aberdeen, Scotland who immigrated to Alberta in the early 1900s. She joined the Club in the 1920s and was actively involved in CFUW affairs. Mrs. Butterworth was Club President (1937–38), chaired numerous committee and study groups and was representative to the Local Council of Women in the 1940s. She served on the National Executive as editor of the CFUW Chronicle. During her time on the Board, Mrs. Butterworth worked hard to gain tenure for married women teachers and in this

Mrs. F. C. (Mary) Butterworth

she had the full support of the Club. For her work as EPSB Trustee and Chair and champion of women's rights, a public school was named in her honour in south Edmonton in the early 1990s. In addition her name graces several streets in an Edmonton sub-division.

Another member who spoke out on behalf of women in education and administration was **Marian Gimby.** As a member of the Alberta Teachers' Association (ATA) Executive in the 1940s, Marian was known to "rock the boat" on many issues regarding the power structure of the ATA Executive. For her determined efforts to effect change, she was elected the first woman President of the ATA in 1951. She was an active member of CFUW Edmonton for many years, serving on the Executive as Corresponding Secretary and as Federation Representative (1939–42).

Dr. Mary Winspear followed Marian Gimby on the Executive as Corresponding Secretary and Federation Representative. Although she was only with the Club for a short while, Dr. Winspear showed a particular interest in Status of Women issues.

In 1943 it was Dr. Winspear who spoke up on a proposal made by the EPSB requiring that women who married should automatically have to resign from the teaching staff. She recommended that the Club actively oppose the move, and the Club voted overwhelmingly to support her recommendation. Mary Butterworth took up this cause during her EPSB commitment. In 1944 Dr. Winspear convened a special

Committee to address the issue of a minimum wage for women, with recommendations being put forward to the Provincial Government Industrial Relations Board.

She also furthered a CFUW inquiry into equity in staff positions at Canadian universities, presumably at the request of the CFUW Academic Appointments Committee (AAC). This was a national Special Committee that existed from 1934 to 1952 to encourage Clubs to submit names of potential candidates to a CFUW registry of qualified women ready to accept appointments in Canadian universities. Unfortunately, this registry and a subsequent CFUW list were never utilized to the full extent of their value. This realization was expressed in the Club Minutes (Exec. Meeting, May 10, 1945) when it was stated: "it was generally felt that there was little chance of a woman getting a posting at the U of A." Nonetheless, the Club sent a letter to the President, Dr. R. Newton, regarding the availability of Dr. Mary Winspear for a position at the U of A. With nothing forthcoming, Dr. Winspear left Edmonton at the end of 1945 for Kingston, Ontario.

The Appointment and Advancement of Women

The appointment and advancement of women on staff at Canadian universities remained an on-going issue with CFUW. In 1950, in support of a CFUW Resolution, the Club wrote to the Minister of Education petitioning for the appointment of more women to positions in the two branches of the Faculty of Education in Calgary and Edmonton. In 1973 they called for a Task Force on the status of female staff at the U of A. The Club also participated in the more wide-reaching CFUW Women in Universities project of the 1990s, as detailed later.

As the effectiveness of the AAC dwindled, it was asked to broaden the scope of its registry "to add to their duties a tabulation of expert women" (CFUW Chronicle, 1951/52). In 1952, the CFUW Legal and Economic Status of Women Special Committee undertook a list of "Competent Women." In preparation for enlarging the registry, several questionnaires were sent to members. In one, asking how many would be willing to sit on Boards or Commissions, the Committee was amazed by the overwhelming interest of members and the calibre and breadth of their talents. Another questionnaire asked if the Clubs would be interested in supporting women at the provincial and federal levels of governments. The Edmonton executive replied that it preferred to keep support to the non-partisan municipal level (Club minutes, April 1953). It was at this level, of course, that the local Club had been successful.

Tax Reform to Benefit Women

Clubs were urged to support other Status of Women issues during the 1950s, including changes to the tax system. Of particular concern was the proposed new federal Estate Tax Bill introduced in January 1958. While designed to replace the Dominion Succession Duty Act, and having some commendable features, women's groups felt it still did not recognize the wife's contributions to the marriage partnership. A letter went out from the CFUW Status of Women Committee to all Clubs asking members to study the Bill carefully and to make presentations to the Federal Government requesting amendments to the revised Estate Tax Act. The Club complied. They also forwarded a Resolution for consideration at the 1958 Triennial Conference concerning income tax exemption for professionally employed women's expenses for a housekeeper or nurse.

Some of the other subjects suggested for study by the National Status of Women Committee during this period included equal pay, jury service, dower legislation, the working woman with family responsibilities and pension rights for working women. Many of these concerns, including advocacy for day care for working women, became central to the Club's status of women actions through the next few decades. It was the rise of these and other related women's issues that provided the momentum for the so-called second wave of the women's movement that culminated in Canada in the Royal Commission on the Status of Women in 1967.

The 1960s: Equality for Women

Whereas the first wave of feminism was considered to be the enfranchisement of women, the establishment of the Voice of Women in 1960 heralded the second wave of feminism in Canada. This was followed by the reorganization and coming together of a large number of women's groups across Canada. One of these groups was the Committee for Equality for Women, an alliance formed in 1966 to pressure the government for an inquiry into the status of women. This alliance was made up of representatives from 32 voluntary and professional organizations and headed by Laura Sabia, who was then President of CFUW. It is said that Laura Sabia, along with Doris Anderson and like-minded women, energized the second wave of feminism, just as Emily Murphy and her Alberta colleagues had energized the first wave of feminism. Certainly as head of a large national organization with over 10,000 members (CFUW), Mrs. Sabia was well placed to spearhead such a movement. Doris Anderson, an ardent feminist and former Albertan, was editor of *Chatelaine* magazine in the 1960s and she used the magazine as a platform for advancing women's issues. For her support and leadership on behalf of women's rights, the CFUW Edmonton nominated Anderson for an Honorary Doctorate at the University of Alberta, which she received in the 1970s.

Both groups, the Voice of Women and the Committee for Equality for Women, which resulted in the Royal Commission on the Status of Women (RConSW), were to have an influence on the local Club. The Voice of Women connected with peace and environmental issues, and the RConSW had an impact on continuing education for women and led to the eventual establishment of the CFUW Edmonton Mature Women's Bursary Program.

Continuing Education for Women: 1960s to 1970s

In the fall of 1964, Laura Sabia came west to Calgary for a Regional Conference of the Alberta University Women's Clubs. At the time she was seeking support from all the CFUW clubs for the proposed Royal Commission on the Status of Women, but she also had a very strong interest in continuing education for women and was gathering support for that issue as well. (See *Education*)

Continuing education for adults, and especially women, was a subject that had gained recognition during the 1950s, and Mrs. Sabia was not alone in her passion. She was able to inspire others to take up her cause through her very dynamic nature, according to Club members who met her at the time. One of those members was Avery Fleming, who was involved in both the Education and Status of Women Groups in the 1960s. In an interview in 1997, Avery was able to provide valuable information regarding this period in the Club's history.

In 1964 a Continuing Education Study Group, chaired by Avery Fleming, investigated what programs were available to mature women at universities across the country. When the Royal Commission on the Status of Women was established in 1967, the Study Group, at Mrs.

Sabia's urging, submitted six Recommendations based on the results of their investigation. These included the need for flexibility in part-time study, increased financial assistance, adequate day care and alternative ways of teaching, such as home study and radio lectures, the latter two being quite innovative and radical for the time. In the fall of 1970, under Club Past President Enid Crockett, members presented this brief in person to the Royal Commission on the Status of Women in Edmonton. For the Club's Brief of 1968, Joan Wensel developed a case history of a composite woman, Mrs. Rusty Baccalaureate, a woman who had three children and who had been at home for ten years. She then proceeded to show all the barriers this typical woman faced in getting back into the work force and in up-grading her education part-time.

The Club might have left it at that, but they were spurred on by a response from the Commission's Deputy Secretary Monique Begin who, according to Avery Fleming, wrote to the Club telling them that "just because the Royal Commission on the Status of Women was finished it did not mean that the work was done." She presented members with ideas on who to see in the government and where to keep pressuring for change regarding their proposed recommendations. The Group, by now renamed the Status of Women Study Group, followed up on the suggestions and made personal presentations to both the Provincial Government and the University of Alberta regarding changes to the Student Finance Act that would aid mature women.

A young woman student at the University of Alberta whom they had met during their investigations further encouraged the Study Group in their lobbying efforts. This woman had set up a support group among the mature women students on campus and the Status of Women Study Group met with them several times to find out what their needs were. It was through these meetings, combined with the surveys and the resultant Briefs, that the Club determined the need for a bursary program. The creation of the Mature Women's Bursary was an important development in the Club's history. (See *Academic Awards*)

Another interesting development that came out of the work of the Status of Women Study Group was the "Second Look" at the University of Alberta Extension Department. Club members Joan Wensel and Avery Fleming suggested that the department set up a model based on a new concept from the University of Minnesota called Second Look for Women. Under Joan and Avery's persuasion, who referred back to their Mrs. Baccalaureate creation, the Extension Department set up courses in 1969 and had personnel from companies give talks to women on how to present themselves for interviews and other skills needed for re-entry into the workplace.

The 1970s: Putting Recommendations into Action

Implementation of Recommendations

The 1970s were a busy time for women's groups across Canada pressing for implementation of the 167 Recommendations that came out of the Royal Commission on the Status of Women. When it reported in 1970, the Commission outlined four principles that would define it. Briefly, these were:

- that women should be free to choose to take employment outside their homes
- that the care of children should be a shared responsibility
- that society has a responsibility for women because of pregnancy and child-birth and special treatment related to maternity would always be necessary (maternity rights) and
- that "affirmative action" policies be promoted at all levels of government.

The CFUW Status of Women and Human Rights Committee encouraged member clubs to follow up on those recommendations that related to CFUW policy, through Briefs, letter-writing campaigns and organizing or participating in seminars and supporting like-minded groups. The Edmonton Club particularly addressed those issues in which they had some background, such as day care (see *Public Affairs*) and affirmative action.

Affirmative action took the form of a petition to the U of A Senate to establish a task force to look at "the status of all female staff members at the University." This came about after several University of Alberta faculty members had tried unsuccessfully to unearth statistical data on the University's hiring and promoting practices regarding women, and turned to the Club's Status of Women Group for help. With the support of the National Federation, the Club made a successful submission to the University Senate. Dr. Jean Lauber, a University staff member and one of the Club's leading advocates for status of women in the 1970s, was a co-presenter of the Brief. Then in 1973 a University of Alberta Task Force was named with June Sheppard as Chair. She was a columnist for the *Edmonton Journal* and a long-time supporter of the Club.

CFUW members were encouraged to participate in International Women's Year (IWY) activities at the national, provincial and local level. At the national level, it was 'Foster the Roster,' a project designed to encourage and promote the appointment of qualified women by the government to public positions. At the provincial level, it was Family Law Reform, and at the local level Clubs were asked to promote career counseling for girls and the removal of sex-stereotyping from school texts.

As a major project aimed at removing sex-stereotyping, the Edmonton Status of Women Study Group put out a booklet called *They Jumped So High They Reached the Sky: Famous Canadian Women*. It was written for young students and included tales of the Edmonton Grads basketball team (whence the title) as well as stories of nine other exceptional Canadian women. Written in a simple short form, the stories proved to be popular and the book became a moneymaker for the Club.

Another project that members took up in 1976 was monitoring children's TV programs for sex role stereotyping. They (26 members) found that of the 47 programs they looked at, over half were moderately to extremely sexist and many were extremely violent. These results were combined with those of other clubs across Canada to give CFUW a fairly accurate account of stereotyping of the period. Petitions were sent to the Canadian Radio & Television Commission (CRTC).

Family Law Reform

In January of 1978, the Club sent a letter to the Alberta Government through their local MLA stating, "one hundred and fifty members of the University Women's Club of Edmonton strongly support the principle of deferred sharing rather than judicial discretion in the proposed Matrimonial Property Act, Bill 102." They joined in a vociferous call from women's groups for a redress of the Canadian landmark Iris Murdoch case on deferred sharing of matrimonial property.

The 50th anniversary of the famous Persons' Case (October 29, 1929) inspired Club member Marjorie Buckley to write a two-part play called *Twin Pack*. This dealt in the first part with the efforts of Alberta's

Marjorie Buckley

famous five (Emily Murphy, Henrietta Muir Edwards, Louise McKinney, Nellie McClung and Irene Parlby) to get women recognized as persons in the matters of rights and privileges. The second part was an update to 1979 of women's struggles for equal rights, focusing in a moving and visual way on the Murdoch case in Saskatchewan.

Although dated now, this play was presented to some acclaim several times during the year, including at the Canadian Federation of Teachers Convention held in Edmonton, and the CFUW National Meeting held in Quebec City. The play helped build a national awareness of the Persons' Case, which is now widely recognized and celebrated annually by Canadian women. (A statue commemorating the work of the Famous Five Women was unveiled in Calgary on October 18, 1999 and in Ottawa on the same date in 2000. The statue, done by an Edmonton artist and U of A graduate Barbara Peterson, represents the first sculpture of Canadian women on Parliament Hill.)

The 1980s: Another Wave of Activity

Women's rights under the Canadian Charter of Rights and Freedoms was one of the focal points of discussion in the 1980s, along with the impact of microtechnology on women's careers, pension reform and pornography issues. Many of these issues were national in scope, requiring federal legislation. The Club's purposes were often best served by adding their voice to the larger lobbying effort of the national CFUW. In addition, as more members were employed full-time, the Club tended to take on a role of supporting like-minded groups or coalitions, rather than initiating major projects on its own. Women's groups have often sought coalition among each other to foster emerging needs. The need to do so has increased over time.

In the early 1980s, the Club joined with other women's groups to pressure the government to establish an Alberta Women's Advisory Council with cabinet status. For that purpose, a Provincial Committee for Alberta Council on Women's Affairs was formed in 1982, and representatives from various women's groups were named to the committee. The Club nominated member Maureen Towns, a lawyer and young mother. Within the year she was chosen as Chair, and capably led the Committee in their 1984 presentation to the government, noting that Alberta was the only province without such a council at the time. The Club was well represented when the motion to establish an Alberta Council on Women's Issues was brought before the Legislature.

In 1986, the government announced a 15-member Advisory Council which was given a sunset clause of ten years. The purpose of such a Council was to "advise and report to the government on matters relating to the opportunity for full and equal participation of Alberta women in the life of the province and to consult and provide information to the public." These aims were certainly in accord with those of CFUW and the Club supported Maureen and the Council in several ways, including petitions and personal representation. Despite protestations from women's groups, the Council was terminated in 1996, ten years after its inception.

Women and Pensions

Another area the Club was involved in was Pension Reform. As the plight of many older women on fixed incomes living in poverty became evident, groups started calling for better pension benefits for women. In the early 1980s the CFUW Status of Women and Human Rights Committee sent letters to all the clubs urging them to become informed concerning the Canadian pension system so they would be able to have some input into the forthcoming debate. Conferences initiated by the Federal Department of Health and Welfare were held across the country.

Members of a newly formed Pension Reform Study Group attended one of these local seminars organized by the Women's Program of the University of Alberta Extension Department, in conjunction with the Status of Women National Action Committees and other women's groups (1982). The information gleaned from the meeting plus other sources laid the foundation for a Brief the Club presented to the Parliamentary Task Force on Pension Reform in Edmonton (1983). It addressed the actual financing of the Canada Pension Plan as well as proposals to overcome the special problems facing women, including a homemakers' pension.

The spectre of marriage breakdown and old-age poverty detailed by pension reformers encouraged many women, Club members included, to take responsibility for their financial futures. Throughout the 1980s, there were two active investment groups in the Club, both assisted by professional financial advisers. Members also attended numerous financial seminars given for their benefit.

Women and Pornography

CFUW was very active in lobbying for stricter pornography legislation in the early 1980s. With the proliferation of pornography through print, Pay TV and Video, there were calls for changes to the Criminal Code that would make a definition of pornography more meaningful–a definition that could be used in legislation, particularly as it concerned child pornography. Although Edmonton did not take a leading role in the pornography debate, the Club lent strong support to CFUW's lobbying efforts.

In 1978 the United States passed the Protection of Children Against Sexual Exploitation Act, and in the same year the Canadian Justice Department strongly recommended that Canada have some updated child pornography laws. However, it would be many years before any concrete legislation was passed (1993). It was in this political climate that some excellent research on pornography was done by several clubs in Quebec and Ontario.

In 1982, the CFUW Clubs of the Province of Quebec brought a package of resolutions to the Annual Meeting in Winnipeg that they had started working on in 1979. After much deliberation and re-writing, these resolutions were passed, calling for a prohibition of the use of minors in the production of pornography and of their access to pornography. They also included a request for the establishment of criteria for classification of films. As a follow-up the Edmonton Club petitioned locally to have unsuitable material put out of reach of children in commercial establishments.

By 1983 a Canadian Coalition against Media Pornography was formed to demand tightening up of regulations. They claimed the proposed "Pay TV's Guidelines for Adult Programming" were too lax.

In response, the Club wrote again to the CRTC reinforcing their earlier recommendations to the Task Force on Sex-Role Stereotyping in the Broadcast Media.

As the seriousness of the issue increased, CFUW passed an emergency Resolution in 1984 calling for action on legislation regarding violence against women in the media and asking for the passage of Bill C-53, an act to amend the Criminal Code in relation to sexual assault and the protection of young persons. The government was claiming there was inadequate support to pass Bill C-53, and so Clubs were asked to renew a letter-writing campaign calling for changes to the Criminal Code. The government also referred to the fact that they were caught between those who opposed any kind of censorship in the media and those groups appealing for some kind of control on the increasingly violent nature of the pornography being shown. Women's groups were aware of this debate, but were not dissuaded by such arguments, and lobbying continued.

Earlier in January 1984, the Club had made a presentation to the Fraser Special Committee on Pornography and Prostitution calling for a more effective definition of pornography as it applied to the importation of such material. A government bill had made Criminal Code criteria for pornography applicable to include Customs and Excise regulations, but women's groups called the criteria ineffective in addressing the problem of pornography and continued to call for a more effective definition of pornography.

Women and the Charter

Through the 1980s women's groups were very concerned with the equality clauses in the Canadian Charter of Rights and Freedoms, and looked for assurance from the government before the Charter was proclaimed into law in 1982. The provincial and federal governments had been given three years to audit their statutes and amend those provisions that offended the equality clauses (Section 15) of the Charter. Any law that offended these provisions and was not changed by April 17, 1985, could only be defeated by going to court. To prevent expensive litigation, women were asked to scrutinize possible amendments to the Charter and to become informed on the issue.

To help women understand all the ramifications of this, a Charter of Rights Coalition (CORC) was formed. CFUW was asked to appoint a member in each province (preferably in the capitals) to monitor provincial legislation and assist in the planning of a regional conference in October of 1984. The position required someone with a grasp of the Charter's provisions and women's issues, and for this the Club looked to Dr. Jean Lauber.

Following the 1987 Constitutional Accord, women's groups again became concerned about the guarantees of equality, and another letter-writing campaign ensued.

Women and Technology

Throughout the 1980s CFUW national and regional conferences dealt with "the reality of women's work" in the new age of technology. They emphasized the demands placed on women with changing roles, questioned how to motivate women to enter new fields available to them, and ways to encourage younger women to study science and technology.

There were several studies done in the 1980s on the problems confronted by girls in the educational system (re: mathematics and science) including a federally funded Canadian study (1984) for the Canadian School Trustees Association authored by Theodora Foster, a member of the national CFUW Executive at the time. Another study was done by the American Association of University Women (AAUW) who commissioned a study of girls in science and mathematics entitled "How Schools Shortchange Girls." Both studies found that girls started opting out of mathematics and science courses in their teens because they had internalized their limitations, and the numbers continued to dwindle in post-secondary programs.

These education studies, and others done during the decade, helped shape CFUW policy. Clubs were urged to support or initiate programs that would aid girls in continuing with post-secondary studies in mathematics and science. Initiatives such as science programs geared to girls' experiences, mentoring, special awards and scholarships were encouraged.

The Club was a strong supporter of the Women in Scholarship in Engineering, Science and Technology (WISEST) program at the University of Alberta, which encouraged high school girls to take up science by offering in-school lectures and summer research programs. The program was extended to include annual all-day conferences for elementary girls aged 9 to 12 and their teachers.

Two names stand out in regard to the WISEST program at the University of Alberta–Club member Dr. Jean Lauber, and Dr. Margaret Ann Armour, Professor of Chemistry and recipient of many national and international honours. For their roles in mentoring young women in science and for establishing a similar support group for women students and staff in the science and engineering faculties at the University of Alberta, they received Edmonton YWCA Tribute to Women awards in 1982 and 1990 respectively.

Dr. Jean Lauber

In receiving the YWCA award in the category, "Women Helping Women," Dr. Lauber was honored not only for her work at the University, but also for her work in CFUW. She was an ideal role model for young women. She was a wife and mother of three children, she had a distinguished career at the University of Alberta as a Professor of Zoology and was named first woman Associate Vice-President (Academic). She was also Chair of the National CFUW Status of Women and Human Rights Committee (1973-76) and locally helped initiate CFUW projects concerning the environment and the status of women.

Dr. Jean Lauber

Women Honouring Women

The YWCA Tribute to Women Awards of Distinction were given as a means of honouring the contributions of women in the community and grew out of the affirmative action of the 1970s. When an Awards Dinner was established in Edmonton in 1982 to celebrate the 75th Anniversary of the Edmonton 'Y' (following in the steps of successful dinners held by the YWCA across the country), the Club was an early supporter and made a point of nominating members for recognition–thus the cluster of Club awards between 1982 and 1988.

In addition to Dr. Jean Lauber, three other Club members were honoured: Saretta Sparling for Community Service in the Volunteer sector (1982), Violet Archer for Women in the Arts (1985) and Jessica Hanna for Community Service (1988). The activities of each have added to the advancement of women in unique ways.

Saretta Sparling, a former Dean of Women at U of A, believed that University women owed leadership to the community because of their knowledge. Her legacy of volunteerism is enshrined in her motto— "volunteerism is the rent we pay for inhabiting the earth." This philosophy is remembered and practised by Club members who were students under her tutelage.

Violet Archer was nominated for her work as composer and teacher, and also for her precedent-setting role in the music world. More than anyone else she cleared the way for female composers in Canada when they were not taken seriously (U of A New Trail, 1999).

Jessica Hanna was nominated primarily for her work with the Edmonton and Alberta Women's Shelters. Under her guidance in 1970 storefront facilities for homeless women were developed. After the Province took over the facilities, she recognized the need for and promoted the establishment of the Edmonton Women's Shelter (WIN House) and WINGS (Women in Need Growing Stronger). She also served as President of the Alberta Women's Shelters Organization.

The work on the Edmonton Women's Shelter provides an example of the co-operative efforts between the Club and the YWCA. When the 'Y' opened the first women's emergency accommodation in 1970, requests came to the Club for overnight volunteers and clothing. According to the Club Minutes (1970), these requests were met as much as possible, but as demands increased the Club recognized the growing need for some kind of permanent accommodation and supported lobbying efforts in this direction.

During this period, the Club also assisted with the Rape Crisis Centre at the YWCA. Through the years, many CFUW Edmonton members served on the YWCA Board of Directors, and several were given YWCA of Edmonton Honorary Life Memberships for their extensive contributions to the organization, including Louise Johnson, Margaret Brine, Betty Mullen, Margaret Thomas and Rita Calhoun. Members who are currently involved with the 'Y' represent a long association that has lasted since the 1910s.

Women in Universities Project (WIU)

In the fall of 1991, the CFUW Status of Women and Human Rights Committee launched a national survey involving female faculty and students called the "Women in Universities Project." The objective of the project was to raise awareness of inequalities that still existed at Canadian universities, to identify creative solutions to the problems, to share them with the institutions and to support initiatives for reform.

> "The purpose of the survey was to examine the status of women at Canadian universities in ten areas of academic life. We hoped that our external concern would assist the internal efforts of Status of Women Coordinators and all members of the University community concerned with reform–the survey was developed as a result of frustration at the glacial pace of change for women at Canadian Universities. Being women graduates in a national network of clubs, we resolved to press politely but firmly for change ourselves."
>
> *(CFUW Journal, Vol. 26, No. 7, 1992).*

It was certainly true that there had been little change at the University of Alberta in the decade following the University of Alberta Senate Task Force on the Status of Women, which was prompted by the University Women's Club Brief in 1973. In 1984 the Academic Women's Association presented an update on the Status of Women to the University of Alberta Senate. The Club President was invited as a representative of a group with a vested interest in the issues. It was not a flattering report. It showed that the status of women had in fact lost ground.

Areas of concern identified by the Women in Universities 1991 Report included many of the same issues raised in the 1984 presentation–salary discrepancies, employment equity (tenure remained a problem), lack of support for women willing to enter non-traditional fields, and lack of female mentors and role models. It was encouraging to note, however, that many of the issues that CFUW and the Edmonton Club had addressed in their Status of Women Briefs in the late 1960s and 1970s were now accepted practices–opportunities for part-time study, flexibility of course scheduling, availability of daycare for faculty and students at most institutions, a decrease in sexual harassment and increased awareness of campus safety measures designed to safeguard women.

Although some concerns may still exist for women academics on campus, there has been vast improvement since the 1920s when **Dr. Silver Keeping** started her career in research at the U of A.

Long-time Club member (1925 to 1957), Dr. Eleanor Silver Keeping, was recipient of a CFUW Travelling Fellowship in 1928 which gave her the opportunity to do post graduate study in England. The following year she received a PhD from the University of Manitoba, and then returned to Edmonton and married Frank Keeping, Mathematics professor at the U of A. Although encouraged by her husband to continue with her research, Silver found that as a wife of a faculty member, she could not receive a salary. Recognizing both her talent and her plight, the Dean of Medicine hired her in 1933 and gave her room in the Medical Building on campus where she set up a diagnostic service for human fungus disease in association with the Alberta Provincial Laboratory of Public Health.

In 1954, she turned over her appointment with the Provincial Lab to a young male PhD assistant and for the next twenty years kept her interest in research as an honorary research associate in the Departments of Medical Bacteriology, Botany and Genetics at the U of A. The appointments carried no salary or tenure. Despite this, Dr. Keeping established a reputation as a renowned specialist in fungi (mycology) and was one of the founding sponsors of the U of A's Devonian Botanic Gardens. (U of A, New Trail, Summer, 1991).

By the mid-1960s it was agreed that spouses at U of A could both be appointed even to the same faculty if qualified in competition with other candidates, the only stipulation being that neither spouse could be paid from a research grant administered by the other.

Dr. Jean Lauber addressed the latter two areas in her role as Associate Vice President (Academic) at the University of Alberta. To help women feel more secure from sexual assault, Dr. Lauber arranged better lighting and more emergency telephones on campus. After studying sexual harassment, she lobbied for changes in the university code of ethics to discourage attempts to trade academic advancement for sexual favours.

In 1990, the Club President presented a Brief to the President's Commission for Equality and Respect on Campus (March, 1990), commending the initiatives to promote only that behavior which would result in mutual respect and equality within the University community.

It also reaffirmed the Club's commitment to groups such as WISEST that works to promote an interest and awareness of the opportunities available to young women in science and technology.

Women and History

Although the Club had made the establishment of a Provincial Archives its Centennial project in the early 1960s, thus recognizing the value of archival material, the Club's own archivists had trouble until the 1990s convincing members of the importance of their own history.

In fact, little was considered history in Western Canada until recent times–few pioneer women had the inclination to write of their day-to-day experiences and it wasn't until the 1960s and 1970s that Alberta women's groups collectively started to formulate a means for getting women's history in writing. The recent efforts of groups such as the (Northern) Alberta Women's Archives Association, which produced an *Introductory Guide to Preserving Archival Records about Women: What's Cooking* (1992) and the Alberta Historical Resources Foundation, which published *How to do Oral Histories* by Judy Larmour in 1994, were helpful. The impetus to finally add CFUW Edmonton's history owes much to the work of these groups, and others, such as the Edmonton YWCA. It was the core members of the 'Y's history project *Retrospect: The Edmonton Y.W.C.A. 1957–1991* that brought their own invaluable experience to the current project.

In addition to piecing together the lives of the early CFUW Edmonton members through archival research, the History Group conducted and taped over 30 oral interviews with the senior members of the Club and a picture of their early pioneer experiences has been added to the files.

With the knowledge acquired from researching and writing the Club history, as well as skills gained through trial and error in the interviewing process, members have been called upon to give workshops on the "Writing of a Club History" and women's history at provincial, regional and national CFUW Conferences over the past few years.

One of the important aspects of writing the Club history has been to trace the development of women in Edmonton and Alberta through the years, giving examples of the strides and setbacks of the women's movement locally. It is not surprising that the membership in the early days was made up almost exclusively of teachers, librarians and housewives. It is rewarding to note how the dynamics of the Club membership has changed. Today it includes university professors, lawyers, senior government officials, city councilors, school board trustees, accountants, investment advisors, systems analysts, as well as teachers, librarians and homemakers. This diversity of professions illustrates the tremendous advantages that have accrued to women through the years, due in large part to the lobbying efforts of status of women groups, such as CFUW Edmonton.

$\mathcal{N}$ational and International Affairs: CFUW and IFUW

Purpose Four: to take action in concert with the International Federation of University Women, of which the Canadian Federation of University Women is a member, to effect change at the international level; to encourage friendship, cooperation and understanding among university women graduates worldwide.

Although the Canadian Federation of University Women Edmonton is an autonomous organization registered under the Societies Act of the Province of Alberta, it is also one of over 123 clubs in Canada that constitute the Canadian Federation of University Women. CFUW is one of the 70 federations and associations that constitute the International Federation of University Women (IFUW). Already ten years old by 1919, the Club (at that time called the Women's University Club of Edmonton) was one of the founding members of CFUW in Winnipeg that same year. Later in 1919 the International Federation of University Women had its organizational meeting in Europe, and CFUW was present.

The Edmonton Club has purposes similar to both CFUW and IFUW. The wording has changed somewhat over the years, but the concerns remain the same. All groups are interested in education (to encourage advanced study and research by women, and to cultivate excellence in education), the advancement of human rights and the improvement in the status of all women, the encouragement of participation of its members in all aspects of public affairs, and all attempts to bring about global understanding and co-operation among women university graduates.

CFUW

In the decade leading up to the formation of the national federation, the Edmonton Club took a leading role in organizing co-operative efforts among the university women of western Canada. As early as 1910 the Club, then called the Alberta Women's Association, encouraged women in other parts of Alberta to form similar organizations. In March of 1911 a letter was received from Red Deer about starting an organization in that city and the possibilities of affiliating with the Edmonton Association. In January of 1912 a letter from Calgary revealed that an organization with the same general aims had been formed there.

Cooperation with other university women in western Canada continued when in March 1915, the Club wrote letters to the university women of Saskatchewan and to the Vancouver and Winnipeg University Women's Clubs suggesting that the groups combine in an effort to raise money for the colours (flags) for the Western Universities Battalion. Saskatchewan was willing, but the others were not and the plan fell through. The Edmonton Club then proceeded to raise money locally for a similar but smaller project.

Another attempt to work together was made in the fall of 1916, this time to obtain guest speakers. The Edmonton Club wrote to University Women's Clubs in British Columbia and Manitoba and much correspondence ensued. Some of it was about the large fee ($400) requested by one speaker to extend his speaking tour from Winnipeg to Edmonton. Despite their best efforts, attempts to work together once again collapsed.

While the Club was attempting to co-operate with other university women's groups in western Canada, another group of Edmonton women, of which Eleanor Broadus was a member, was attempting to form a women's alumnae organization solely for graduates. Mrs. Broadus had been the first President of the Club, but was no longer a member. On March 18, 1919, a special Executive meeting was called to discuss a letter received from Mrs. Broadus, in which she suggested that the Women's University Club of Edmonton join with the fledgling alumnae group in forming a single club of women university graduates that in future might join the proposed Federation of Women's Clubs in Canada. The Executive members were alarmed at this turn of events because they highly valued the non-graduate members of their Club and did not want to exclude them. They were also concerned that Mrs. Broadus' group might want to usurp the name of their Club. The Executive therefore endorsed the actions of Mrs. Race, then Club President, who had earlier rushed to file a letter with the provincial authorities to protect the name of the Club.

A reply was sent to Mrs. Broadus stating her proposal would entail a change in the Club's constitution and that the Club wanted to find out more about the details of the proposed federation and its membership requirements. At the regular meeting of April 12, it was stated that no general appeal had yet been made to various existing clubs and the federation idea was still tentative. A motion was passed that the Executive of the Women's University Club of Edmonton communicate with the secretary of each of the University Women's Clubs in Canada to request that a conference of representatives from all those clubs be called at some central place as soon as possible to consider the drafting of a constitution for a national federation of University Women's Clubs of Canada.

A letter came from Miss Addison of Toronto saying that there was a suggestion in Toronto about a conference in April, June or September. Eventually a letter was received in July 1919 from the University Women's Club of Winnipeg asking that delegates be sent to a conference of university women to be held in Fort Garry Hotel in Winnipeg on August 26/27, 1919. The Edmonton Executive sent a night lettergram to Kathleen Teskey, who was in Ontario at that time, asking her to go to the conference, giving her full voting powers and promising to pay her expenses. Geneva Misener was also named a delegate. The Canadian Federation of University Women came into existence at this organizational meeting.

Edmonton was one of six founding Clubs. The others were: Victoria, Regina, Winnipeg, Toronto and the McGill Alumnae. The first Federation meeting was held in Toronto in 1920, where the Club's delegates were Mrs. S. A. Dickson and Miss Girdler.

From the national perspective, the formation of the Federation is described thirty years later by its first President, Mrs. R. F. (Margaret) McWilliams:

> Some of the leaders among university women in Canada had been dreaming of a national federation for years, but the effective impulse towards it came from Great Britain. Early in 1919 Dr. Winifred

Cullis, well-known in Canada by reason of the time she had spent during the war lecturing at Toronto University, suggested that the national federation should be organized at once, so that Canada might become one of the first group of countries in the coming International Federation of University Women. This suggestion was reinforced by a companion one from Dr. Virginia Gildersleeve of the American Association of University Women to the effect that, while she hoped the Canadians would form their own federation, they might if they preferred, be allied with the American Association.

Canada's response was immediate. A conference of four of the leaders in university organizations–Mrs. J. A. Cooper, president of the Toronto club; Mrs. R. F. McWilliams, president of the Winnipeg club; Miss May H. Skinner, then representing Canada on the American Association's Committee on International Affairs; and Miss Laila Scott–took place in Toronto in March, 1919.... The various clubs responded enthusiastically to the appeal and the organization meeting took place.

Calendar 1981–1982 revised edition, **Sixty Years of CFUW,** *which in turn is quoting from an account written by Mrs. McWilliams, the first CFUW President, in the 1949–50* **CFUW Chronicle.**

Back in Edmonton, at the September 24 Executive Meeting, a letter from Mrs. McWilliams was discussed. In it the appointment of Jessie Montgomery as Convenor of the Committee on Library Work was announced. Mrs. McWilliams also said that she had received a letter from Mrs. Broadus on the matter of the tentative organization of University Alumnae in Edmonton. The Edmonton Executive decided to write a letter to Mrs. Broadus explaining the steps taken during the summer concerning the formation of CFUW.

During the fall of 1919 there was much correspondence between the Edmonton Club and the newly formed CFUW. A draft copy of the constitution was received, a list of Club officers was sent, Miss E. Chauvin's name was sent as the elected Convenor of the Interassociation Committee of the Federation, and Kathleen Teskey's name was sent as the Edmonton Club's delegate to the Executive Federation meeting. In December the Club's by-laws were changed to conform to CFUW's and three classes of members established: federate, local (i.e. without degrees) and non-resident members. Miss Teskey became the Federation Representative.

Mabel Patrick recalls this period in the Club's history:

The first meeting I attended, I remember clearly as one which made a vivid impression. It was held in the lounge of Athabasca Hall on April 12, 1919. I was upstairs, preparing to spend a leisurely Saturday afternoon when someone came to my door and urged me to join the meeting downstairs as one more person was needed to make a quorum and most important business was to be dealt with. I recall that Mrs. Cecil Race, the vice-president, was in the chair.

The important business was whether or not our organization, known since February 13th, 1917, as the Women's University Club of Edmonton, would join with a group of graduates who wished to form a University Women's Club. Mrs. Broadus, who had chaired our first meeting in 1909, was the organizing Secretary, if not the leader in the new movement. It was felt that our club was unique in having non-graduates as members and that, as a result, we might be excluded from that proposed Federation...I might add that it was learned subsequently that there were other clubs with non-graduate members and provision in the Federation was made to include these...Not gaining our support, the matter of a single club, as sponsored by Mrs. Broadus and others was dropped...

From a talk given at the Club's 50th Anniversary

Organization

From its inception, CFUW operated on a triennial system. The Triennial Conference meetings held every three years included the number of delegates from each club proportional to the size of its membership. Smaller meetings were usually held during the Triennium. Sometimes these were Council Meetings (with one delegate from each club) and sometimes Executive Meetings. This system worked reasonably well, but by 1988 women were finding it difficult to devote three years of their lives to the Executive, especially the Presidency. Moreover, it was realized that the Federation would benefit from having a general meeting every year. In 1988 the triennial system was changed to biennial. Today three-day general meetings are held annually, with the number of delegates from each club still dependent on the size of its membership.

For most of its history (1919–1988) CFUW's head office was in the hometown of the President, usually in accommodation provided by the local university or college. Every three years massive files and equipment were moved across the country, a new secretary was hired and trained, and the wheel was re-invented. In 1988 all this changed. No longer were universities able to provide office space, and the system had become unwieldy. At last a Head Office was established in Ottawa, with a very small, but permanent, staff. This was convenient for talking to government, and for its proximity to other national women's organizations and to the National Archives, where CFUW's records are deposited.

Other changes came about in 1988. After many attempts to find a designation more gender neutral than "chairman," the term "chair" was adopted. CFUW also wanted to make Clubs' names more uniform, and to get away from the term "Club" which some non-members regarded as elitist. As a result, most clubs changed their name to "Canadian Federation of University Women [insert location]." A few, particularly those with clubhouses, kept the old name of "University Women's Club." With all these changes CFUW did become more business-like, efficient and up-to-date, but it may also have lost a bit of its old charm.

Meetings and Conferences

Strongly individualistic and Edmonton-centred, CFUW Edmonton nevertheless has always been very much aware of its wider interests and responsibilities. Through the years, the Edmonton Club hosted several national meetings and conferences including Triennial Conferences in 1934 and 1955, Federation assemblies in 1969 and 1989, a Western Canadian Conference in 1981, and numerous smaller national executive, regional and provincial meetings. The 1969 Council meeting was the Golden Jubilee of CFUW, as well as the sixtieth anniversary of the Edmonton Club, therefore it was a slightly more celebratory affair than usual. Gold-coloured tablecloths graced the banquet tables and Klondike-style clothes were provided for some of the distinguished delegates and guests at the barbeque, including the IFUW President from the Netherlands. Although the weather was cold, the barbecue itself was a great success.

In May of 1981 CFUW Edmonton held a Western Conference on "Energy for the 80s" at the University of Alberta. This was an ambitious and successful affair with many experts speaking on various kinds of energy and numerous workshops on environmental and energy issues. In 1989 the Edmonton Club was pleased and honoured

1955 CFUW Triennial, Edmonton Planning Committee

Seated, L to R: Lucile Kane, Kathleen Morrison (Chair), Inez Calhoun, Mrs. G. A. Bright

Standing, L to R: Mabel Patrick, Mrs. W. S. Scarth, Ruth Hyndman, Mrs. F. de C. Evans

1989 CFUW AGM, Edmonton

L to R: Co-Convenors, Win Mellon and Joyce Law with CFUW President, Tammy Irwin

1989 CFUW AGM, Edmonton

Hostesses dressed in Klondike attire for barbeque at Fort Edmonton Park

L to R: Margaret Skelley, Bonnie Danyluk, Georgie Scafe, Jill Barnicoat, Rose Rosenberger, Joyce Law, Janet Meikle, Robin Robinson

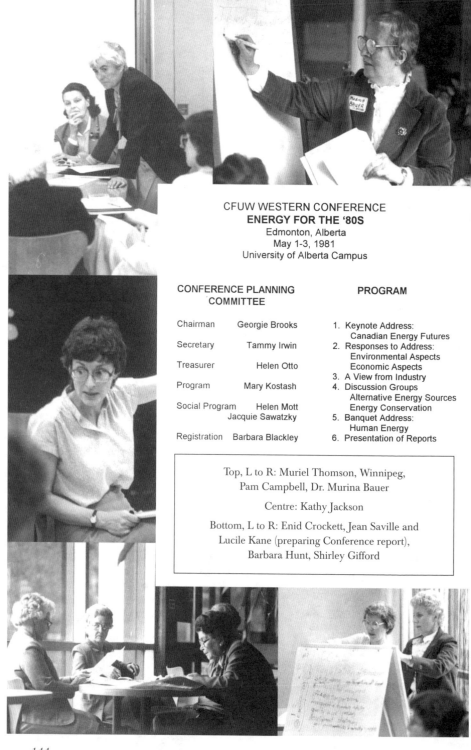

CFUW WESTERN CONFERENCE
ENERGY FOR THE '80S
Edmonton, Alberta
May 1-3, 1981
University of Alberta Campus

CONFERENCE PLANNING COMMITTEE

Chairman	Georgie Brooks
Secretary	Tammy Irwin
Treasurer	Helen Otto
Program	Mary Kostash
Social Program	Helen Mott
	Jacquie Sawatzky
Registration	Barbara Blackley

PROGRAM

1. Keynote Address:
   Canadian Energy Futures
2. Responses to Address:
   Environmental Aspects
   Economic Aspects
3. A View from Industry
4. Discussion Groups
   Alternative Energy Sources
   Energy Conservation
5. Banquet Address:
   Human Energy
6. Presentation of Reports

Top, L to R: Muriel Thomson, Winnipeg,
Pam Campbell, Dr. Murina Bauer

Centre: Kathy Jackson

Bottom, L to R: Enid Crockett, Jean Saville and
Lucile Kane (preparing Conference report),
Barbara Hunt, Shirley Gifford

that the CFUW Annual General Meeting (AGM) was held in Edmonton during the national presidency of Club member Thomasine (Tammy) Irwin.

Club Member Involvement

CFUW Edmonton's links with other Clubs in Canada and with the national body as a whole have been kept strong and vital through the involvement of members on national and international committees. In the years since 1969, four members have chaired National Standing or Special Committees: Jean Lauber (Status of Women and Human Rights), Robin Robinson (Publications, and Finance and Structure), Murina Bauer (Fellowships) and Barbara Blackley (Resolutions, and Constitution and Bylaws). Several have been provincial Directors, and Tammy Irwin was both Provincial Director and Western Vice-President before becoming President in 1988. During her CFUW Presidency, Tammy was a busy person. During a six-week period in 1989 she presided over the CFUW AGM in Edmonton, represented CFUW at the American Association of University Women's annual meeting in Washington, D. C., was a panelist in an environment workshop in Washington, and led the Canadian delegation to the IFUW Triennial Conference in Helsinki. Following her term as President, Tammy was the CFUW Chair of International Relations, and from 1995 to 1998 the Resolutions Chair for IFUW. She was re-appointed to the position of Chair of Resolutions, IFUW, for the triennium 1998 to 2001.

The only other Club member to serve as National President was Mrs. W. J. Melrose (1937–1940). This was an especially difficult time, just before and during the first year of World War II. Mrs. Melrose had the unpleasant experience of sailing for home from the IFUW Conference in Stockholm after the war had been declared in 1939. With the turmoil in Europe and the disappearance of many of the European Federations, IFUW was doing what it could to keep communications open and to help members in dire circumstances.

Mrs. W. J. (Charlotte) Melrose
CFUW President (1937–1940)

During her term of office, "refugee funds for displaced graduates were set up and plans made to receive children of British graduates into 300 Canadian homes. These plans were abandoned in 1941 after the sinking of the ship *City of Benares* with the loss of many lives. Heart rending stories about Polish refugee women and the plight of the IFUW President, Dr. S. Adamowicz, were told at the meetings." (from *Calendar, 1981–1982* revised edition, **Sixty Years of CFUW**).

Policy/Resolutions

National policies are created through Resolutions proposed by Clubs or national committees and debated by delegates at annual CFUW meetings. Every year each Club receives and debates proposed national resolutions, proposes amendments if necessary, and then votes on them, thus providing guidance to the Club's delegates as to how to vote at the national meeting. When a club sends a delegate to a CFUW annual meeting, that delegate is part of a process that has been on-going during the previous year. With an even broader perspective, international policies are established in a similar fashion at IFUW triennial meetings to which CFUW sends delegates.

Resolutions are a vital link which allows local clubs to advocate on issues relevant to their area, but with broad national scope. To be considered, topics must also initiate new policy or re-affirm existing policies, conform to CFUW's purposes and direct CFUW and its member clubs as to what action is to be taken. Some of the categories of the Resolutions passed at general meetings concern: Status of Women, Human Rights, Economic Security, Peace, Education, Libraries, Environment, Consumer Protection, Pensions, Health, Children and Youth, and Pornography.

A special committee to handle Resolutions was formed in 1939; it was changed to the current status of Standing Committee in 1955. Prior to that time, any Resolutions to be discussed by the conference delegates were usually handled by the National President and the Corresponding Secretary. The Resolutions are to be found in the CFUW Policy Book available from Head Office and recently on CFUW's web site.

By the 1980s, the number of Resolutions began to escalate. A survey of CFUW Policy in 1993 showed that 209 policies in 35 categories had been established, 157 of which had been passed between 1982 and 1993. There were 16 resolutions in 1982 alone. Witness to this increase was Club member, Barbara Blackley, who was Chair of the Standing Committee on Resolutions in 1982–85. She and her committee, including several local members, worked hard to make order out of the numerous and often poorly constructed resolutions being brought forward. Some of the procedures now in place to ensure better wording, research and documentation, as well as consensus among Clubs with similar Resolutions, were initiated during this period.

The Edmonton Club, besides dealing with Resolutions from other clubs, has initiated several of its own for adoption by the national body. In the 1930s one supported a national radio system and urged the CBC to have a western Canada CBC station as soon as possible (1933). Another prodded the government to carry out an investigation of the poor conditions in a federal penitentiary (1937). Two Resolutions foreshadowed World War II. One asked the Government of Canada for an embargo on the export of war material to Japan and reiterated support of moves to take the profit out of manufacturing of war materials (1937). The other asked the Government to instruct delegates to the World Disarmament Conference to do everything possible to obtain a mutual agreement that all nations prohibit private manufacture of war equipment and assume control of the export of all war material.

In 1944 the Club supported a Calgary recommendation urging the Federal Government to give grants-in-aid to the provinces to help defray rising education costs. Another recommendation supported the Canadian Broadcasting Corporation and asked that the CBC direct all broadcasting in the Dominion. A third urged the Federal Government to make the establishment of a National Library one of its most important post-war projects.

In the 1950s and 1960s the Club's interests lay largely with education, libraries including school libraries, and day care. Accordingly, most of its Resolutions and Briefs went to the Provincial Government of Alberta. Nevertheless, some Resolutions did go to the Federal Government. Long before the Canada Council was actually established, recommendations went from the Club to the Prime Minister urging the establishment of such a body. One Resolution went to CFUW itself, asking that the age limit on CFUW awards be abolished (previously the Professional Scholarship had been reserved for women under the age of 35).

By 1970, CFUW Edmonton was actively involved in the pollution debate. It prepared a Resolution that was global in intent calling for true intergovernmental co-operation and immediate action on a worldwide basis to decontaminate and protect from further pollution, polluted air, soil and water. Dr. Jean Lauber, the Edmonton member instrumental in researching and formulating this Resolution, first took it to the CFUW Triennial Conference in 1970, and then to Philadelphia where she put it forward to IFUW on CFUW's behalf. The Resolution was adopted. Since then, CFUW Edmonton has proposed and had adopted by the national organization a Resolution on drinking water quality (1988) and one on sovereignty over domestic water resources and opposition to the diversion of water between water drainage basins (1993).

Other special interests in the 1970s were cable TV and its use of advertisements, the disposal of solid waste, matrimonial property rights and family law. CFUW Edmonton participated in the submission by CFUW of a roster of "qualified women" to the Federal Government, a response to the Government's claim that it didn't appoint many women to positions of influence because it didn't know many eligible women. A grant was received from the Secretary of State (1974) to support a central bureau at CFUW Head Office listing qualified women. This project continued, with varying degrees of success, for many years. Another project, part of a national CFUW project, was a survey of children's TV programs concerning sexist stereotyping of roles.

CFUW Edmonton and CFUW had strong opinions about Canada's proposed new Constitution. Letters were sent in November of 1981 insisting that Clause 28 (which says that the rights and freedoms guaranteed in the Charter of Rights and Freedoms are for both male and female persons) must be binding on all provinces and not open to modification or negation through provincial legislation. Along with the Federation, the Club opposed any possible attempts to legislate notwithstanding clauses that would have discriminatory applications.

Fellowships and Awards

IFUW has a fellowships and grants program, which makes awards every two years. In 2000 awards totaling between 22,000 and 32,000 Swiss francs were made, and one award of $8,000 Canadian and one of 2,500 pounds sterling were also given. Similarly, CFUW has always given fellowships and awards to Canadian and landed immigrant students and in 2001 these awards totaled $32,900. CFUW awards are administered by a Fellowships Committee, which each year sifts through hundreds of applications for these much sought-after awards, including a special award, the Polytechnique Commemorative Award. It was established in 1991 as a memorial to the young women murdered in Montreal in 1989.

Since 1976 money for these awards has largely come from a Charitable Trust set up for this purpose by CFUW. The Club's Executive headed the drive in Alberta to raise initial funds for the Trust, and through fashion shows the Club raised $1,500. The Club continues to contribute to the Charitable Trust.

Two other CFUW awards are also made from the Charitable Trust. One was originally the Reading Stimulation Grant, begun in 1946 to help small regional libraries buy children's books. It has now evolved into the CFUW Public Library Grant, awarded to the National Public Library to assist with publications of its Read-Up-On-It Program booklet. A second award was the Creative Arts Awards, established in 1970 as the Golden Jubilee Award which gave money to music composers "under 30 years and on the threshold of a career in composition." It has become the CFUW Creative Music Award, which is presented yearly by the Banff Centre to an exceptional student in the Centre's music program.

Not only is CFUW Edmonton fully committed to its local academic awards program, but a small group also devoted a great deal of energy to the CFUW National fellowship program during the 1990s. Between 1988 and 1998 various Edmonton members served on the CFUW Fellowship Committee either as part of a core group or as outside evaluators. In 1990 Dr. Murina Bauer, herself a recipient of a CFUW Fellowship in the 1950s, assumed the Chair of the National Fellowship Committee for the biennium. Together with three local members, she supervised the initial processing of close to 500 applications in each of the two years. The group was overwhelmed with the number and caliber of women seeking advanced degrees and it reinforced their commitment, and in turn the Club's, to assisting women in their quest for higher education that has always been central to CFUW Edmonton efforts. The history of the Club's commitment to its own awards program is discussed in Academic Awards.

Special Projects

During World War II one of the Club's main efforts was helping women graduates in Europe. A special refugee fund was set up for this purpose, supported by savings made through simplifying the Club's expenditures and from members' donations. There are continuous records of parcels and money being sent to the Club's special protegee, Dr. Marianne Weill, as well as to others. The refugee fund was closed in 1946 and monies left in it went to an IFUW fund for their continuing relief work. Money was sent fairly regularly to the fund, named the IFUW Hegg-Hoffett Relief Fund to honour Madame Hegg-Hoffett of Switzerland who was among the first to visit and report on displaced university women in refugee camps after the war. She continued to advocate on their behalf for over twenty years. Later in 1960, the Club adopted Dr. Fluger, an ill and destitute refugee. Until her death four years later the Club frequently sent her letters, clothes, books, food and money.

Money was sent fairly regularly to Crosby Hall, home until 1993 of the British Federation of University Women. Crosby Hall is an historic sixteenth century building moved and reconstructed (the work beginning in 1926), then repaired and renovated after World War II. Members of the University Women's Clubs all over the world were able to stay there while in London.

Over the years CFUW has had many special projects to which the Edmonton Club has contributed. One was the centennial project, a book of biographies of outstanding Canadian women, *The Clear Spirit*. It was edited by Vida Peene and published in 1967 by the University of Toronto Press and immediately went into a second printing.

For many years CFUW held a creative writing contest, with the winning entries printed in a booklet distributed throughout the country. In 1988 it sponsored a Peace Essay Contest in two categories, ages 12–14 and 15–18. Eight hundred essays were submitted from all over Canada on the topic, "What I Am Prepared to Do for Peace." The winners were introduced and awarded their prizes at the Annual General Meeting held in Edmonton in 1989.

Provincial Affiliation

CFUW Edmonton is a member of a provincial organization of CFUW clubs, called the Provincial Council. Before 1985 there was a loosely organized provincial association of the University Women's Clubs of Alberta (Calgary, Lethbridge, Edmonton, Medicine Hat, and Red Deer). They met irregularly but enthusiastically. This informal association was formally organized into the Provincial Council in 1985. In a snowy January of 1986, eleven Club members pooled their resources, rented a van complete with chauffeur, and traveled to Calgary to attend the first meeting of the CFUW Alberta Provincial Council since its formal organization in the previous August. The trip was a huge success. Meetings have been held since in individual homes, historic sites, and campuses of the Universities of Alberta and Calgary and Red Deer College.

The provincial organization was registered as a society in 1988. It meets once or twice a year to exchange ideas and hold discussions and workshops on topical subjects. It also acts as a central body representing all CFUW Alberta clubs to the Provincial Government of Alberta. As of 2001 it comprises Calgary, Calgary North, Edmonton, Lethbridge, Red Deer and Strathcona County Clubs. The Provincial Council assists in the formation of new clubs, and is supported by one dollar per member from all Alberta clubs.

The Dandy Bunch

Through the years, various clubs have disagreed with the internal organization of CFUW and its effect on the local clubs. At times this resulted in the establishment of committees to improve the operation of the federation itself. For example, exasperated that CFUW was presenting a deficit budget at the 1993 national Annual General Meeting, Edmonton President and Club representative, Robin Robinson, managed to get a motion passed asking for a balanced budget. She then formed an Edmonton group of seven like-minded members who wanted to restructure CFUW so that it would be more efficient and less costly. The group was locally known as the "Group of Seven," but among themselves as "The Dandy Bunch" (so named by their most faithful correspondent, a member of the Vancouver University Women's Club). After much consultation with clubs across Canada and at their own expense, these seven were officially appointed by CFUW as the CFUW Task Force on Finance and Structure.

Second IFUW Conference

The Conference met in Paris, July 11, 1922 in Reid Hall, the American Women's Club House. Many of us lived there, and there the meetings were held. Seventeen countries were represented. Our Canadian Membership was then about 1000; the Americans numbered 14,000; the Belgians 80, to give you some idea of relative numbers.

Discussions were carried on in French or English.

It seemed strange that women in Britain, in Canada and in the US were in a much poorer position than were continental women as to professional training and position; equal pay for equal work; legal status; and the position of married women workers and their pay. Many of the continental groups entered the IF to lend the weight of their

Continued on page 155

They took their final recommendations to the 1994 Annual General Meeting in Winnipeg. There they met with partial success. Some recommendations were accepted, others amended. The fact that those seven members were willing to spend an enormous amount of time and money in an effort to improve CFUW indicates the value each places on the organization. From this one can also understand that individual members *can* make a difference.

CFUW Edmonton and CFUW attempt to be open, friendly groups, where new members are welcome. The advantages of membership are many. With their CFUW affiliation, members can get an introduction to Clubs all over the world. A move to a new Canadian city means an instant circle of friends in the local CFUW club. Members can attend Annual General Meetings held in different parts of Canada–in 1996 it was Newfoundland, in 1997 Kelowna, BC, in 1998 Sudbury, Ontario, in 1999 Calgary, Alberta, in 2000 Guelph, Ontario, in 2001 Montreal, Quebec–and find old and new friends.

International Federation of University Women (IFUW)

The International Federation of University Women (IFUW) held its first official meeting in London in 1920, with Canada as a charter member. Delegate Gwynethe Tuttle, MSc, became the first member and U of A graduate to represent the Club at an International Federation Conference. The second IFUW Conference was held in Paris in 1922. Kathleen Teskey, who was spending the year in Europe in travel and study, was asked to be one of the six Canadian voting delegates. At least twenty other Canadian women, including Mrs S. A. Dickson of Edmonton, also attended.

Three IFUW Triennial Conferences have been held in Canada, the first one in 1947 in Toronto when Dr. A. Vibert Douglas of Kingston, Ontario, was installed as the first Canadian IFUW President. Many Edmonton members attended the second Conference in Vancouver in 1980. A workshop was held in Edmonton during the previous spring to make maple leaf coasters to sell as souvenirs in the Relief Shop at the Conference. A third Triennial Conference was held in Ottawa in 2001, home of the second Canadian IFUW President, Linda Souter.

The following has been excerpted from two columns by June Sheppard that appeared in the Edmonton Journal, October 8th and June 9th, (Section A7 in both cases) 1980. The information was provided in an interview June had with Tammy Irwin and Jean Saville, both of whom attended the IFUW Conference in Vancouver. June, a well-known columnist for the Journal, was a strong supporter of CFUW activities. Although the article was written 20 years ago, the spirit of IFUW remains unchanged.

Those who judge the impact of events by the size of the headlines or the decibel-level of the early morning news announcer's voice seem to have decided that the women's movement is hanging weakly on the ropes. Or as one writer put it recently, "looking a little yellow around the edges."

Continued from page 154

experience and their numbers to the efforts for recognition of their anglo-saxon sisters.

The effort to promote international understanding and friendliness involved discussion as to furthering: interchange between countries of professors, teachers and students; the endowing of international scholarships; the founding of Club houses and the promotion of peace through all these means, and in particular through interest in the League of Nations.

The Conference closed with an eloquent appeal from Mrs. McWilliams for the exercise of the 'dispassionate, impersonal and understanding mind' that is the best fruit of University training.

(excerpted from a typed copy of Kathleen Teskey's talk given at CFUW Edmonton's 50th Anniversary celebration.)

The fact is that, while its objectives in too many cases are still far short of realization, the effects are being felt in countless ways that are not daily headline material, and in an astonishing number of remote corners.

The movement has cut across age groups, lifestyles, educational backgrounds, religions and the political spectrum in a way I wouldn't have believed possible 25 years ago. Interestingly enough, some of the most vivid evidence of its impact comes from women who preface their remarks with words like "I'm not part of any movement" or "I'm not a libber," and then proceed to reveal such changes in their thoughts, attitudes, hopes and priorities in recent years that theirs becomes the most dramatic testimony of all to how deeply this revolution has touched every life in one way or another.

I was thinking these things as I read material provided me about a non-headline event held in Vancouver this summer when 950 women from 45 countries attended the 20th Conference of the International Federation of University Women. I suppose had it been a gathering of extremists, saying and doing loudly outrageous things to grab headlines, few people in Canada would have been unaware of its presence. As it was, it passed with scarcely a ripple on the Canadian consciousness and little effect in puncturing the myth persisting (even encouraged) in some quarters that the fight for women's rights is dead or dying. The prime interest of this international organization has traditionally been the education of women around the world. That hasn't been lost sight of in the much broader range of issues that now are its concerns.

The Australian federation is interested in literary programs for aboriginal women in that country; Bangladesh members want to help educate village women; the Turkish affiliates hope to assist migrant women and those in squatter settlements. There is appreciation in IFUW for the enormity of the world population problem with all the hardship it implies, especially for women. Programs in family planning and sex education are an international need.

Most of the branches have had programs to give the better-educated women more knowledge about their legal rights and to encourage them to get into national organizations and the economy generally.

From many parts of the world, delegates brought their anxieties about the continuing deterioration of the environment through atmospheric, water and land pollution—the destruction of so many plant and animal species and the denuding of millions of acres through deforestation. They believe expansion of forest conservation to be imperative.

The IFUW is greatly interested in the care of the elderly within their homes as long as it is feasible, and in medical care that is less dehumanized and recognizes the dignity of the human person.

The encouragement of 'women-elect-women' campaigns was recommended to get women on decision-making bodies so their voices are heard, their viewpoints contributed and their energies, intelligence and priorities as women given equal status. Top priority at Vancouver was given to the UN Convention on the Elimination of all Forms of Discrimination Against Women—to its study with a view to bringing about its early ratification and implementation.

A movement that's a "little yellow around the edges?" Doesn't sound like it to me!

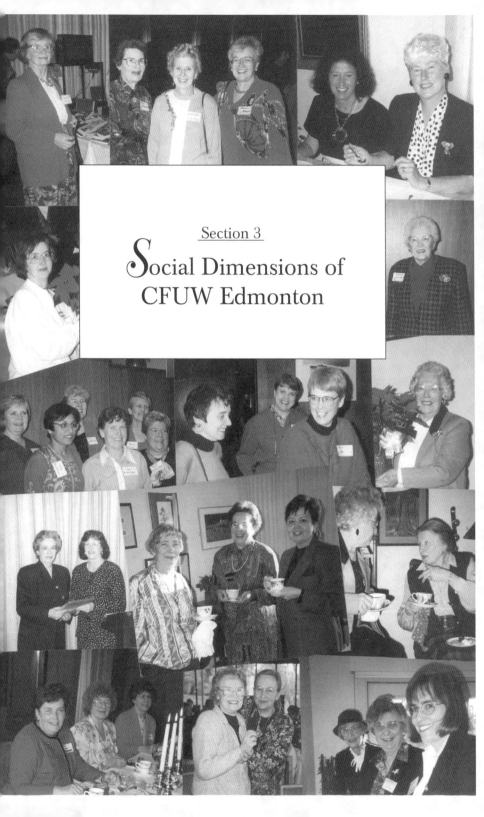

Section 3

*S*ocial Dimensions of
CFUW Edmonton

Social Dimensions of the Club

The work of the Standing Committees and Study Groups and how they fulfill the purposes of the Club illustrate one dimension of CFUW Edmonton, but there is another dimension of the Club that is equally important–the social fabric of the Club. In interviews, members expressed their enjoyment of the fellowship in coming together with women of similar interests and goals. They also told of the importance of having stimulating speakers at the monthly meetings. Not only did women become members of CFUW Edmonton to participate in the opportunities for social activism, but they also came because they enjoyed the company of other like-minded women. In short, they had *fun*.

In 1966 a U of A Master of Arts thesis (Puffer, 1966) describes these two aspects of the Club. The basis of the thesis (Friendship and Commitment in a Voluntary Association: the University Women's Club of Edmonton) was that there are two kinds of associations(those that are "expressively oriented," or sociable, and those that are "instrumentally oriented" or socially active. Although the expressed goals of the Club are instrumental in nature, Puffer learned that members are equally committed to the importance of teas, dinners, social get-togethers and meetings. The Club has components of both a social club and a socially active organization.

In the previous section we have provided details about the social action component of the Club. Here we elaborate on the social aspect of the Club, including members' reasons for joining, the speakers program, various Interest Groups and some of the social events held over the years.

Chapter 6

*M*embership

Who were the women who joined CFUW Edmonton and what were their reasons for joining? From research and interviews, it appears that most joined to have the opportunity to meet with like-minded women in a spirit of cooperation, and to gain intellectual stimulation through projects, study groups and the speakers' program. Until the late 1960s many women who obtained their university degrees got married and settled for a role in the home. Membership in the Club gave them an opportunity to collectively support women's issues and participate in community affairs. Interestingly, the goals the Club espoused regarding the status of women working outside the home aided such women, but membership in the Club declined during the same period. Still, many of the current members, including those with full-time careers outside the home, feel that the sharing of mutual goals and ideals and the social interactions are important to them, and have continued their membership in the Club.

Graduates in the early days came mainly from the British Isles, Eastern Canada and the United States. Today, membership is made up of women university graduates from around the world, although the majority are from Canadian universities.

Early years

At its inception, membership in the Club was made up of university graduates and women whose husbands held positions of prominence in Edmonton, such as the wife of the Lieutenant-Governor (the Official Visitor of the University), wives of the Minister and the Deputy Minister of Education and some wives of the University of Alberta faculty and senate. When the Club became part of the larger Federation (CFUW) in 1919, membership was changed to Federate Members (university graduates), Local Members (i.e. without degrees) and Non-resident Members. At some point Local Members became Associate Members and eventually Associate Members were wives of University of Alberta staff only. The wives of the university faculty were still eligible to become Associate Members of the Club until the early 1960s and as such they had all the privileges available except voting on Federation matters. At the most there were approximately 35 Associate Members in the 1960s, but in an average year there were between 20 and 30 such members. Each one was an active and valuable member of the Club.

Advisors to Women Students at the U of A

Because of the Club's early concern for the welfare of women students on campus, it is not surprising that a close association developed between the Club and the women advisors (Deans, Wardens) at the University of Alberta. At least six of the eight women advisors figure prominently in the Club's history. They were Helen Sheldon, first advisor to women students (1911 to 1912), Dr. Geneva Misener (1913 to 1920), Dr. Mary Winspear (1942 to 1945), Maimie Simpson, an active and long-term member (1946 to 1960), Saretta Sparling (1960 to 1968), and Isobel Munroe Smith (1968 to 1975) who was instrumental in the development of the Club's Mature Women's Bursary.

From the Club's earliest days, there had been an attempt to entertain the freshmen and graduating girls at get-togethers in the members' homes. For these events, the Club often sought the help of the Advisors/Deans for compilation of lists and for contacting the girls. This shared experience led to some Advisors joining the Club. This socializing continued through the 1950s, with the Dean of Women facilitating the get-togethers. Then in 1960 Saretta Sparling announced that it was becoming too time-consuming and involved too many students to continue the practice. Her 1960 list would be the last. As the population of the university increased substantially after the 1960s and as women came to be represented on the campus in greater numbers, the role of the Dean of Women was changed to Dean of Students.

Rise in Membership

Membership rose slowly but steadily through to the 1930s, from 64 members in 1914 to 137 in 1929/30. For the next decade, it leveled off to between 140 and 150, and although there were several new members each year, others must have left in equal numbers. In a 1941/42 Membership Report, Convenor, Grace Studholme, reported that there had been a slight decline due to the war; three members had left to undertake war work, two with the RCAF and another with a munitions company in the East. At the same time two honorary members whose husbands were with the RCAF had been welcomed. During this period, the Club made an effort to invite wives of servicemen who were university graduates to become honorary members.

Libby Frost graduated in 1925 and worked for 10 years in the Registrar's Office at the U of A during the Depression. She remembers she was very glad for the job, but after she was married in the 1930s, she said that she was embarrassed to say that she had a job— there were so many unemployed. Thus she retired to the home, raised a family and took up volunteer work.

By the end of the 1942/43 season, there was a significant increase in membership to 185 (158 Federation, 26 Associate and 1 Honorary). This may have been due in part to the increase in the city's population, itself, for there was a large influx of service personnel in the early 1940s connected with the Alaska Highway project and the British Commonwealth Air Training Plan. Membership in the Club continued to rise each year until it peaked in 1961 at 374 members (343 Federation and 31 Associate).

Among the many members who joined the Club during the war years, several were to remain active members for over 50 years. These women included Ruth Hyndman, Mary Dodds, Kay Wark and Norma Freifield. All related similar reasons for joining. They were, and remained single career women, but at the time they were trying to establish themselves in jobs related to their training and were looking to meet women of similar interests. Although there were informal social groups where they met and had dinner with associates and friends, the women said that they found the study and interest groups of the Club both challenging and worthwhile. Ruth Hyndman said that she was encouraged to join by Norma Freifield, a librarian at the U of A and a recent member herself who was very enthusiastic about the Club's work.

Ruth Hyndman also related that some joined at this time because their mothers had belonged. One of the first daughters to join was certainly Libby Frost whose mother, Mrs. Cogswell, was one of the Club's earliest members. Mrs. Cogswell fit the profile of the educated woman, expecting to stay home following marriage. Thirty years later, her daughter was still bound by the traditions of an earlier era and was expected to stay home after marriage. For these women, the Study Groups and work of the Standing Committees provided a great deal of stimulation. Although little is known of Mrs. Cogswell's activities within the Club, her daughter Libby Frost (President from 1968 to 1970) was active in several major studies, including saving Rutherford House and laying the groundwork for Strathcona Place for Seniors.

Another member felt that she had no option but to join in the 1950s–not only was her mother a member, but so was her mother-in-law. That was Fran Reynolds, whose mother was Cora Casselman and mother-in-law was Mrs. G. G. Reynolds, both active and long-time members of the Club. Fran joined as a recent grad in 1957, and remains an active CFUW member.

Post World War II

After the Second World War, there was a boom in enrollment at the U of A and many of the Club's new members came to Edmonton as wives of new professors. Among the 34 who joined in the Fall of 1946, there were graduates from Oxford, England, the four Western Canadian provinces, Ontario, Indiana, Washington State, Columbia, Chicago, Smith University and California. This diversity added to the vitality of the Club.

In the 1940s and 1950s, the Club also invited exchange teachers and foreign students to become guest members. At the same time they made efforts to try to contact displaced persons and immigrant women qualified for membership in the CFUW.

Membership rose steadily from the 1940s to early 1960s and peaked in the period of 1959 to 1961. This period represented the halcyon days for the Club as well as for many other Alberta women's clubs. With the advent of the oil boom in Alberta (1947) there was a dramatic increase in the population of the province and a corresponding rise in Club membership.

One of the local members who joined in the 1950s recounted how she saw an ad in the paper about a Fall tea of the then University Women's Club of Edmonton, and decided to attend. "I was from a small town, and had found university life so stimulating, so that when I found myself married and living outside of Edmonton on an acreage, I thought the UWC would be a good group to get into–it was quite exciting to come back and find all these other [like-minded] people. The meetings were large and the speakers interesting–there were lots of things going on."

Another member who had a similar experience said that it was a fellow staff member at the school where she taught who recommended the Club. "Being interested in talking to people and finding out what was going on appealed to me, rather than belonging to a strictly 'social' club and baking cookies," she related. Joining in the mid-1950s, she said that she was swept into the Education Standing Committee because of her teaching background and soon found herself making recommendations on school curriculum. She ended up being the Club's representative on the Provincial Curriculum Committee.

Mrs. Margaret Greenhill (President 1962 to 1964) who joined in the 1950s said she thought "many women who had graduated were frustrated to think that they had spent all those years [studying] and were now spending their time changing diapers."

Membership Peaks in the 1960s

According to membership lists of the 1960s, new members continued to come from across Canada, the United States and Europe. Again, many came as wives of the newly recruited professors hired to staff the ever-burgeoning University of Alberta. Also, by this time quite a few of these members came as transferees from other CFUW and IFUW Clubs. One of the women who came from the United States in the late 1960s was Dr. Jean Lauber, who was to have a profound influence on the Club and whose activities are detailed in *Status of Women.*

Dr. Lauber had been a member of the American Association of University Women (AAUW) and looked forward to joining its counterpart in Canada when she and her husband came to teach at the

U of A. She stated in an interview that when she attended her first meeting of the AAUW, she was pleased to be introduced for who *she* was, a zoologist, and not as Professor so-and-so's wife. She felt that recognition in one's own right was and is an important aspect of both organizations.

Another member who joined in the late 1960s was Tammy Irwin, who came to Edmonton via the CFUW Clubs of Vancouver and Winnipeg. As a young mother, she found the work of the Club suitable to raising a family—you could do as much or as little as you wished, but still feel a part of the process. However, with her background and commitment to CFUW, she soon found herself on the Executive and immersed in several study projects which eventually led to the National Presidency in 1988.

Still others joined the Club after having belonged to the Newcomer's Club, an active organization that made a point of introducing the women to activities in Edmonton.

By the end of the 1960s membership began to decline. One factor was the discontinuation of Associate Membership in the Club. There were several reasons for this change. The Faculty Women's Club (FWC), when formed in 1933, was a purely social club (as it still is) open to wives of staff and female staff. Through the years many women belonged to and enjoyed the opportunities offered by both the CFUW and the FWC. However, when the latter extended its program to include a number of similar interest and study groups, some of the wives no longer felt they needed the CFUW. At the same the time, the Club thought the time was right to become a club purely of university graduates. Thus some of the FWC members withdrew to concentrate on their own organization, while others continued to belong to both clubs. Existing Associate Members without degrees could remain, but no new ones were accepted after the new Constitution was drawn up in 1964.

Other factors that led to the decline included the rise in special interest groups in the City, many dealing with issues that the Club had previously addressed. Also relevant was the fact that more and more women were working outside the home. The membership has remained fairly constant since the beginning of the 1970s.

In the end the reasons for joining are many. Some women join at the invitation of a friend or associate; others for the community outreach aspect of the Club or to support women at university through the scholarship and bursary program. Still others support the national and international aspects of the Club. Some have given of their talents for a period of time and then have gone on to other areas in teaching, politics, law or administration. Still others have remained members throughout their time since graduation and have given the Club much of its continuity. And some have returned to the Club after an absence to resume their friendships and re-kindle their interest in new and interesting subjects of study.

Honorary Membership

In the early years there was a policy of asking distinguished women to become Honorary Members of the Club. The Honorable Irene Parlby was one of these for several years, as was Dr. Allison Proctor for as long as she lived (see also *Public Affairs*). During the Second World War, the Club extended Honorary Membership to graduate wives of service men as well as to exchange teachers, even if these teachers were not graduates. More recently, Lois Hole, former Chancellor of the U of A and current Lieutenant-Governor, was made an Honorary Member (1998), as was the Honorable Anne MacLellan, Federal Minister, who was a member of the Club in the 1990s.

Club member Johanna Michalenko was named an Honorary Member of CFUW in February 2000 for her contributions to the community, especially in the areas of consumer advocacy and status of women and human rights. As a graduate of the U of A in Home Economics (Textiles), Johanna joined the Club in 1936. She moved to Saskatoon with her husband in the 1940s, when he became a professor at the University of Saskatchewan. There, she became involved again with CFUW, as well as with the Ukrainian Women's Organization(s) of Saskatchewan and the Consumers' Association of Canada (CAC). Within each organization she assumed leading executive positions. She was President of CFUW Saskatoon, CFUW Provincial Director and on the National Executive as Chair of the Status of Women and Human Rights. A National VP (Western President) of CAC, Johanna was particularly noted as being one of those responsible for initiating the standardized textile labeling that appears in our clothing today. She also advocated for the establishment of a federal Department of Consumer Affairs. After she was widowed, Johanna returned to Edmonton and rejoined the local Club in 1982.

She joins Dr. Roberta Bondar, scientist and astronaut, as the only other Honorary Member of the National Federation, denoting the great honour accorded to her. Both the Edmonton and Saskatoon Clubs collaborated in nominating Johanna for this membership.

Honorary Presidents

At the time CFUW Edmonton was first formed in 1910, it was the practice for societies to ask prominent citizens to be Honorary President. Being a women's group with close connections to the University, it was logical that the President's wife be asked to be Honorary President of the Club. Initially, Mrs. Bulyea, wife of the Official Visitor to the University and Lieutenant-Governor for the Province of Alberta, was Honorary President. In 1918, Mrs. Tory, wife of the U of A's first President Dr. H. M. Tory, was invited to fill the role, as were subsequent Presidents' wives. As well, Mrs. Rutherford, wife of Alberta's first Premier and later Chancellor of the University, served as Honorary Vice-President from 1909 into the1930s. She was very generous with her time and made a practice of entertaining the women students. During the First World War, she entertained women graduates at her home each spring, and those who made their home in Edmonton often became members of CFUW Edmonton.

The wives of the University Presidents not only accepted the role of Honorary President, but also often graciously hosted the Club's "Opening Tea" at the official University residence. This tradition held until the end of the 1960s at which time the University President chose to live off campus.

As an indication of how this role functioned in the life of the Club, the example of Jessie Stewart is pertinent. As wife of President Andrew Stewart, she was an active member of the Club and a valued member of the Drama Group. After retiring to the west coast she kept in contact and sent the Group two books of her poetry. Mrs. Helen Johns, wife of President Walter H. Johns, was another active and very conscientious Honorary President during her ten-year term, paying Club fees in order to participate fully in the CFUW. She attended meetings when her schedule permitted, and hosted a luncheon at the President's home for each new executive. She also hosted a luncheon for the CFUW National Executive when the Golden Jubilee Council Meeting was held in Edmonton in 1969.

The practice of inviting women to be Honorary President was discontinued after 1984 for a number of reasons, but mainly because the image of the honorary "tea pourer" was passé, and the women often had busy schedules of their own.

Honorary Presidents 1909 to 1984

1909–14	Mrs. Bulyea, wife of the Official Visitor to the University and Lieutenant-Governor of Alberta
1916–18	Mrs. R. G. Brett, wife of the Lieutenant-Governor of Alberta
1918–28	Mrs. H. M. Tory
1928–36	Mrs. R. B. Wallace
1936–41	Mrs. W. A. R. Kerr
1941–50	Mrs. Robert Newton
1950–59	Mrs. Andrew Stewart
1959–73	Mrs. Walter H. Johns
1973–75	Mrs. Max Wyman
1975–77	Mrs. H. Gunning
1977–79	Mrs. R. Steinhauer, wife of the Lieutenant-Governor of Alberta
1979–82	Mrs. Jean Forrest, Chancellor of the University of Alberta
1982–84	Mrs. Myer Horowitz

Unless otherwise designated, the Honorary Presidents were wives of the Presidents of the University of Alberta at that time.

Membership Recognition

CFUW Edmonton recognizes members' significant anniversaries of their university graduation. In the early days a large sterling silver maple leaf pin was presented to the 50-year grad and a bouquet of flowers to the 60-year grad. As the cost of silver increased the pin got smaller, and by the late 1970s the Club was giving a small silver maple leaf pin with the lamp of knowledge and CFUW embossed on it to both categories of grads. This pin more accurately reflected the ties to the Canadian Federation.

In 1993, it was decided to honour the 60- and 70-year grads by donating to the U of A Library Special Collections rather than

Life-long teachers

Isabel McRae (right) on the 60th anniversary of her graduation (1934–1994) with Mabel Geary. Both were members of the 1927 graduating class of Camrose Normal School and taught in one-room schools in north-central Alberta in their early days.

Isabel returned to U of A full time (1931–1934) for a BA and later a BEd (1960). Mabel received her BEd in 1951 after several years at summer school. Following graduation, the women taught in high schools in Edmonton and Leduc, respectively, until their retirement. Now in their nineties, they remain active participants in the Club.

duplicate the pin, which many of the 50-year grads already had. A monetary gift was sent for the first time on behalf of long-time members Lucile Kane, Winifred Long (70 years) and Ruth Hyndman (60 years). Unfortunately, what appeared to be a good idea was not to last. The university found it was not cost effective, as the donation only covered part of the cost of the books at the current prices. In 1997, the Club began giving a donation to the Academic Awards Fund in the name of the 60- and 70-year grad recipient, a practice that continues today.

Chapter 7

$\mathcal{P}$rograms

The program of the regular monthly meeting, usually with a featured speaker, has always been a key component of the Club. Interviews with members revealed that a good speaker's program was one of the most important aspects of the Club. Through the years members have been privileged to hear some very fine speakers from the university, the government and the community at large, who generously gave of their time. The following summary of the program gives an indication of the subjects and issues that concerned members through each decade.

Speakers Program

Through its close affiliation with the U of A, the Club was fortunate to have access to some of the leading experts in various fields of endeavor and in the early days relied a great deal on the mostly male staff of the University. The U of A first President, Dr. Henry Marshall Tory, a busy man if there ever was one, addressed the general meetings many times. He and succeeding Presidents of the University were often asked to give the opening remarks at Club events or address the Club at the regular meetings. Other members of the faculty who gave of their time during the period 1910 to 1919 included Dr. R. Allan, Head of Geology, who gave an illustrated lantern slide show on the Rocky Mountains (1913), and Dr. Burgess, who gave a series of lectures on architecture from the Greco-Roman period to the medieval times (1914).

Many of the topics during the Club's early days centred on arts, literature and culture and in this way were much like university courses. This would have appealed to the members who had few other outlets for advanced learning. Each year there were also one or two talks of wider community interest.

The Club often relied on the expertise of its own members, many of whom were distinguished in their own right. In the 1920s, for example, Mrs. E. T. Bishop, the first woman elected as Chairman of the Edmonton Public School Board, and a member of the Club's first Executive gave many addresses on educational matters as did Dr. Donalda Dickie, a curriculum specialist. The April meeting was frequently given over to members of the Education Standing Committee to make their annual report and recommendations. The reports of the members' attendance at the IFUW and CFUW Conferences were also of great value to the members and were well received. Kathleen Teskey and Mrs. Sam Dickson actually reported on the first organizational meeting of the International Federation of University Women (IFUW) in Paris in 1922. One of the aims for the establishment of IFUW was the promotion of international peace and understanding and many talks centred on this issue in the 1920s.

In the 1930s talks continued to stress peace and disarmament. Irene Parlby, as one of the first Canadian women appointed official representative to the League of Nations at Geneva spoke on this issue in 1931. CFUW President Mrs. Thom dealt with disarmament in an after-dinner talk to the Club in 1933, and Dr. Geneva Misener, representative to the Pan Pacific Peace Conference (1934/5) stressed the subject on more than one occasion. A Round Table discussion "Can a League of Nations be Effective?" was one of the program highlights of 1937.

In the 1940s, the Club was privileged to have a few guest lecturers who came on tours to other women's clubs. These guests often spoke in Convocation Hall and the meetings were open to the public. Such prominent women, described by the Club as "outsiders of some distinction," included Miss Julie Matouskova, member of the World Council of YWCA, a refugee from Prague who spoke from personal knowledge on "Conditions in Europe" (1940); Dr. Winnifred Cullis,

Past President of IFUW, described in the Edmonton Journal as one of the great university women of the period (1941); Dr. Lotte Hitschmanova, well-known humanitarian of the Unitarian Service Committee (1946) and Dr. Frances Moran of Dublin, a distinguished lawyer and one of the judges at the Nuremberg Trials (1948).

When one of the speakers was called away to active service in the 1940s, the Club decided to rely on its own members more often. Some of the talks given between 1940 and 1943 included those by the well-known teachers and educators Mary Butterworth, Marian Gimby, Dr. Donalda Dickie and Dr. Mary Winspear. Parliamentarian Cora Casselman gave two talks in 1941; one was on her impressions of Winston Churchill's recent speech in Ottawa, the other on "Notes and Comments of Parliament."

The 1947 program involved two members. One was U of A bacteriologist and university lecturer Dr. Silver Keeping, who spoke on "Mice and Men," dealing with mice as carriers of disease. The other was playwright Elsie Gowan whose talk was entitled "Radio on the Air." Mrs. Gowan's radio plays gave voice to many of the CFUW studies during the period–day care, immigration, domestic disputes and sympathy toward native issues.

In the 1950s members continued to value talks on subjects ranging from literature and art to geophysics as they had in earlier years, and many of the talks continued to be given by members of the U of A faculty. However, as the decade progressed there was an increasing emphasis on issues of human rights, on the Canadian Indian (CFUW was promoting a Commission on the Canadian Indian) and women's affairs.

Traditions Change

"University Women Hear Dean Discuss Beauty" reads a headline in the Edmonton Journal describing a Club meeting of May 1960. The address on the broader meaning of beauty came on the eve of Maimie Simpson's retirement as Dean of Women at the U of A. She was a long-time member of the Club and a Past President (1935–37). The image conveyed by this headline was one of an era fast disappearing. Outgoing President Norma Freifield noted this in her comment to the group, "a judicious blending of the traditions and policies of the past with fresh ideas for the future would be needed" if the Club was to be successful.

Just a Few More Speakers Worthy of Note

1915 – School finance – Mrs. Hill, second woman Trustee on the EPSB

1916 – Women's Educational and Industrial Union – Dr. Forbes of Rochester New York; also spoke on "The Immense Significance of the Enfranchisement of Women" at a special meeting

1917 – Adult Education among the Foreigners [sic] in the Province – Secretary of the YMCA

1923 – Mrs. McWilliams – CFUW's first President who spoke about the Federation

1923 – Miss Duff – Women's Legal Rights in Alberta

1926 – Professor A. L. Burt – series of lectures on the League of Nations

1927 – Honorable Mrs. Irene Parlby – Member of the Alberta Cabinet without Portfolio and only woman in the UFA Government

1928 – Major Newbury – New Tendencies in Art

1931 – Dr. E. A. Corbett – "Songs and Legends of French Canada," illustrated with gramophone records of French Canadian songs

1934 – Professor James Adam – "Modern Drama" and the effects that moving pictures were having on it

1935 – Dr. Silver Keeping, member and CFUW Scholarship winner, "Fungi I Have Met"

1941 – Charlotte Whitton, CFUW Ottawa member, on "Women in the War Effort"

1944 – Dr. E. A. Corbett, Director of Canadian Association for Adult Education on "Future for Fighters," referring to future education of service personnel

1945 – Douglas Homersham of CJCA Radio Station on "Microphone Techniques and General Production of Plays"

1946 – Mr. H. J. Wilson, Deputy Attorney General on "Juvenile Delinquency"

Through the 1960s, the program emphasized continuing education for women, family welfare and day care. Another major theme of the 1960s was Canada's Centennial (1967). One of the featured speakers during this time was the Honorable A. R. Patrick, Provincial Secretary and Provincial Representative to the Centennial Committee, who was not only speaker at the Club's banquet in 1962, but also assisted the Club immensely in their effort to have the Provincial Archives become part of Alberta's centennial project. At the end of the decade, the new Provincial Archivist spoke to the Club.

The 1970s saw a continuation of issues arising out of the Royal Commission on the Status of Women (1967 to 1970), tax reform, petition on matrimonial property and funding of advanced education for mature women. Concern about children's welfare included talks on the battered child syndrome and education of disadvantaged children. An increased awareness of environmental issues led to the first major talk given to the Club on the subject of pollution and the environment by Dr. W. A. Fuller of the U of A (1970). Members of the new Anti-Pollution Study Group presented a panel discussion on recycling and the Ecology Caravan.

Major themes during the 1980s dealt with the Canadian Constitution, the North American Free Trade Agreement (NAFTA), and the advent of the personal computer. The Club was again fortunate to have some of the U of A's leading experts to address members. For instance, from 1985 to 1990 the Program Committee committed one evening each year to a lecture by associate members of the Boreal Institute for Northern Studies, U of A. These popular lectures by experts on political science, forensic science, zoology and the environment always drew a large turnout (approximately 100 people for each event). There were also talks on stress management and the fundamentals of Alberta Healthcare, including women's health issues and palliative care. In a more-light hearted vein, there were demonstrations by local wine merchants and gardening experts. The latter was especially popular as it was often given by Lois Hole.

There was a wealth of talent within the Club and members were called on again to participate in the program of the 1980s. Who better to give a talk on travels to the Galapagos Islands and on its fauna than Zoologist Dr. Jean Lauber, or to illustrate "Women Artists from Renaissance to Present," with appropriate music for each period, than educator and long-time docent at the Edmonton Art Gallery Mary

Kostash, or to speak about wills or the constitutional debate than lawyers Maureen Towns and Diana Goldie?

In the 1990s the issues of adult literacy, biotechnology and bioethics were addressed. An innovation in the 1990s was the featuring of the graduate women scholarship winners as speakers at the January meeting. This proved to be a popular idea, for the enthusiasm and talent of the women students were an inspiration to the members. Also of inspiration was a visual presentation by long-time member Kay Wark on the Peaceful Valley Project (a 12 acre day-use park and an environmentally protected area) which she and her brother designated to the Alberta Land Trust for use by the elderly, disabled and terminally ill, and which officially opened in June 1996. Assisting the Warks in the development of the park was member Hiske Gerding (President 1995 to 1997) in her position with the Alberta Government.

In the first two decades, male professors at the U of A gave many of the talks, but over the years that gradually changed. A survey of speakers in the 1940s shows there were 28 talks given by men and 26 by women guests, plus 13 given by members. By the last decade of the century, out of approximately 68 speakers, 54 were women, many with PhDs.

It is the Club's policy to give a small honorarium in the speaker's name to the Academic Awards Fund (AAF). Prior to starting this gesture in the 1990s, the Club often gave gifts such as books or a nominal monetary honorarium to the speaker.

The Play's the Thing

Whether participating, promoting, reading or just being in the audience, members of the Club have had a long-standing love affair with the play. In the early days, plays were a popular form of entertainment because they were one of few choices, particularly in a community such as Edmonton.

The Club was assisted in putting on plays by its close affiliation to the staff and students at the U of A. Professor James Adam of the Engineering Department is credited with giving invaluable assistance to the Club in the early days, as were the students of the Dramatic Society and the CKUA players. Later the Studio Theatre players took part in some of the plays. To raise money for the First World War efforts and for scholarships, the Club put on a half dozen plays between 1914 and 1920, productions by such well-known playwrights as A. A. Milne, E. M. Barry, and George Bernard Shaw.

At times the Club put on productions for their own enjoyment, such as the one-act play *Double Demon* by A. P. Herbert, which was done under Dr. Adam's direction in 1930. Also in the 1930s the Modern Trends Group presented several skits for the membership, including one called *The Harem* for the annual Club Banquet. The ladies considered it a rather daring attempt at the time but they felt that something light-hearted was needed at the height of the Depression.

The Club had among its membership one of the leaders in the Drama Community of Edmonton, Eva Osyth Howard (1892-1972). Eva Howard was a graduate of the Royal Victoria College for Women at McGill in 1913 and began teaching in Edmonton the following year. In 1927 she was assigned to Victoria Composite High School to teach literature and composition and while there became the first person to introduce drama into the school curriculum. The theatre in the new Victoria Composite High School was named in her honour in 1985. For her contributions to the students and to the Edmonton Community Theatre, Miss Howard received the Canadian Drama Award in 1940.

Another member of talent was Agnes Teviotdale, one of the Club's early members, who wrote and directed several revues for the Club. For the Christmas Party of 1946, she put together a skit called *The Spotlight Shifts Backward,* and for the Club's 50th Anniversary in 1960 she co-wrote a medley of songs and skits for a historical revue called *Salad Days.* The revue combined the talents of the Choral Group and others and was a great success, as described in the Edmonton Journal, January 19, 1960:

> The club's history was a clever presentation by narrator, choral group, dancers and various members giving live drama to the events since 1910 when the Women's Association held its first meeting. The script for the review was written by Mrs. D. J. Teviotdale and Mrs. Hugh Campbell. Mrs. Angus Macdonald was narrator and Miss Elizabeth Filipkowski led the choral group who punctuated the story by a version in song. Mrs. H. T. Coutts was pianist.

On various occasions, the study groups put on skits for the general membership to illustrate a particular social issue, such as education, child psychology or family welfare. In the late 1970s, member Marjorie Buckley wrote and produced a well-received play called *Twin Pak,* a two-act play dealing with the Person's Case, (the story of Alberta's Famous Five Women) including a contemporary update (see also *Status of Women*).

Through the Just-For-Fun Group of the 1970s and 1980s and the Lively Arts Group of the 1990s, members have continued their interest in the play with numerous theatre outings. These groups and the Club's Drama (Play-Reading) Group that survived for sixty years are further described in the next chapter on Interest Groups.

Chapter 8

*I*nterest Groups

Why join an Interest Group? "New skills, new friends and broadened horizons are the extra benefits from participating in Interest Groups." This was written by a Coordinator of Interest Groups in the 1980s, but could just as well have applied to any period in the Club's history. The Interest/Study Groups have always played a major role in the life of the Club. For the most part, the Groups lasted for several years or more. It would be impossible to list all those that appeared during the Club's history, but describing some of the main ones provides a general picture of members' interests.

From the beginning the interests that brought members together were reading, drama, French conversation, world studies and art and music appreciation. Although other concerns came and went with time, these remained constant for almost five decades and the Drama Group lasted even longer. Periodically courses were offered on child care, decorating or gardening. Lucile Kane recalled in an interview taking a course for young mothers on child care and home decorating in the 1920s but the general membership never showed much interest in these topics. The literary and cultural interests generally prevailed.

In the 1930s, the Interest Groups remained much the same, but the prefix "Modern" was added to some—Modern Fiction, Modern

Biography, Modern Trends. Clearly, 'modern' is a relative term! The Modern Trends Group designed their own program for the year within the Club's framework. One year it was a series of lectures on geology, another year on interior decorating, and yet another involved the group putting on a play for the Club's annual banquet.

Another group, Recent Grads, was formed in 1933 for the benefit of newly graduated women. Members designed their own program, ranging from service to the community (hospital visits to read and write letters for the patients) to preparing papers of an intellectual nature for presentation to each other. Recent Grads was convened as needs arose; in some years there was more than one Group, while at other times there was none.

A popular group of the 1930s through to the 1960s was the International Affairs Study Group. Members especially remember attending meetings under Convenor Chrissie Wootton. Libby Frost recalled that it was the best that she belonged to. "It was a marvelous group. We worked so hard and we learned an awful lot; we studied different countries, their politics, what was going on, that sort of thing." Chrissie and her husband were very involved with the League of Nations and, after the War, with the United Nations where she maintained a great interest in international affairs. As was so often the case, the success of an interest or study group lay in the leadership and passion of its convenor.

This was also true of the Choral Group that was introduced in 1942 under the direction of Conductors Cornelia Higgin and later Elizabeth Filipkowski. Grace Studholme was usually the piano accompanist. This Group performed at all the banquets and Christmas teas in the 1940s. One didn't have to have any great musical talent to join, just enthusiasm, according to members of the group who were interviewed in later years.

In an Annual Report in 1960, the first VP and Convenor of Study and Interest Groups, stated that some Recent Grads, "feeling not too recent," had gone on to form other groups in the Club, including Family Welfare and World Affairs (which studied Africa, South America, etc.). Several members recalled this period in their interviews. As she remembered it, Sheila Campbell thought that the core group of the Family Welfare/Day Care Group of the late 1950s and 1960s had been made up of the Recent Grads alumni. These groups put together several excellent Briefs on Day Care Standards. (See *Public Affairs*)

Another not-so-recent-grad recalled her preparation for a report to her peers, most likely a World Affairs Group of the late 1950s. She said that, "each person took a topic and researched it just as if they were doing a paper at university. I remember thinking that I had spent more effort on my report than I ever did at university. It was on the leaders in Africa, when the countries were going through the transition to independence."

Although there have been several Art Appreciation Groups through the Club's history, during the 1950s there was an active Art Group which painted under the instruction of a professional. They displayed their work at various CFUW meetings, as did Art Groups from other Clubs during the period. At the 1955 Triennial Meeting in Edmonton, the paintings of the various members filled several rooms.

In the 1960s, when Club membership was at its peak, there were 32 Interest and Study Groups. To some degree, the increase was due to the duplication of existing groups. There were seven circulating book groups, three each of play-reading groups, biography, world studies and conversational language groups (French, Spanish and German). By the end of the decade, however, a major change in the type of Interest Groups began to emerge. With advances in information technology, cultural interests that were formerly central to Club life were being taken care of in other ways. Groups such as biography, world studies, art and music appreciation and language conversation became less and less popular while others were phased out all together. New groups arose reflecting current topics and interests. The Club continued its role of being a vehicle for the pursuit of knowledge and fulfillment.

New Trends, New Groups

Members of the first Gourmet Cooking Group rented kitchen space in the Home Economics Building on the U of A campus for a series of eight cooking demonstrations in the late 1960s. These followed the pattern of the popular cooking shows put on by the local utilities company in the 1960s. Gourmet Cooking reappeared as Hospitality Cooking in the 1970s, and remained popular. It was so popular that by the 1980s there were several groups including day and evening groups, couples gourmet, dining out and by the 1990s a slim cuisine group.

With more women working full or part-time, members looked for more relaxed forms of entertainment. Another group, Just-For-Fun, was formed in the 1970s. In light of the intellectual bent of some of the earlier Study Groups, the name says it all. The group met monthly, day or evening, with group activities including theatre, light opera, museum tours and special luncheons with guest speakers. The tours included two bus trips to the Glenbow Museum in Calgary. In 1982, 43 members attended artist Judy Chicago's "The Dinner Party," a celebration of women's achievements throughout history depicted by 39 place settings set on a triangular table. Then in 1984 members viewed a world-class Pre-Columbian Art Exhibit at the museum. Guest speakers included author and U of A writer-in-residence Maria Campbell. Just-For-Fun evolved into the Lively Arts Group, which remains popular today.

Another trend contributed to women's financial awareness. Two Investment Groups were established which met monthly under the direction of professional investment brokers. Both Groups lasted for over fifteen years (1978 to the 1990s). There were also several short-course seminars on finance for members. Part of the interest stemmed from widespread discussion on pension reform throughout Canada, prompting greater individual responsibility for retirement planning.

A further challenge of the 1980s was the rise in new technology, especially the personal computer. Members attempted to keep up-to-date in this area through a group called Fun With Computers. Through specially designed courses offered at the U of A and other courses at Grant MacEwan Community College (GMCC), members gained access to some of the earliest PC computer programming courses in the city. Over 40 women took the several courses offered; a few went on to advanced "basic-language" programming and one member, Pam Laing, went on to become an instructor at GMCC. Both the Investment Group and the Computer Group demonstrate once more the function of the Club in channeling an interest in a constructive way.

A wide range of topics reflected both the serious and recreational through the 1980s and 1990s. For instance, the increased interest in fitness was reflected in the active cross-country ski group of the mid 1980s, and the several walking groups of the 1990s. There were also short course seminars on topics as varied as fashion, finance, public speaking and parliamentary law, cardio-pulmonary resuscitation (CPR), calligraphy and origami. One group that appeared intermittently throughout the Club's history is the Bridge Group, now a current favorite. In 1997 a Health Care Study Group was formed to look at the ramifications of health care cuts made in the province and to determine their effects, especially on women. The Group also studied the viability and efficiency of the Edmonton Home Care System.

One of the constants through the years has been the members' love of reading. There have been different forms of book groups, such as Circulating Books, Modern Fiction, Great Books, New Books, Living Library and Random Readers. Whatever the name, members have always had an appreciation for reading and for sharing the experience.

Drama–Play Reading Group

During the 1920s and 1930s Edmonton had a lively amateur "Little Theatre," supported by the U of A's Faculty of Extension, which not only gave training and advice to local theatre groups throughout Alberta, but maintained a library of scripts for their use. In 1924, it is noted that the Department provided scripts to over 200 communities (History of Alberta, p. 238). The U of A's own radio station, CKUA, which operated out of the Department of Extension, also broadcast numerous plays after its inception in 1927.

Members of Drama Group–1992 (founded 1931)
Standing, L to R: Barbara Blackley, Winnifred Long (charter member), Libby Frost, Jean Monckton, Peggy Rootes
Seated, L to R: Lucile Kane, Norma Freifield, Grace Studholme.
(absent, Louise Johnson, Edith Whidden)

Thus, the environment was ripe for the formation of a Play-Reading Group. What makes the Club's group unique is that it continued to exist for so many years. For over 60 years (1931 to the mid 1990s) one particular Drama Group met regularly and one of its original members, Winnifred Long, attended meetings into the 1990s.

This is a testament to the members' devotion to theatrical plays. It also combined a longing to keep up tradition among the older members with the competitive spirit and interest of the younger members who were known to search the shops of London, New York and other places on the lookout for new plays. Their story also provides an insight into a group of women who strongly supported local theatre and formed a core audience, and who gave voice to a city that today prides itself on its rich theatrical traditions.

On the occasion of the Drama Group's 50th anniversary Jean Monckton wrote and presented a wonderful account of the group, and it is reproduced here in its entirety. It provides an exceptional glimpse into the lives of the women of the early 1930s when the Group started. Not only does it describe a specific Group, but equally important is the way in which it sheds light on the humour, commitment and intellectual lives of the women who participated in CFUW Edmonton.

Drama Group 1931–1981

Imagine if you will, a sitting room arranged for an informal meeting–dining room chairs dotted about amongst the normal furniture. Punctually at 1 p.m. a group of women begin to arrive–there will be sixteen in all. Chatting quietly they perform an obviously familiar ritual making sure that the member who is reader for the day is in a chair with plenty of light and that everyone else has a really comfortable chair. "Comfortable" usually means a hard, straight-backed chair, and the squashy modern creation will be left severely alone, untenanted for the whole afternoon! Everyone then relaxes and has dessert and coffee. They will have come despite the weather–a few years ago meeting day dawned with weather warnings on all sides, temperatures already well below zero [Fahrenheit] and blowing snow everywhere. As group leader for the year, I phoned Grace, hostess for the meeting, "Grace, do you think we should cancel the meeting in view of the weather?" A pause, then Grace, "Well, Jean, we never have cancelled a meeting yet." I thought, "And I'll be damned if I'll be the first," and so we went ahead. Everyone got there–how I'm not sure, but I do know that Enid, Margaret, and I floundered through the snowdrifts from Windsor Park to Garneau, walking backwards for most of the way to save our faces it seemed, giggling hysterically or occasionally shouting above the wind, "This is crazy you know!" Fortunately, apart from our intrepid selves there was no one else in sight. Sometimes, too, the weather has become part of the play: a clear afternoon, Edith Whidden, her back to the window absorbed in reading Agatha Christie's *Mousetrap,* the tale of people trapped by a snowstorm in an English country house. The plot thickens and the eyes of those seated opposite the reader widen with alarm as a totally unforecast storm blots out the landscape, and the real world outside and the imaginary world within seem to become one. We were not stranded, but the drive home was a little too exciting for my taste!

Coffee finished, the group leader brings us to order and there are a few minutes of business—arranging future hostesses and readers, the reading of a letter from an old member—and then the reader begins the play. It follows no "theme for the year" being entirely a matter of the reader's taste limited by the very practical considerations that one voice will be reading all the parts (so it must not have a large cast) and it will be a play that she has been able to edit to such length that it can be read in one and a half to two hours at most, still maintaining the style, flow, and comprehensibility (no mean task with some modern plays). Halfway through, she will organize a break for coffee; for example, recently, Enid, "Louise, when I get to the bit about stones rolling down the mountain, you will know I'm near the coffee break."

At the conclusion of the play we disperse rather quickly into the late afternoon, still discussing the play but now determined "to beat the traffic rush."

This is the Drama Group and this is what it has been doing in one way or another for the last fifty years. Other groups have come and gone, some, like Biography, French, and even other playreading groups have lasted many years but none has achieved this long, unbroken record. Why? It is difficult to say, but perhaps you may find the answer somewhere in its history.

That history begins on November 14, 1931, when, at a general meeting of the University Women's Club, Mrs. Butterworth announced the formation of three new Study Groups—Modern Fiction, French, and Drama. The Drama Group to be led by Mrs. Wallace, wife of the President of the University, in whose home, Number 1 Campus, the first meeting was held. Apparently it was suggested that the refreshments served should be "Johnny cake and an apple"!

The group was an instant success and by 1933 it had "more members than could study together effectively and so a second group had to be formed. The group meets every two weeks. At each meeting papers are given by members and general discussion follows. Membership is between 12 and 20."

The study of Drama was taken seriously–1934–35 was devoted to Elizabethan Drama, Jonson, Shakespeare, and Marlowe amongst others. Winnifred remembers that, "it was like doing a university course. You must remember that we were all young women, recent graduates or wives of faculty members and we looked on these meetings as a chance to continue the kind of experience we had enjoyed in University."

In the early years the group met for luncheon provided by one hostess. There were also lavish Christmas parties given by Mrs. Wells. Mrs. Wells was the senior member of the group (old enough to be a mother to most members) and everyone deferred to her. When reading plays members carefully omitted all words which they felt might offend her. However, when she read her play she read everything, steaming ahead without any embarrassment saying, "Well, that's how it's written!" Mrs. Wells's tradition of hospitality was carried on into the seventies by her daughter, Helen Sutherland, who, though never a member of this club herself, always had the Drama group's first fall meeting in her home.

Later on all meetings became dinner meetings–one hostess again providing the meal. Such a prospect appalls me, but Winnifred assures me that, "then anyone with any kind of income had a maid. You could get a live-in maid all found for a top wage of $20 a month"!

Husbands were invited to the Christmas parties and took part in the plays. Later, although she vehemently denies responsibility, Inez Calhoun is widely credited with the introduction of very active, even riotous, party games, and Lucile Kane remembers playing Sardines at her home. Kathleen Morrison (a charter member of this club and a devoted member of the Drama group until her death two years ago) was discovered squeezed under the piano which was a very elderly instrument and in imminent danger of collapse!

As time passed, what Winnifred calls "maidlessness" arrived, with the result that only the Christmas dinner remained a dinner meeting and in fact became a pot-luck supper remembered for deadly struggles to carve turkeys with blunt knives in strange kitchens, and mashing mountains of potatoes!

So much for private frivolity, but the group throughout its life has also "put itself before the public" or at least the meetings of this club to provide entertainment. In the thirties most club programs were "homegrown"–members of the Faculty talked on all kinds of subjects, frequently on the theatre and literature, and Dr. Silver Keeping gave a memorable address on "Fungi I have known"! Study groups regularly gave skits at the Annual Banquet held in March, and for a number of years the Drama group alone put on plays in Convocation Hall for the Annual Meeting (then a separate event from the Banquet).

The first skits, under the title "Study Groups Grave and Gay," were done in 1935. Each group was expected to "take off" its work for the year, and the Drama group, which had been deep in Elizabethan plays, presented a morality play. Mary Elliott recalls a large wooden cradle in a crèche setting where peasants were trying to hide a pig they had stolen. Winnifred and Grace remember Mrs. Wallace (the director) cavorting about clad in a leopard skin to everyone's great amusement! Incidentally, in those days, again quoting Winnifred, "the Corona Hotel was the place for a banquet. The meal which included everything from soup to nuts with real linen and waitresses for every table of six cost only 50 cents a plate with a 10 cents tip per person!" The executive's decision to give each waitress a dollar must have seemed lavish indeed!

In April of 1934 the Drama group presented two short plays at the general meeting–*Everybody's Husband* and *Brothers in Arms*. The latter you will see later this evening.

In 1936 Mrs. Wallace wrote a 45-minute play called *Poisoned Prunes* for performance at the Annual Meeting. Jessie Stewart has recalled rehearsing in Con Hall–"We depicted various types of women and I was supposed to be the modern, smoking cigarettes etc. Kenneth Neatby looked in as we were rehearsing and gave me some tips on smoking! I haven't made use of his advice!" The minutes state that, "In it, Tendencies of Modern Literature and Thought appeared as personalities. It was thoroughly understood and enjoyed." The group received a grant of $10 for make-up and costumes. Later that year Mrs. Wallace departed for Kingston where she still lives and at the age of 93 still keeps in touch with us. To mark this jubilee of the group whose success owed so much to her talent and enthusiasm we have today sent her flowers.

Even without her lively presence the group continued to prosper and produce plays for the club–*Dixon's Kitchen* (a Carolinean play of country courtship under the direction of Stella Cameron),

The Treasurer's Report, now thought to be a spoof on the Annual Meeting! Many skits and charades followed until the late fifties.

Meanwhile meetings of the group had assumed their present format and the tone was perhaps not quite so serious, for there was no annual theme and members made their own choice of plays, sometimes playing records of them (*Medea and Don Juan in Hell,* but most often reading, as we do now, a wide variety of plays then being produced on the London or New York stage (*The Heiress, The Lady's Not For Burning, The Rainmaker, The Glass Menagerie,* and a number of musicals like *Brigadoon*). To obtain recent plays was not easy and members relied on Inez, who worked in the Library, to hunt them up, and they also made good use of Burns Mantle Plays of the Year, which published synopses of current plays (and still does) accompanied by long illustrative dramatic extracts. Today, plays can still be a problem. Fortunately, our members travel a lot, and wherever they go they scour local bookshops for plays, and there are friends, relatives, and old group members who also send us offerings; so we have read in the last ten years alone plays from New Zealand, Australia, China, Nigeria, and London. A recent visit to Toronto produced a modern Russian play. You name it and we have probably read it. After all, in the last fifty years there have been five hundred plays read (ten per year). Subjects range from the mediaeval *Everyman* to the modern marginally understandable *The Effects of Gamma Rays on the Man in the Moon Marigolds* and of late many Canadian plays such as French's *Leaving Home,* Sharon Pollock's *Walsh, Overlaid* by Robertson Davies. We feel rather smug that John Aubrey's *Brief Lives* was a hit with us long before it reached the Citadel!

We end the year with a pot-luck luncheon to which we invite the club president and vice-presidents. In 1973 the president, Marjorie Buckley, read her own play, *The 5,000 Year Mortgage.* That was a unique event and we can assure the president today that she is not expected to follow suit. The final ritual of the year is the presentation of a silver coffee spoon to the group leader if it is the first time she has served as leader. It was the custom to give a spoon however often a member led the group, but the inflation in silver prices has cramped our style! Even so many members have two or three spoons, which really emphasizes one extraordinary thing about this group—not only has it continued for so long but we still have members who have belonged to it since the thirties, forties, and fifties as well as mere membership babes of the last ten years We are not a closed group, exclusive (as I had certainly imagined when I first heard of it). From the very beginning numbers have been limited to a comfortable roomful, and sixteen (our present number) is certainly that! No one drops out of the group—they may die or move away and only then is there room for a new face. In the last eleven years there have been only eight new members, which is probably a faster rate of change than in previous decades since it is only now that people are retiring and moving to warmer climes.

We keep in touch with past members by Christmas cards, letters, and visits. There is a pleasant sense of continuity and, unless you are the reader of the day and all keyed up to read, there is an endearing cosiness and relaxation in the meetings. They are important to us. They are fun. Long may they continue!

Jean Monckton, November 16, 1981

Chapter 9

$\mathcal{F}$undraising

Though substantial energies went into raising money for community projects in the early days, the Club was not primarily a fundraising group. The main focus of the fundraising was and remains the development of the Club's own scholarship programs. The methods of fundraising over the years represented what was popular at the time, be it plays, public lectures, magazine sales, fashion shows or wine-tasting, as well as the always popular used-book sales.

At the time of the First World War, plays and public lectures were a popular means to raise money for war relief efforts. In 1916, *You Never Can Tell* by G. B. Shaw was put on with the help of the U of A's Dramatic Society and raised enough to give $140 towards the purchase of musical instruments for the U of A Company of the Western Battalion and $33.25 to the Red Cross. Other plays put on in conjunction with the Dramatic Society between 1916–1920 averaged $200, although the popular play *Alice-Sit-by-the-Fire* raised over $300. Monies went towards the U of A Soldiers' Comforts Club or the scholarship fund. A substantial amount was also raised by the public lectures with noted poets such as Bliss Carman and Vachel Lindsay and through several dansants that raised $150 each.

Vanishing Teas

The following description of a Vanishing Tea from the late 1940s gives an insight as to how these long since vanished fundraisers worked.

"We are planning to have a series of vanishing teas. One of the schemes the committees considered was assessing each member $2.00, but that would give us less than $500, while this scheme will raise $2000.

You probably all know how this is done. The first hostess invites 5 people to tea (or it may be in the morning or evening), each of those five agrees to invite 4, each 4 invites 3, each three, 2, and each two asks 1 person, and each person pays 25 cents for her tea. We want to have 25 of these chains and the members of the executive and of this committee have already agreed to be starters.

It is quite probable that some of you may be invited to several teas–but at 25 cents, it will take a while to be giving even $1 or $2.

Also it is possible some of you may not be invited to any. That will be too bad, but you could still consider yourself responsible for a donation. Some of you may not want to take an active part in this plan. In that case, figure out your share of the $2000, and give."

Another method of raising funds was by tightening the purse strings on the Club's social outlay. This in effect meant 'tealess' teas at the height of the war, and restrictions on the goodies.

Fundraising in the 1920s included the presentation of several more plays, as well as book showers and personal donations. By the 1930s, new fundraising projects were initiated in order to support the University Hospital Library which the Club had taken over in 1935. One project was the Club's sponsorship of magazine subscriptions among the membership. This successful idea was established on a trial basis in 1947 under Mrs. S. Dickson, and was continued into the 1960s. Funding for various war relief efforts in the 1940s again came from simplifying the social expenditures and from personal donations. The main efforts were directed towards helping graduate women war refugees in Europe. At the end of the Second World War the Club held Vanishing Teas to support the University Memorial Fund.

Members addressed and stuffed envelopes for Federal elections in 1979 and 1980, netting over $2000 for each event.

PAA CFUW Edmonton 87.340.2

Fashion Show
Models from Peggi Adams participated in 1977 Fashion Show to raise money for Club's Academic Awards Fund and CFUW Charitable Trust.

Sewing Team Prepares for DINOFAIR
L to R: Ann Malcolm, Patricia Giffen, Noreen Brownlie, Jill Barnicoat, Joan Weston

Through the 1950s and 1960s, fundraising went towards building up and maintaining the inventory of books at the Hospital Library and towards the undergraduate scholarship that was increased several times during the period.

Scholarships, Bursaries

When the Mature Women's Bursary was established in 1971, the initial funding for it came from the collection of telephone books (a first for the City, and initiated by the Club), personal donations (including one of $1000) and donations from other organizations. In 1972, the Club sought charitable status for the Academic Awards Fund (AAF). With that in place, the Club began several major fundraising activities and a formal Ways & Means Group was formed.

Ways and Means

A special Executive Meeting was held in September 1974 to discuss fundraising projects. A definite goal of $10,000 was set and a modus operandi outlined, including letters soliciting donations to be sent to associations, a fashion show, a book sale and display at Rutherford House, a spring garage sale and bridge and dessert parties. The Fashion shows became a major fund-raiser in the 1970s.

Swing Into Spring Fashion Shows

The Club held five fashion shows between 1975 and 1980, each a successful venture and the highlight of fundraising during the 1970s. "I remember when we oversold tickets to one show" related Cathy Haysom, one of the Convenors, "knowing that we'd have to bring in our own folding chairs and lawn chairs if it was sold out–and that's exactly what happened." Cathy, along with Jacquie Sawatzky, co-chaired several of the Club's Swing Into Spring shows. They were professional affairs featuring models from Peggi Adams and John Casablanca's Elite Studios, with the very popular Vernis McCuaig as commentator.

The first fashion show with Robin Robinson as Convenor was held in the auditorium of the Misericordia Hospital Nurses' Residence (1975) and subsequent ones at the Mayfield Inn. Each show raised between $1500 and $2000. After the success of the first few, the Club elected to hold an additional show in 1978 to raise money for the newly established CFUW Charitable Trust as well as for the Academic Awards Fund. A final show, Fashions for Fall, was held in 1980 which again raised money for both funds.

Fundraising in the 1980s and 1990s

A major fund-raiser in 1980 was the addressing of envelopes for a federal election, which raised $2,248. As the AAFund became more firmly established, personal donations started to come in, followed by endowments in the early 1980s. This allowed a Graduate Women's Scholarship to be added to the Club's AAFund. Although personal donations were still sought for community-related gift giving or special projects, the main emphasis on fundraising focused on the bursaries and scholarships. Numerous mini-fundraisers to support the AAFund included in-house auctions, raffles, wine-tastings, and the ever-popular used book sales.

Some of the ideas in the **25 Alive Campaign** were quite creative. Here's a sampling:

- Have your children or grandchildren pay you to do the chores that are usually theirs
- Sell something: that opera, ballet, theatre or sports ticket you can't use, your own handiwork, Great Aunt Matilda's antimacassar, your belly-dancing outfit...
- Turn down the thermostat and donate the saving
- Put aside $1 a week for 25 weeks
- Donate $2 of your weekly salary for 12 weeks. Then add $1
- Walk the neighbour's dog, pig or llama for $3 a time. Six outings and you're almost there!
- Buy an airline ticket on a seat sale and donate part of the $$ saved.
- Do something outrageous and people pay you to stop!

From the brochure: 25 Alive

By the 1990s fundraising projects included some interesting events, such as:

- Luncheon with her Honour, Mayor Jan Reimer at the Hilton Hotel–1992
- DINOFAIR–held at Hawrelak Park in connection with an Enviro-Fair, June, 1993; members organized playground activities for children and sold stuffed dinosaurs that they had sewn. They were to highlight the World Dinosaur Tour held in Edmonton
- 25 Alive promotion–members were encouraged to think of creative ways to raise $25 each
- Sale of Entertainment Books–promotional coupon book for dining, accommodation and other events, with the Club receiving a percentage of sales
- Book sales held at the meetings
- The major fund raiser of the period was a Casino held in the summer of 1999
- Donation and raffle of a Yardley Jones painting.

As the AAFund grew into a sizeable amount through the 1980s and 1990s, management of the money became a major concern. The investments were eventually handed over to the University of Alberta Endowment to maximize the return on the money and provide additional exposure for the Club. The Club retained responsibility for administering and distributing the awards.

Chapter 10

Meetings: From Theatre Rotunda to Church Basement

The Club has met at various places in Edmonton through the years for its general meetings, teas, receptions and banquets. A general outline of these venues is given, with special acknowledgment to the wives of the U of A Presidents who so generously welcomed new members and women students to their homes for many Club teas and receptions.

General Meetings

The earliest meetings of the Club pre-date the campus buildings themselves and were held in the Strathcona Collegiate Institute where the University of Alberta had temporary quarters. By 1911, Athabasca Hall was completed and members met in its lounge. Two years later they moved to a classroom in Assiniboia Hall and after that to Pembina Hall.

During the 1930s and 1940s, the Club met in classrooms or Wauneita Lounge of the Arts Building and sometimes in the Medical Amphitheatre. Members recall these settings as less than ideal, for they say it wasn't easy serving even light refreshments. They had to use either the janitor's little kitchenette in the Arts Building or a small room next to the Amphitheatre, where they heated their tea and coffee on bunsen burners. Older members recall, with some amusement, entertaining guest speaker Charlotte Whitton in such a manner in the 1940s.

There was some feeling among the members who lived on the North Side of the Saskatchewan River that all meetings shouldn't be held at the University, and an effort was made in the 1940s to satisfy them by holding two meetings at Talmud Torah Hall and three at the Macdonald Hotel. Although the meetings were well attended, it was found that the cost was going to be more than meeting at the University, and in the days when there was good street-car service and no parking problems, the advantage lay in continuing at the University. Talmud Torah was suggested because a city-wide Women's Forum had held meetings there regularly in the 1930s.

In the Fall of 1950, the new Students' Union Building (now University Hall) was completed and the Club had the use of the women's new Wauneita Lounge. According to members, this was one of the most popular meeting places, although it lacked an elevator, which was an important consideration for the older members! When a new SUB was built in the late 1960s, the Club again had to look for a new meeting place (a room in the new building was offered to them but it didn't fit their requirements). In 1970 the Club arranged to rent one of the rooms at the Faculty Club on Saskatchewan Drive. Space was not always available at the Faculty Club, however, and the general meetings had to be held in various venues from church basements and annexes to the Clinical Sciences Lounge for several years. Since the mid 1980s the Club has met regularly at the Faculty Club.

The purpose for the meetings was the same then as it is today–to provide the opportunity to come together socially and to hear talks from experts in various fields of endeavor thus keeping up-to-date on current issues. In the early days meetings were held monthly–usually Saturday afternoon at 3:00 p.m. It wasn't until the 1970s that the general meetings were held in the evening, and then only after much discussion and debate.

Annual General Meeting (AGM)

For the Annual General Meeting, the Club looked to a larger venue on campus in the early days–often using Athabasca Hall, the convocation halls of St. Stephen's College, the Arts Building or even the old University Cafeteria. For special meetings, the Club continued to use the lounge in Athabasca Hall until the Air Force took it over in the early 1940s. (The Hall was the centre of graduate student social activity in the early days.)

For much of the Club's history, the AGM and Banquet were held separately, the more formal Banquet often being held in February. However, in the early 1960s the two events were combined and became the focus of the year-end meeting. This arrangement lasted until the early 1990s when it became obvious that it was far too much for one evening's event and they were once again held separately. The Banquet remained the year-end May/June event.

Banquet

The Banquet was the highlight of the Club's social activities each year, especially during the period it was held at the Macdonald and Corona Hotels (1930s to early 1960s). It was a formal affair complete with gloves and long gowns. Cost of the dinner in the mid 1930s was $1.10. A proposed menu for a dinner in the early 1940s was not considered adequate and the revised offering came to $1.70!

The Macdonald Hotel was the centre of social activity in Edmonton for many years and visiting dignitaries were often entertained by the Executive with tea at the Macdonald. In 1941, after questioning the advisability of having a banquet at the height of the war, the Club opted for a Christmas Tea at the Macdonald instead. This proved to be a most successful event and was continued for the duration of the war. After the war, members went back to the former custom of having banquets. However, the Christmas Tea also became an annual event.

Club's Golden Anniversary Dinner at the Macdonald Hotel, Jan. 19, 1960, included Mrs. W. H. Johns, Honorary President, standing left, and Winnifred Long
Seated, L to R: Cora Casselman, Mrs. G. G. Reynolds, Ruth Hyndman, Convenor

After the era of the Macdonald, the Club looked to other venues for the banquet, and the following list gives a good indication of the expanded social facilities of the City by the 1960s: Mayfair Golf and Country Club (1960s), Lister Hall and the Faculty Club on the U of A campus (1970s), Derrick Golf and Country Club and Downtown Centre Club and (Shaw) Convention Centre (1980s). In the 1990s,

It was because she served tea so well that **Mrs. Lucile Kane** was invited to join the Club in 1927 by Mrs. A. C. Rutherford, wife of the University Chancellor. In a humorous account of her early days, Lucile told how Mrs. Rutherford always had teas for the women students at the U of A and her daughter, Hazel had become tired of having to help her mother. It was suggested that she bring another girl or two to help at the teas and so Lucile was asked since she knew the family. Mrs. Rutherford thought that she showed possibilities, and that she had the "poise and polish to be a good tea pourer, since she came from a University town such as Stanford." Lucile was thus invited to become a member. She not only joined, but was a valued member of the Club for 70 years!

mainly as a consequence of escalating costs, the Club returned to the U of A campus and to the Faculty Club for the banquet.

Opening, New Member's and Senior's Teas

Throughout much of the Club's history, an opening tea was held on a fall afternoon (3:00 p.m.) to welcome new and returning members back after a summer hiatus. In the early days, it was a tradition to ask the wife of the University President to be Honorary President and she often hosted the tea at the official university residence. The importance of teas in the early days was very significant. Being asked to be a tea pourer was a great honour. "You always asked the Honorary President first, plus at least three other women of note," recalled a President of the 1960s. "We did a lot of pouring at teas–in addition to the Opening Tea and the Christmas Tea, we often were asked to pour at the social functions of many other women's groups it the City."

In addition to the Opening Tea, a New Member's Tea was held later in the year (January–March) to give the new members an opportunity to meet with each other and the Executive and was usually held in a public place. During World War II, it was held in the foyer of Garneau Theatre because of limited space on campus. Now named the New Member's Reception, it has become a fall event and is most often held in the homes of the Executive members. Even the original Opening Tea, now called the Membership Reception, is an evening event (since 1983).

Teas for graduating senior students were held regularly into the 1950s. On occasion there have been special teas for the university girls, such as the one-time event in 1943. The Club extended its interests to the freshmen girls and decided to entertain them in small groups by holding teas in the homes of members in a sense fulfilling the original mandate of the Club. Club member and Dean of Women, Dr. Mary Winspear, organized the event which was considered a great success. This liaison between the students and the Club proved to be beneficial and through the interaction many new members became interested in joining the Club. Unfortunately, with the increased enrollment at U of A after the 1950s it was not possible to continue the practice of entertaining the women students through teas and socials.

The idea of an Afternoon Tea was revived in the 1990s when Robin Robinson hosted several Spring Teas for "senior members who can't always make it to meetings." The events were very successful and will hopefully be continued to accommodate the older members.

Although the level of formality has declined and members are no longer expected to don formal gowns and gloves for the banquet, nor hat and gloves for the Teas, the value of the social occasions remains as important to members today as in years past.

Chapter 11

Communication: Records of the Club, Newsletter and Publicity

The minutes of the Club tell a story in themselves. For the first decade of CFUW Edmonton, the minutes were all taken down in longhand, some in green ink which are very difficult to read. As time progressed, the Club paid to have the minutes typed (1920s to1940s) and eventually bound, so that they are well preserved. From the 1940s on they were typed by the Recording Secretary and filed. Various other reports of these early years were done on foolscap (legal size) paper, having been run off on a Gestetner machine (these were pre-photocopy days!) From the 1980s on there has been a revolution in printing and today the Recording Secretary has been known to type the minutes on her laptop. It is doubtful anyone is nostalgic for the old days of recording the Club Minutes.

Newsletter

The evolution of the Club newsletter tells a similar story. It wasn't until the 1970s that a full-scale newsletter was sent out. Prior to then members just received a notice of the up-coming meetings in the mail. Today, the newsletter editor puts together the copy on a computer and scans in extra material, including photos, so that a professional looking product is produced. Although most newsletters are mailed, some are e-mailed to members, and the Club envisages many more members coming on-line in the future. The whole aspect of communication has completely changed from the old days.

It's a far cry from the 1970s and early 1980s when the newsletter was put together and mailed out by the Association for the Handicapped (Rehabilitation Centre) at their downtown location. The names and addresses were all typeset and the Membership Secretary had to check with the Association and go over all the changes of address and membership many times, which was a very time-consuming practice. In addition, CFUW and IFUW publications are also produced several times a year and are available at meetings. In this way members are kept informed on the wider Federation issues as well.

Publicity

Publicity in the early days was not a problem when coverage of the Club's activities was on the women's or society page of the local newspaper. In one write-up in the 1920s, the names of every member attending the AGM, the executive and convenors of all the Interest/Study Groups were given, as well as a brief history of the Club. For the Club's 50th anniversary celebration at the Macdonald Hotel, there was a full write-up, complete with photos. Such is not the case today. When one of the authors took a description of the Club's 70th anniversary to the local paper in 1980, she was told "we don't do women's groups anymore."

What did generate news were major projects, such as the Club's environmental projects–the paper bin collections, telephone book pick-ups and Ecology Caravan–which received good coverage in the 1970s. The establishment of the Mature Women's Bursary Program received coverage during that same period; however, by the time the later Graduate Women's Scholarship Program came into being (mid 1980s) the award activities of the Club were no longer unique.

The lack of publicity is a lament heard from other women's groups and CFUW Clubs. Creative ways have to be employed to gain a wider audience. One new way, of course, is through the Internet, and both the CFUW and the Club have gone on-line with positive results.

Past Presidents gathered with honored guests and current President, Robynne Healey, at Club's 90th Anniversary celebration at Rutherford House, November 22, 1999.

Front Row, L to R: Rita Calhoun, Robynne Healey, Robin Robinson, Ruth Hyndman, Johanna Michalenko (guest) Betty Gravett and Georgie Brooks

Back Row, L to R: Win Mellon as Dr. Geneva Misener, Hiske Gerding, Tammy Irwin as Mrs. Melrose, Cynthia Boodram, Ann Stewart (hidden), CFUW President Mavis Moore, Peggy Giffen (guest), Barbara Blackley, Alberta Boytzun, Jean Lund, Melvina Gowda, Joan Cowling

Afterword: Looking Back, Looking Forward

The women of CFUW Edmonton did not start out in altruistic fashion to bring education and culture to the community. They started out, by degrees, with a desire to assist and encourage young women at university, based on their own experience as among the first women in Canada to receive a higher education. Soon after they sought to advance women's position in the community at-large by the promotion of women to the U of A Senate and to the local school boards and then to promote the betterment of public education in general.

By 1919, when the Club became part of the Canadian Federation of University Women (CFUW) it was able more clearly to define and enlarge its original purposes. The communication networks and organizational structure of CFUW undoubtedly helped focus the Club's goals and activities. The continued existence of the Club and Federation is based largely on the ability to work for common goals, to maintain a constant set of values and to provide fellowship and a positive learning experience for women with common interests. The latter objective is summed up in the CFUW motto "Knowledge is growth, Come Grow with us".

CFUW Edmonton's preference for reasoned debate has led to a non-partisan, inter-faith Club which has encouraged the exploration of varied points of view and of emergent problems. As an organization it is neither radical nor conservative, although among its members there may be a whole spectrum of views. Attached to the value placed on reason are two further characteristics. Firstly, education in all its forms is taken to be of paramount importance and secondly, it is agreed that words are a form of action, and therefore briefs, studies and public representations at hearings are used to help achieve the Club's goals. This affection for reason has been the mainstay of the Club throughout the past ninety years, during which time its members, singly and as a group, have made a significant and durable contribution to the community.

By detailing the activities of CFUW Edmonton over the past ninety years, and highlighting some of its major accomplishments, it is hoped that current and prospective members may be encouraged to meet new challenges just as past members did. As we enter the 21st Century, the idea of women's equality is no longer novel, but it is still disputable. It has been important to document the longevity of some of the problems and the ways in which ordinary women have struggled to solve them and to bring about change.

Submissions

The following list includes some of the major Briefs, petitions, reports, recommendations and Resolutions submitted by CFUW Edmonton to various levels of government, education officials, CFUW and concerned citizen's groups. Unless specified otherwise, government Briefs or recommendations were addressed to the Alberta government.

1909-1919

1912   Resolution passed by Club to be brought before the Local Council of Women (LCW) that "a Censor or Board of Censors be appointed for Moving Pictures."

1912   Resolution passed by Club to be brought before the LCW that "cleanliness, ventilation, and overcrowded conditions in the Strathcona street-cars, plus expectoration, be investigated."

1914   Petition for extension of "the franchise equally to women," in response to the LCW's Standing Committee on the Franchise for Women which sought support from women's groups.

1915   Petition to Edmonton Public School Board (EPSB) protesting proposal to curtail positions of Supervisors of Music and of Art.

1917   Recommendation to EPSB that a thorough course in Manual Training and Household Arts be given in public schools and be optional in high schools, also that no homework be required in public school until Grade V and that there be shorter hours in public and high schools.

1917   Recommendation to EPSB that action taken by the Board prior to the war regarding the education of backward children be resumed as early as possible. Further request to LCW to investigate provision for custody and training of those who leave the Red Deer School for Feeble-Minded at age 16.

1920s

1920   Recommendation to Minister of Education asking the Department to purchase school textbooks in England or in Canada rather than the United States, especially for Literature and History.

1920   Support of LCW Resolution that "the Federal and Provincial governments be approached in regard to the matter of giving equal representation of women and men on all Boards dealing with women and children."

1922   Resolution to LCW encouraging it to establish an Educational Standing Committee which would encourage study and discussion of educational questions and serve as a medium for circulating information among its affiliated organizations.

1924   Resolution to Department of Education regarding raising the standard of secondary education in the Province of Alberta by requiring the passing grade of 50% on each subject for entrance to High School and in all succeeding grades.

1928   Recommendation to EPSB that should a new school be formed it be named Chegwin in honour of the teachers, the Misses Chegwin.

1930s

1930   Recommendation to Minister of Education, Hon. Perren Baker, that qualifications of teachers be raised requiring the successful completion of Grade XII for entrance into the Normal schools of Alberta.

1930   Recommendation to EPSB regarding the current School Reader, that at the conclusion of the contract for supply of the present reader, the new one be better graded, more interesting, with a more modern approach and that peace be stressed rather than the glorification of war.

1933   Recommendation to Dominion Government urging that CBC have a western Canada CBC station as soon as possible; also support of CFUW (Vancouver) Resolution calling for a children's program on CBC.

1933   Resolution to Prime Minister urging the Dominion Government to instruct delegates to the World Disarmament Conference to do everything possible to obtain a mutual agreement that all nations prohibit private manufacture of war equipment and assume control of the export of all war material.

1933   Recommendation to Mayor and Edmonton Library Board regarding the appointment of a permanent librarian for Public Library and urged that only a qualified person be appointed.

1937   Resolution on Prison Reform to Dominion Government arising from concern over poor conditions in Federal Penitentiary and asking government to carry out an investigation of such conditions.

1937   Resolution to EPSB stressing strong opposition to proposed motion "that elementary schools of more than five rooms should not have women as principals."

1937   Resolution to Dominion Government asking for an embargo on the export of war material to Japan and reiterating support of moves to take the profit out of manufacturing of war materials.

1939   Petition to Prime Minister deploring the shipment of scrap iron to aggressor nations.

1940s

1943   Letter to EPSB expressing disapproval of proposed changes to the School Act which read "women teachers would automatically surrender their contracts when they married." Based on refusal of Edmonton teacher to resign after she was married (October 4, 1943), citing that the School Board Act as written did not permit discrimination between men and women.

1943   Resolution to Dominion Government asking that women be represented on all committees concerned with government policy affecting women either directly or indirectly (in support of CFUW Calgary Resolution).

1943   Resolution to Minister of Health and Welfare, Dr. W. W. Cross, and Committee investigating Child Welfare Work in the Province of Alberta calling for:

> • an independent investigator or social worker well recommended by the Canadian Welfare Council,

- efficiency of foster home placement by the addition of more trained and experienced inspectors and probation officers,

- compilation of complete records and statistics so that they may be comparable with other provinces.

1944   Letter to Premier E. C. Manning, Government of Alberta, expressing concern for adequate nursery school facilities in the province due to increasing number of working women.

1944   Resolution to Dominion Government urging that a competent commission with Indian representative be appointed to make a survey of all Indian Reservations and communities in Canada for purposes of recommending immediate needs and laying plans for future development giving special attention to education (in support of CFUW Calgary Resolution).

1944   Recommendation to Provincial Government urging it to secure gifted students for teacher training and to give them generous financial assistance (in support of CFUW Calgary Resolution dealing with the problem of the probable shortage of teachers after the war).

1944   Recommendation to Dominion Government to give grants in aid to the provinces to make the recruiting and training of students possible. Report of the Education Committee (April 1944) regarding the relationship between federal and provincial governments in the field of education concluded that:

- federal aid to finance education was essential,

- a minimum standard of not less than the existing average of educational opportunity in Canada be a condition of such aid,

- federal aid, while still maintaining provincial control of education, could include subsidies for building and equipment, percent of income and corporation taxes turned back to the provinces be earmarked for education, and extension of the existing Dominion-Provincial training scheme.

1944   Resolution to Parliament of Canada urging it to take immediate steps to:

- give CBC authority, free from political or other interference, to direct all broadcasting in the Dominion,

- appoint a competent person as general manager and fill vacancies on the Board of Governors,

- empower the Prime Minister to make a public declaration that the independence and integrity of CBC be assured and a high standard be maintained.

1944   Resolution to Parliament of Canada urging it to make provision for the establishment of a National Library as one of its most important post-war projects. Stated that Canada was one of the few countries in the world without a National Library and its existence would be one of the strongest factors in the stimulation of better library services throughout the Dominion.

1945   Brief to Minister of Economic Affairs recommending the appointment of a library commission, the establishment of a system of regional libraries and the need for a library building at the U of A.

1945   Recommendations to EPSB dealing with revised salary schedule for teachers, petitioning for adequate clerical help in the schools and a funding program for improving educational facilities.

1950s

1950   Resolution to Dr. Swift, Minister of Education, petitioning for the appointment of women to executive positions in the Department of Education, including superintendents and inspectors, and for more women staff in the two branches of the Faculty of Education (Calgary and Edmonton).

1953   Brief to U of A in support of Friends of the Indian Society urging the University to accept responsibility for preserving (Canadian) Indian history and folklore by setting up an Indian Museum with a curator who would do research and give lectures.

1954   Resolution to Provincial Government opposing any action that would lower entrance requirements for the Faculty of

Education, U of A or shorten the training period required for certification of teachers.

1955   Request to Provincial Government to enact legislation providing that women be given equal opportunity to work and that no employer be permitted to discriminate between male and female employees by paying a female employee a lesser rate of pay for work of comparable character (in support of Business and Profession Women Resolution and CFUW).

1956   Recommendation to Prime Minister urging the establishment of a Canada Council.

1957   Resolution to CFUW Education Standing Committee to undertake a comparative investigation of secondary school standards and university entrance requirements in all provinces with a view to promoting a uniform high standard. Letters sent also to Premier, Minister of Education and Dean of Arts & Science at U of A.

1957   Submission to Special Committee on Crime Comics, Attorney-General's Department recommending the setting up of a committee to investigate the matter and emphasizing the need for greater availability of reading material for youth by extension of library facilities with proportionate increase in number of trained librarians.

1958   Letter to Prime Minister, Hon. John Diefenbaker and certain members of Parliament of Canada requesting revision to the Bill concerning Succession Duties.

1958   Brief to Royal (Cameron) Commission on Education dealing with special services category, including guidance counselling, teaching of gifted and handicapped students and financial aid to students.

1958   Brief to Royal (Cameron) Commission on Education re libraries:

> • protesting combined use of libraries as study halls-arising from fact that construction grants for new schools given only where joint use was designated, and
>
> • urging appointment of a Provincial Supervisor of Libraries under the Department of Education. Stated that

purpose of a supervisor was to help set standards for libraries and give encouragement and advice to school boards and teachers.

1959   Brief to Child Welfare Commission titled "Day Care of Children in Edmonton and Jasper Place" asking for specified minimum requirements and licensing of day nurseries and that regulations be more strictly enforced.

1959   Brief to Alberta Education Council and Department of Education "Who Should go to University–Who Should Pay the Fees" arising from survey of financial assistance to talented students in Canada, especially in Alberta. Stating that Cameron Commission's recommendations on this matter be adopted and that available financial assistance to students be better publicized.

1960s

1961   Brief to EPSB concerning school library development in the Edmonton Public School system. Recommendations included upgrading of the Library Specialist to a Supervisor of School Libraries, adequate space for a central library in every school with over 200 pupils, at least one course in library management for teachers in charge of libraries and an increase in the book budget.

1961   Recommendation to Premier and Government of Alberta, regarding Increased Grants for Education.

1962   Brief to Hon. A. R. Patrick, Provincial Secretary regarding a Provincial Archives outlining the following recommendations that the Province:

  • appoint a fully qualified provincial archivist

  • form a Public Documents Committee and an Independent Board of Trustees

  • pass legislation safe-guarding public documents and

  • begin a program of micro-filming

1962   Brief to City Council regarding a Central Registry for Handicapped stating that the old Royal Alex Hospital was completely inadequate for the purposes of a treatment centre and school for multiple-handicapped children and urging that it serve as a basis only for the eventual setting up of a complete and adequate treatment and schooling facility.

1963   Brief to EPSB regarding School Guidance Services noting lack of guidelines, especially in high schools and under-staffing of department of special services and provincial guidance clinic.

1963   Brief to Department of Education asking for improved provincial library facilities (in support of CFUW Calgary recommendations).

1964   Brief to Hon. Aalborg, Minister of Education regarding the appointment of a Supervisor of School libraries.

1965   Brief to federal Royal Commission on Bilingualism and Biculturism (B&B).

1965   Brief to U of A Senate re "Use and Extension of University Facilities for Continuing Education." Pertained to use of university facilities for part-time study and night courses.

1966   Brief to Minister of Welfare, Hon. L. C. Halmrast re: "Standards for Training of Custodial and Supervisory Personnel in Day Care Services in the Province of Alberta and Public Education with Respect to Same." Summary of Recommendations:

- A supervisor of a day care center having more than five preschool children should be specially qualified as to training, experience and personal abilities.

- Ratio of staff to children, grouping of children and assistant qualifications should be made similar to existing standards in British Columbia.

- The Department of Welfare should establish certification for day care personnel and encourage the development of training courses throughout the province.

- Department of Welfare should educate the public on day care services.

- The Department of Welfare should establish a Branch of Day Care with a specially trained director to help solve day care problems.

1966   Brief to Board of Governors, U of A, regarding "Training Courses for Custodial and Supervisory Personnel in Day Care Services." Summary of Recommendations:

- That a short-term program of evening and summer courses in day care, similar to those presently available at the Extension Departments of the Universities of British Columbia, McMaster and Carleton, be made available at the Department of Extension, U of A.

- That admission requirements for such a program include present employment in day care services, or a Grade XII Diploma or its equivalent, or the age of 25 years for candidates not now employed as day care personnel but having good personal qualifications.

- That certification should be given for completing the minimum program of four courses, and advanced certification be given for additional courses to be added in the future.

- That the University of Alberta seek the cooperation of a local day care center to provide practice teaching for candidates. Any such center should meet the educational and physical standards of a model day care center as set out by the Child Welfare League of America.

- That the University of Alberta give consideration to introducing a degree program in pre-school education and child care.

1968   Brief to federal Royal Commission on Status of Women– "Recommendations to Aid Women Re-entering University and Ultimately the Labor Force." Recommendations included:

- counselling services with a mature individual who recognizes needs of women graduates

- availability of part-time study

- new methods of study such as home study through TV lectures, employing the best techniques and best professors to produce university credit instruction

- provision for greater flexibility in day care

- financial support: the community, and women's groups in particular, should be made aware of the total lack of financial aid for part-time women students

- loans, bursaries, fellowships and scholarships should be made available to part-time students.

1969   Letter to Board of Governors, U of A regarding the use of Rutherford House for Club purposes and asking for postponement of Board's decision to demolish House in order to prepare a detailed financial feasibility analysis.

1969   Brief/Letter to Minister of Public Works regarding the Preservation of Rutherford House citing public support and feasibility of preservation. Copies of letter sent to Premier and all members of the Cabinet, as well as the Leader of the Opposition and the Lieutenant Governor.

1970s

1970   Letter to Minister of Social Development, Hon. R. A. Speaker, asking for continued support and improvement of day care services. In response to a fact sheet issued by the Homes and Institutions Branch of the Department of Social Development (1970) indicating a desperate need for more day care services in the province.

1971   Report titled "A Guide to the Operation of the Edmonton Public School System" from which a pamphlet was produced and made available to the public.

1972   Brief to Federal Government for use by the Canadian Preparatory Committee for the Stockholm Conference on the Human Environment "Quick Action to Improve the Human Environment" regarding air and water pollution.

1973   Brief to Minister of Health and Social Development, Hon. Neil Crawford, titled "Recommendations Regarding Single-Parent

Women on Social Allowance at Alberta Universities." Recommendations called for extra assistance under the Student Finance Act.

1973   Brief to Student Finance Board, Department of Advanced Education, "Recommendations Regarding Single-Parent Women on Social Allowance at Alberta Universities" recommended that extra assistance under The Students Finance Act, Part XII (Appendix) should be made readily available and known to qualified applicants and the terms of reference should be extended or clarified to ensure that social allowance recipients are specifically included.

1973   Brief to Mr. W. Thorsell, Executive Officer of the U of A Senate, urging Senate to establish a Task Force to study the status of all female staff members at the University.

1975   Brief to EPSB, "Proposals for a Program of Affirmative Action regarding the Employment and Promotion of Female Professional Staff by Boards of Education." Drew attention to the disproportionately small number of women in administrative positions in the school system.

1976   Recommendations to City Council requesting that a Provincial Grant of $460,000 be spent on library system.

1979   Brief to Task Force on Children with Learning Disabilities.

1980s

1980   Brief to CRTC Task Force on "Sex-Role Stereotyping in the Media."

1980   Brief to the Environment Council of Alberta's Public Hearing on Hazardous Wastes, Edmonton.

1982   Brief to Task Force on Gifted and Talented Students, Alberta Education, recommending that provincial legislation be enacted to ensure that special education is available to gifted and talented students throughout Alberta and that provincial funds be provided to support special training of teachers at university, to help establish innovative programs and to help classroom teachers acquire necessary materials.

1982   Brief to Task Force on Mature Students, U of A Senate, citing ten years experience in administering the Club's Mature Student Bursary Fund and emphasizing special financial needs of single student parents.

1983   Brief/Presentation to Parliamentary Task Force on Pension Reform concerning reform of Canada Pension Plan with special focus on women.

1984   Brief/Presentation to Fraser Special Committee on Pornography and Prostitution.

1987   Letter to Premier Don Getty, Intergovernmental Affairs Minister and MLAs regarding the Meech Lake Accord and the issue of equality of women as guaranteed in the Charter of Rights.

1989   Brief/Presentation to Canada/Alberta AlPac Environment Impact Assessment Review Board.

1990s

1990   Brief to President's Commission for Equality and Respect on Campus at U of A.

1990   Brief to Hon. Ralph Klein, Minister of Environment, re vision statement "Alberta's Environment: Toward's the 21st Century."

1990   Brief to Royal Commission on New Reproductive Technologies.

1993   Brief to Minister of Education, Hon. Halvar Jonson, regarding budget cuts to education.

1993   Letter to Minister Responsible for Women's Affairs, Hon Gary Mar, asking how the government plans to address women's issues when funding for Alberta Advisory Council on Women's Issues expires at the end of 1996.

1993   Letter to Premier Ralph Klein urging Alberta Government to ratify the UN Convention on the Rights of the Child.

1994   Letters to Premier Ralph Klein and to Minister of Environmental Protection, Hon. Ty Lund, regarding Advisory Committee Report on Special Places 2000: Alberta's Natural Heritage, stating lack of commitment from government for Special Places 2000.

1994   Presentation to Review Committee on Libraries, Alberta Community Development. Response to provincial government request for public input into funding of public libraries. Recommendations included opposition to user fees and further cutbacks to funding of public libraries, emphasis on helping adult learners and in eliminating illiteracy and more effective co-operative arrangements between public libraries and educational institutions (schools, colleges and universities).

1994   Brief to Axworthy Special Committee on Human Resources, Job and Growth "Improving Social Security in Canada." Brief referred to CFUW policies regarding issues which address the difficulties faced by women in overcoming poverty, the need for adequate daycare, literacy programs, tax reform, education funding, loans.

1994   Letter to Hon. Gary Mar, Minister Responsible for Women's Issues protesting the cancellation of the Person's Case Awards given to mature women upgrading their education.

1996   Brief to Hon. Ty Lund, Minister of Environmental Protection, protesting hazardous waste storage near designated Shorebird Sanctuary at Ryley, Alberta.

1997   Petition and Brief to Hon. Sergio Marchi, Federal Minister of the Environment, re Canadian Endangered Species Protection Act - Bill C65 asking for stronger legislation.

1998   Letter to Hon. Shirley McLelland, Minister of Community Development, protesting relocation of the Provincial Archives. Motion made to support retention of the Provincial Archives in Edmonton.

1999   Letter to Hon. Anne McLellan, Minister of Justice and Attorney General of Canada and MP, Edmonton West concerning viability of CBC, citing lack of adequate stable, long term funding and lack of politically independent and dynamic leadership at the helm of its operations.

Appendix

Survey of Club History by Decades

This survey provides a guided tour of ninety years of the life of CFUW Edmonton. It lists activities of the Club, actions representative of its purposes, stage markers of Club change and items of historical interest. As such it allows a glimpse into the scope of Club life, and the changes in that life as the 20th Century progressed.

Overall the material is organized by decades. Within a decade, items are grouped under topic heads that may vary somewhat from decade to decade, reflecting a shift of Club focus.

Name Changes Through the Years:

1910 –Alberta Women's Association

1917 –Women's University Club of Edmonton

1941 –University Women's Club

1968–University Women's Club of Edmonton

1989–Canadian Federation of University Women Edmonton

List of Abbreviations used in Survey:

AAFund (AAF)	Academic Awards Fund
AEA	Alberta Education Association
AEC	Alberta Education Council
ATA	Alberta Teachers' Association
CAC	Consumers' Association of Canada
CFUW	Canadian Federation of University Women
CFUWE	Canadian Federation of University Women Edmonton
CRTC	Canadian Radio and Telecommunications Commission
CIR	Co-ordinator of International Relations - CFUW

EPSB	Edmonton Public School Board
Prov. Gov't.	Provincial Government of Alberta
Fed. Gov't.	Federal Government of Canada
IFUW	International Federation of University Women
IODE	Imperial Order of Daughters of the Empire
LCW	Local Council of Women
RConSW	Royal Commission on the Status of Women
RH	Rutherford House
SUB	Students' Union Building, U of A Campus
U of A	University of Alberta
UFWA	United Farm Women's Association
UN	United Nations
UNESCO	United Nations Educational, Scientific and Cultural Organization
UWC	University Women's Club of Edmonton, later renamed CFUW Edmonton
YWCA	Young Women's Christian Association

1909 to 2000

1909 to 1920

Organizational Meeting Nov. 30, 1909 a small group of women laid the foundation for an Educational "college club." First meeting held January 8, 1910.

Aims of Organization

"The object of the organization shall be to promote educational interests, especially those of women in the province of Alberta" (Article 2 of the Constitution). Original objectives were to "assist in giving to the women students of the University a social life that would be both cultural and wholesome and offer a scholarship of

$50 to the woman in the freshman class whose record of scholarship was highest."

Membership & Fees

Initial membership approximately 40 with 83 by end of decade. Fees $2 plus a $1 initiation fee for new members. Membership included both graduate and non-graduate women, including the wives of U of A and government officials.

Executive

First Executive included: Honorary President, Mrs. Bulyea, wife of the Lieutenant-Governor (Official Visitor to the University), Honorary Vice Presidents, Mrs. Tory and Mrs. Rutherford President Mrs. E. K. Broadus First Vice President Mrs. W. D. Ferris Second Vice President Mrs. Muir Edwards Secretary Mrs. E. T. Bishop Treasurer Mrs. H. Riley Corresponding Secretary Mrs. R. B. Wells Three elected councilors, Mrs. Knight, Dr. Synge, Mrs. Beck Standing Committees established by 1911-1912: Social, Membership, Program and Education

Names Committee

Alberta Women's Association chosen from list of seven proposed names, 1910. Changed to **Women's University Club of Edmonton** in 1917.

Meetings/Program

First meetings held in the Strathcona Collegiate Institute (old Strathcona High) where University had temporary quarters. Moved to present U of A campus 1911. Met first in Athabasca Hall, then in newly built Assiniboia Hall in 1913, and later in Pembina Hall. Meetings held every second Saturday of the month at 3:00 p.m. Featured speakers were often U of A professors. Topics included women's franchise, the war effort, history, culture and educational issues.

Study/Interest Groups

Reading Groups with leaders first set up in 1913.

Scholarships

Three awards: $50 award, Gold Medal 1912, and $25 to a Grade XI matriculating female in the province, 1917.

Student Aid

> Student Aid Fund (later known as the Student Loan Fund) established from $1 initiation fees, 1914.

Education

> Sponsored public forum, 1915 at McKay Avenue School. Special meeting with eight school board candidates speaking, 1916. With YWCA initiated classes in English for immigrants, provided $25 grants to the 'Y' for educational programs, 1910–1914.

Public Affairs

> Special projects to raise money for war relief efforts included theatrical productions and lectures. Arranged series of public lectures on European War with U of A History Department.

Women's Affairs

> Furthered the election of women candidates for the EPSB and the U of A Senate. Worked on petition for women's enfranchisement with LCW. Standing Committee set up to help compile the "Laws of Alberta which relate to women" 1914. Organized Girls' Conferences in conjunction with YWCA, UFWA and Church Sunday Schools, 1918–1920.

Associations

> Local Council of Women, YWCA, representation at convention of United Farm Women of Alberta in Calgary, 1918.

CFUW

> Founding member of **Canadian Federation of University Women** (CFUW) along with Toronto, Winnipeg, Regina, Ottawa, Victoria and McGill Alumnae. Organizational meeting held in Winnipeg, 1919.

1920 to 1929

Membership & Fees

> Membership 137 by end of decade. Fees raised to $3, 1925.

Executive

> Positions of Federation Representative, 1920 and Library Standing Committee Convenor, 1922 added to Executive.

Meetings/Program

> Meetings held in Arts Building or Pembina Hall, Saturday 3:00 p.m. followed by Tea in Wauneita Rooms, Arts Building. Program: speakers with emphasis on international peace and understanding, League of Nations, history, literature and women's legal rights in Alberta.

Study/Interest Groups

> League of Nations, Circulating Book Club, Literature Groups (modern poetry, plays and novels).

Education

> Monitored public school curriculum. Major study of educational systems led to resolution to raise exam standards in province, 1924. Taught and read to shut-in children at University and Royal Alexandra hospitals, 1926 to early 1930s.

Scholarships

> Over $1000 raised through fundraising. Major projects included four plays, lectures and an exhibition of Canadian art.

Public Affairs

> Surveyed school libraries in province and prepared draft for new Library Act for Alberta, 1923, 1924. Set up library in Pembina Hall Women's Residence, 1927. Assisted in furnishing Reading Room for YWCA. Presented gift of $50 painting to Edmonton Museum of Arts (now Edmonton Art Gallery).

Women's Affairs

> Charter member Mrs. E. T. (Thyrza) Bishop elected to EPSB, 1921 and first woman appointed as its Chair, 1923.

Associations

> Local Council of Women, YWCA, Alberta Education Association, League of Nations Society, Edmonton Social Service Council.

CFUW

> Calgary Club formed 1924, Medicine Hat 1929. Two members, Dixie Pelluet and Eleanor Silver Dowding (Keeping) recipients of Federation Scholarships, 1922, 1928. $100 loan given by Club to Dixie Pelluet to help her with continuing studies in England, 1923.

IFUW

Organizational Meeting of **International Federation of University Women** (IFUW) held in London, England, 1920. Canada, Great Britain and the United States were founding organizations. Purpose was to promote peace and international understanding. Club participated in European Student Relief Fund 1922.

1930 to 1939

Membership & Fees

Decade began with membership of 137, 150 by 1940. Fees $3. New category of Recent Graduates created with reduced fee of $1.50.

Meetings/Program

General meetings in classrooms of the Arts Building or the Medical Amphitheatre, U of A, Saturday 3:00 p.m. Annual banquets usually held at the Macdonald Hotel, occasionally at the Corona Hotel. Dinner at the Corona in 1937 was 75 cents. Program emphasized peace and disarmament, family and child welfare.

Study/Interest Groups

Study Groups expanded to include: Vocations, Social and Economic Problems, Child Study, League of Nations (peace and disarmament), Juvenile Delinquency, Current Events, Drama (Play Reading), Art, Circulating Books, Modern Biography, Modern Fiction, Modern Trends, French Conversation and Recent Grads.

Education

Brief regarding upgrading of teachers' qualifications sent to Minister of Education, 1930. Studied preschool child development, changes to high school curriculum. Worked actively with U of A Committee in securing employment for women students, 1930 to 1934. Sponsored public meeting on vocations for young women, 1931. Joined city groups in planning for a school for unemployed, 1933.

Scholarships

Scholarship Fund established incorporating all awards being given by the Club to U of A students.

Public Affairs

> Supported a national radio system and advocated for children's radio programming, 1933. Sponsored talks on world peace including an open forum on League of Nations, 1935. Investigated library services in high schools and urged that only a qualified librarian be appointed to permanent position at the Public Library, 1933. Established Women's University Club U of A Hospital Library, 1935 to 1967.

Women's Affairs

> Strongly opposed suggestion by EPSB that schools of more than five rooms not have women as principals, 1937. Concentrated on status of women in administrative positions in education, 1937.

Associations

> Local Council of Women, YWCA and League of Nations Society (although many and various peace groups came on scene during the decade, Club decided to affiliate with the League of Nations only).

CFUW

> 6th Triennial Conference held in Edmonton, August, 1934. Mabel Patrick, Convenor of local arrangements, 50 cents to attend any session. Resolutions dealt with International Peace and Disarmament, Canadian Foreign Policy and Public Radio. Charlotte Melrose elected President of CFUW, 1934–37.

IFUW

> Relief Fund of University Women refugees established.

1940 to 1949

Membership & Fees

> Fees remained $3 through the 1940s. $1.50 for Recent Grads. Membership went from 150 to 245.

Name Change

> Name changed to **University Women's Club,** 1941.

Meetings/Program

> General meetings in classrooms of Arts Building or Medical Amphitheatre, Saturday, 3:00 p.m. Christmas Teas held at Macdonald Hotel in place of banquets at height of war; banquet reinstated in 1948.
> Program: Women and the war effort, reconstruction, social welfare (child welfare, juvenile delinquency), adult education and Indian affairs.

Study/Interest Groups

> Reconstruction, Postwar Problems of Women, Canadian Affairs (Penal Reform), International Relations, Social Welfare, Recent Grads, Choral (new), Drama (Play Reading), World Studies, Modern Biography, Modern Fiction and Circulating Books. Choral Group organized in 1942 under direction of Cornelia Higgin, performed at all banquets and Christmas Teas throughout the 1940s and early 1950s.

Education

> Studied new trends in education and revision of the public school curriculum. Stressed need of financial aid from all levels of government in order to improve teaching conditions and secure gifted students for teacher training after the war, 1944.

Scholarship Fund

> Gold Medal discontinued, scholarship changed to bursary. Amount increased to $150 in 1943.

Public Affairs

> War Effort: Local participation included entertaining servicemen at the Garrison Hostess Club and YMCA United Services Club and volunteering at Red Cross Depot. Refugee Fund helped graduate women war refugees in Europe with clothes and money including Club's special protegee, Dr. Marianne Weill. Submitted recommendations to Committee to Investigate Child Welfare Work in the Province of Alberta, 1943. Supported CFUW Resolution on Public Broadcasting, also Calgary Club's proposal for an investigation into Indian Affairs, 1944. Initiated CFUW Resolution urging the Parliament of Canada to make provision for the establishment of a National Library, 1944. Urged province to

appoint a Library Commission and to establish a system of regional libraries, 1945. Continued active involvement with University Women's Club Hospital Library.

Women's Affairs

Expressed strong disapproval of changes to School Act which would have women teachers automatically surrender their contracts when married, 1943. Compiled list of qualified women to act on government committees, boards, 1945. Mary Butterworth elected to the EPSB, 1946–1957, second woman elected to Chair Board, 1955–1956. Worked to gain tenure for married school teachers. Stressed need for availability of information on retraining for women in postwar period.

Associations

Local Council of Women, YWCA, League of Nations Society, Alberta Association of Adult Education, Alberta Education Council, Canadian Association of Consumers, forerunner of Consumers' Association of Canada.

CFUW

Triennial held in Quebec City, 1943. Per diem rate for delegates to cover train and hotel expenses was $8.00. 1945 AGM to be held in Wolfville, N.S. was cancelled. Triennial held in Winnipeg, 1946. National Federation Executive Meeting held in Edmonton, May, 1944. Charlotte Melrose convenor of local arrangements.

IFUW

Triennial Meeting, Toronto, August, 1947. First IFUW meeting held in Canada and first Canadian, Dr. Vibert Douglas, named International President.

1950 to 1959

Membership & Fees

Membership increased from 251 (1950/51) to 367 (1959/60). Fees $5.00 (1952), first increase in 12 years.

Meetings/Program

General meetings Wauneita Lounge, old SUB, U of A, Saturday 3:00 p.m. Program: forums and talks highlighted educational aspects of federal Massey Report (early 1950s) and provincial Cameron Commission on Education (1958), Canadian affairs, Status of Women and Indian affairs.

Club Archives

Archives Committee set up to look into preservation and storage of Club records, 1958.

Study/Interest Groups

Canadian Affairs (Juvenile Delinquency and Penal Reform), International Affairs, New Horizons (Studies of the North), Legal and Economic Status of Women, Women in the Modern World, Citizenship and Immigration; also Recent Grads, Drama, Circulating Books, French Conversation, Biography, Choral, Music Appreciation and Art.

Education

Brief to Provincial Government opposing lowering of entrance requirements to the Faculty of Education or shortening of training period of teachers, 1954. Brief to Cameron Royal Commission on Education emphasizing need for improved library facilities in schools and changes to high school curriculum, 1958. Brief to Department of Education requesting that financial aid to students be better publicized.

Scholarship Fund

Loan Fund discontinued, 1959. Grade XII Bursary raised to $300 from $200 in 1959.

Public Affairs

Edmonton Citizenship Council: participated annually in New Citizen's Tea and had two representatives on their Library Committee, 1958 to mid 1960s. Recommendations to Attorney-General's department regarding "Obscenity in Literature," 1954. Resolution to federal government urging the establishment of a Canada Council, 1956. Brief and recommendations to provincial government's Child Welfare Committee regarding "Care of Children in Edmonton and Jasper Place," 1959.

Status of Women

> Resolution to 1958 CFUW Triennial Conference concerning income tax exemption for professionally employed women's expenses for a housekeeper or nurse. Resolution to provincial government protesting wage discrimination. List of names submitted to the City Appointments Committee, two of whom received posts, 1959–1960.

Social

> President Norma Freifield and First Vice-President Barbara Blackley represented Club at luncheon in honour of Queen Elizabeth and Prince Philip at the Legislature Building, summer 1959.

Associations

> Edmonton Citizenship Council, UN Association, YWCA, Council of Community Services, Allied Arts Council, Alberta Education Council, CAC.

CFUW

> Triennial Conference held in Edmonton, 1955. Kathleen Morrison in charge of local arrangements.

IFUW

> Conference in London, England, 1955 coincided with 50th Anniversary of British Federation. Lucile Kane attended as official CFUW representative. Hegg-Hoffett Refugee Relief Fund (for university women refugees in Europe) supported by annual Club donations.

1960 to 1969

Membership & Fees

> Highest membership in Club's history, 374 in 1961 including non-voting associate members, declined to 280 in 1967. Fees $8.

Name Change

> **University Women's Club of Edmonton,** 1968. Major changes to Executive, fiscal year, criteria for membership.

Meetings/Program

Wauneita Lounge, old SUB 1960–1967, off campus 1968-1970. 50th Anniversary Celebration held at Macdonald Hotel, January 1960. Programs: Canadian Centennial, Royal Commission on Status of Women, continuing education.

Study/Interest Groups

32 groups at beginning of 1961 season: Canadian Affairs, Indian Affairs, Family Welfare, Status of Women, Citizenship and Immigration, Participaction (Public Affairs), Archives, Fund Raising; also Drama (Play Reading), Circulating Books, Biography, Choral, French Conversation, Music Appreciation, New Members' Group (replaced Recent Grads, 1963). Several groups duplicated such as Play Reading, Circulating Books and Biography.

Education

Brief to EPSB regarding Guidance Counselling. Based on extensive fact-finding study of Edmonton and area schools, 1965. Active involvement with AEC through decade. Prepared a program called "Research in Mathematics" for TV series, Education Week, 1965.

Scholarship Fund

Grade XII Bursary given over to U of A to administer entirely, 1968. Reassessment of focus of Club's support for education led to the establishment of an Academic Awards Fund to be administered by the Club.

Public Affairs

Motion at Club meeting to support efforts of the community to establish an Edmonton Friendship Centre for Indians, Eskimo and Metis passed, 1962. Libraries: Brief to EPSB regarding the need for supervisor of school libraries with adequate staff to carry out city-wide programs, 1961. Two Briefs to Minister of Education regarding improved provincial regional library facilities, 1963 and appointment of a provincial supervisor for school libraries, 1964. Archives: Brief to Government of Alberta calling for the establishment of an Alberta Provincial Archives as a Centennial project, 1962. Club Archives deposited at Provincial Archives, 1969.

Hospital Library: After 35-year involvement, Club transferred large inventory of books and magazines to the University Hospital Women's Auxiliary, 1967. Proctor bequest of $1000 donated to Rare Books Collection at U of A.

Club provided leadership in restoration and preservation of first Premier's House, 1967-1970.

Day Care: Two Briefs regarding Day Care Services were sent to Minister of Welfare, Provincial Government and Board of Governors, U of A, 1966.

$50 donations given annually in the 1960s to UN Summer School Scholarship at Banff and to UNESCO Science Seminar Scholarship.

Status of Women

Brief to Royal Commission on Status of Women entitled "Recommendations to Aid Women Re-entering University and Ultimately the Labor Force," 1968. Briefs to Provincial Government and U of A Senate regarding financial aid for mature students, 1968–1969.

Associations

Edmonton Citizenship Council, UN Association, YWCA, Council of Community Services, Allied Arts Council, Alberta Education Council, CAC.

CFUW

Provincial Meetings of Alberta University Women's Clubs: Lethbridge, 1963 focused on improving library facilities in province, Calgary, 1965 emphasized continuing education for women. CFUW Council Meeting, 1969–50th Anniversary of CFUW held in Edmonton. Barbara Blackley in charge of local arrangements.

IFUW

Dr. Fluger, European university woman refugee, adopted as Club protegee.

1970 to 1979

Membership & Fees

Membership ranged from 199 in 1970 to 147 in 1979. Fees raised from $10 in 1971 to $12 in 1974 to $15 in 1976.

Executive

New position of Public Relations (Publicity), 1979.

Meetings/Program

General meetings in Wauneita Lounge, old SUB, U of A; other venues from 1976 to 1979. First 60 years of Club celebrated in song and dance at AGM, 1970, dinner tickets were $4.75. Club History "As It Happened–The First 60 Years" published, 1973, Editor, Marjorie Buckley. Program emphasis on pollution and the environment, status of women, bilingualism and biculturalism, and continuing education.

Study/Interest Groups

Education, Anti-Pollution, Status of Women, Cable TV-Media, Participaction (Public Affairs), Ways & Means (Fund raising), Drama, Circulating Books, Les Abeilles Francaises (French Conversation), Music Appreciation, Modern Biography, Great Books, Just-For-Fun (new), Hospitality Cooking (new).

Education

Compiled extensive survey of the school system titled "A Guide to the Operation of the Edmonton Public School System," 1970. Brief to Task Force on Children with Learning Disabilities, 1979.

Academic Awards Fund

Offered first Mature Women's Bursary, 1971. Perpetuating Academic Awards Fund established to support bursary program, 1972. Charitable status received.

Public Affairs

Promoted expansion of paper bin collections in city schools and initiated collection of telephone books. Set up a popular slide show presentation for schools. First Club representative to the Public Advisory Committee of the Environment Conservation Authority, 1971. Cable TV-Media Study Group formed. Club representative attended monthly meetings on "Cable TV As It Affects the Community" and CRTC hearings in Banff.

Status of Women

Brief to U of A Senate urging establishment of a Task Force to study the status of all female staff members at the University, 1973. Report titled "Single Parent Women on Social Allowance at U of A" 1973 gave rise to Brief to government regarding the Student Finance Act and assistance to needy students, 1973. Lobbied for a program of affirmative action regarding employment and promotion of female professional staff by Boards of Education, 1975. Lobbied provincial government on behalf of matrimonial property legislation, 1976. Brief to the CRTC Task Force on Sex-Role Stereotyping, 1979–1980. To honour International Year of Women, **They Jumped So High** was published in 1975. **Twin Pack,** a play to celebrate the 50th Anniversary of Persons Case was written by Marjorie Buckley.

Associations

Supported Alberta Women's Shelters, YWCA programs.

CFUW

Club voted to support CFUW's drive towards self sustaining Fellowship fund, The Charitable Trust, 1977.

IFUW

Club member Dr. Jean Lauber named an official CFUW delegate to IFUW meeting in Philadelphia, 1971.

1980 to 1989

Membership/Fees

Membership: 179 in 1980, 220 in 1989
Fees: $20 (1980), $27 (1983), $35 (1986)

Name Change

Canadian Federation of University Women Edmonton, 1989.

Bylaws

> CFUW change to Roberts' Rules of Order from Bourinot necessitated rewriting of Club Bylaws, 1982. Executive: Social Secretary added 1983, First Vice President and Interest Group Convenor become separate positions 1986.

Meetings/Program

> General meetings in Saskatchewan Room, U of A Faculty Club, 8:00 p.m. Christmas holiday season celebrated at Rutherford House in the tradition of the Rutherford family with member Hazel McGuaig, daughter of the first Premier in attendance, 1986. Program: emphasis on new technologies, computer education, Canadian Charter of Rights and Freedoms, North American Free Trade Agreement (NAFTA), environmental awareness.

Interest/Study Groups

> Drama, Circulating Books (3), Just-For-Fun, Hospitality Cooking (3), Couples Gourmet, Investment (2), Random Readers, Antiques, Fun With Computers, Crafts, Environmental Concerns, Les Abeilles Francaises, Music Appreciation, Public Speaking & Parliamentary Law, Pension Reform, Boreal Circle (studies of the North), Creative Writing and Cross-Country Skiing.

Education

> Ad Hoc Committees formed to present briefs on Gifted and Talented Students, 1982, and Mature Students, 1982. Played active role in elections of two school boards elections (public and separate). Co-sponsored public forum to discuss Provincial Education Bill 59, 1988.

Academic Awards Fund

> To honour the Club's 75th Anniversary, three $1000 Jubilee Scholarships awarded to graduate women, 1985. Permanent scholarship for women graduate students established, 1987. Academic Awards Fund AGM held separately from Club's for first time January, 1988.

Public Affairs

> Ad Hoc Committees formed to present Briefs on Pension Reform 1983, Pornography and Prostitution 1984.
>
> Participatory and financial support to community causes included

WIN House, WINGS (Women in Need Growing Stronger), A Safe Place, Youth Emergency Shelter, Edmonton Food Bank, Christmas Bureau and Alex Taylor School. Two awards given to Project Morningstar for native students at St. Paul, 1981.
Received Edmonton Historical Board Annual Recognition Award for leadership in preservation of Rutherford House, 1987.
Undertook CFUW Resolution on Drinking Water Quality, 1987.
Brief to Provincial Alberta Pacific (AlPac) Environment Impact Assessment Review Board, 1989.

Status of Women

Dr. Jean Lauber named CFUW Alberta liaison to Canadian Charter of Rights Coalition (CORC), 1983. Co-sponsor of "Women and the Charter" Conference at U of A October, 1984. Maureen Towns named Chair of Provincial Committee for an Alberta Council on Women's Affairs, 1983.

Associations

Representation on Public Advisory Committee of the Environment Council of Alberta, Provincial Committee to Establish an Alberta Council on Women's Affairs, Alberta Women's Shelters.

CFUW

CFUW Western Conference "Energy for the '80s" held at U of A, May, 1981 emphasized alternative forms of energy. Georgie Brooks, Convenor. UWC Clubs of Alberta formally became The Alberta Provincial Council, 1985, official incorporation, 1987.
Tammy Irwin elected CFUW President for two year term, 1988-1990. CFUW changed to a biennial system (from triennial), 1988.
CFUW AGM hosted by Edmonton, June 1989, theme "Stewardship of our Earth–An Environmental Imperative." Joyce Law and Win Mellon in charge of local arrangements.

IFUW

20th Triennial Conference held in Vancouver, August 1980 (second time in Canada). 950 women from 45 countries attended.

1990s

Membership & Fees

Membership averaged 150 throughout decade.
Fees: $45 (1990), $50 (1992), $55 (1996).

Bylaws

Revisions included new fiscal year end May 30, change of AGM to April from May.

Meetings/ Program

U of A Faculty Club 3rd Monday of month at 7:30 p.m. 90th Anniversary celebration of Club held at Rutherford House, November 22, 1999.
Programs: adult literacy, healthcare funding, biotechnology, Canadian unity.

Interest/Study Groups

Environmental Concerns, IFUW, Current Issues, Health Care, Club History, Circulating Books (3-4), Random Readers, Investment Portfolio, Drama, Video Flicks, Hospitality Cooking, Couples Gourmet, Slim Gourmet (2), Ladies out to Lunch, Lively Arts and Bridge.

Education

Brief to Provincial Minister of Education regarding proposed budget cuts to education, 1993. Presentation to Library Review Committee, Department of Community Development regarding funding for public libraries, 1994.

Academic Awards Fund

Graduate Women Scholarship winners were featured speakers for first time at January AGM, 1991. Two separate categories for scholarships established, Master's and PhD, 1996.

Public Affairs

Letter to Premier urging Alberta Government to ratify UN Convention on the Rights of the Child, 1993. Brief to Axworthy Special Committee on Human Resources on Improving Social Security in Canada, 1994. Letter to Minister of Community

Development protesting relocation of Provincial Archives of Alberta to site outside Edmonton, 1998.

Participatory and financial support to community causes included Kids Help Line, books for inner city school, Christmas Bureau. Members and families participated in judging exhibits of Edmonton and area school children at regional Heritage School Fairs, May, 1999. Members assisted at National Heritage Fair in August, 1999. Environment: initiated CFUW Resolution on Canadian Water Transfer, 1993. Participated in discussions and workshops on Federal Green Plan 1990, Alberta Environmental Protection and Enhancement Act 1992, Alberta Water Resources Act 1990–1996 and Special Places 2000 initiative 1992–1999.

Status of Women

Briefs to the President's Commission for Equality and Respect on Campus, U of A and to Baird Royal Commission on New Reproductive Technology, 1990. Letters to Provincial Minister Responsible for Women's Issues protesting cancellation of the Persons Case Awards, and questioning termination of funding for the Alberta Advisory Council on Women's Issues, 1994. Workshops on Writing Women's History/Club History presented at Provincial, Regional and National CFUW Conferences, 1998–1999.

Associations

Alberta Heritage Alliance

CFUW

Honorary member, Dr. Roberta Bondar, carried CFUW logo into space on NASA flight, June 22, 1992. 75th Anniversary of CFUW and IFUW celebrated at AGM in Vancouver, August, 1993.

IFUW

Tammy Irwin attended Triennial in Palo Alto, California 1992 as CFUW Past President and Convenor of International Relations (CIR). Appointed Chair of IFUW Resolutions Committee for triennials in Yokohama, Japan 1995 and Graz, Austria 1999.

CFUW Edmonton Presidents

Mrs. E. K. (Eleanor) Broadus 1910–1912

Mrs. N. D.(Louisa) Beck 1912–1913

Mrs. E. K. Broadus 1913–1914

Geneva Misener 1914–1915

Mrs. R. A. King 1915–1916

Mrs. Cecil (Annie) Race 1916–1917

Kathleen Teskey (May–Sept) 1917

Edith Chauvin 1917–1918

Mrs. Evelyn Muir Edwards 1918

Mrs. Cecil (Annie) Race 1919

Mrs. S. (Evelyn) Dickson 1919–1921

Vacant 1921–1922

Jessie F. Montgomery 1922–1924

Mrs. J. Gillespie 1924–1926

Mrs. F. C. (Cora) Casselman 1926–1927

Mabel Patrick 1927–1929

Mrs. W. J. (Charlotte) Melrose 1929–1931

Mrs. F. C. (Cora) Casselman 1931–1933

Mrs. I. F. (Kathleen) Morrison 1933–1935

Maimie Simpson 1935–1937

Mrs. F. (Mary) Butterworth 1937–1939

Mrs. E. Stansfield 1939–1940

Mrs. H. C. (Elsie) Newland 1940–1942

Mrs. E. W .S. (Lucile) Kane 1942–1944

Mrs. S. H. (Nell) Gandier 1944–1946

Mrs. W .P. (Inez) Calhoun 1946–1948

Mrs. R. L. (Myrtle) Anderson 1948–1950

Mrs. M. H. (Winnifred) Long 1950–1952

Mrs. W. S. (Lorna) Scarth 1952–1954

Mrs. D. J. (Agnes) Teviotdale 1954–1956

Mrs. Ruth Hyndman 1956–1958

Miss Norma Freifield 1958–1960

Mrs. F. D. (Barbara) Blackley 1960–1962

Mrs. S. H. (Margaret) Greenhill 1962–1964

Rita Calhoun 1964–1966

Enid Crockett 1966–1968

Libby Frost 1968–1970

Marjorie Buckley 1970–1972

Thomasine (Tammy) Irwin 1972–1974

Georgie Brooks 1974–1976

Melvina Gowda 1976–1978

Joyce Law 1978–1980

Karen Stevens 1980–1982

Jean Lund 1982–1984

Win Mellon 1984–1986

Pat Mackenzie 1986–1987

Marion Gee 1987–1989

Cynthia Boodram 1989–1991

Betty Gravett 1991–1992

Ann Stewart 1992–1993

Robin Robinson 1993–1994

Alberta Boytzun 1994–1995

Hiske Gerding 1995–1997

Joan Cowling 1997–1999

Robynne Healey 1999–2000

Margaret McInall 2000–2002

NOTE: Until 1964 Presidents were named using their husbands' initials. We have added first names when known.

Selected Bibliography

Books

Armour, Margaret–Ann. "WISEST–An Initiative at the University of Alberta to Encourage Women into the Sciences and Engineering." Standing on New Ground–Women in Alberta, edited by C. Cavanaugh and R. Warne. Alberta Nature and Culture Series. Edmonton: University of Alberta Press, 1993.

Babcock, Douglas R. Alexander Cameron Rutherford: A Gentleman of Strathcona. Calgary: The Friends of Rutherford House and The University of Calgary Press, 1989.

Burt, Sandra, Lorraine Code, and Lindsay Dorney, eds. Changing Patterns–Women in Canada. "The Canadian Women's Movement: The Second Wave," Chapter 4. Toronto: McClelland and Stewart, 1988.

Chalmers, John W. Teachers of the Foothills–The Story of the Alberta Teachers' Association. Toronto: University of Toronto Press, 1968.

Cole, C., and J. Larmour. Many and Remarkable–The Story of the Alberta Women's Institutes. Edmonton: Alberta Women's Institutes, 1997.

Coulter, Rebecca Priegert. "Patrolling the Passions of Youth." Edmonton: The Life of a City, edited by B. Hesketh and F. Swyripa. Edmonton, NeWest Publishers Ltd., 1995.

Johns, Walter H. A History of the University of Alberta. Edmonton: University of Alberta Press, 1981.

Kinnear, Mary. Margaret McWilliams: An Interwar Feminist. Montreal: McGill–Queen's University Press, 1991.

Kostek, M. A. A Century and Ten: The History of Edmonton Public Schools. Edmonton: Edmonton Public Schools, 1992.

Kostek, M. A. Looking Back: History of the Edmonton Public School Board. Edmonton: M.E. Lazerte Composite High School Press, 1982.

Macdonald, John. The History of the University of Alberta, 1908–1958. Toronto: W. J. Gage, 1958.

Orenstein, Peggy, in association with the American Association of University Women. School Girls: Young Women, Self-esteem and the Confidence Gap. New York: Doubleday, 1995.

Palmer, Howard, and Tamara Palmer. Alberta, A New History. Edmonton: Hurtig Publishers Ltd., 1990.

Pierson, Ruth R., and Marjorie G. Cohen, eds. Canadian Women's Issues, Volume II: Bold Visions. Toronto: James Lorimer & Co., 1995.

Rooke, P .T., and R. L. Schnell. No Bleeding Heart: Charlotte Whitton – a Feminist on the Right. Vancouver: University of British Columbia Press, 1987.

The Y.W.C.A. History Project Group. Retrospect: The Edmonton Y.W.CA. 1957–1991. Edmonton: The Y.W.C.A. History Project Group, 1993.

CFUW Edmonton, CFUW, and IFUW Publications

Batho, Edith C. A Lamp of Friendship, 1918–1968, A Short History of the International Federation of University Women. Eastbourne, England: IFUW, 1968.

Berton, Janet, and Claire Coates, eds. Calendar/Calendrier 1981–1982, revised edition, Sixty Years of CFUW. Montreal: CFUW, 1981.

Buckley, Marjorie W., ed. As It Happened: The University Women's Club of Edmonton: The First 60 Years. Edmonton: CFUW Edmonton, 1973.

Farnham, K., ed. They Jumped So High. Published for International Women's Year. Edmonton: University Women's Club of Edmonton, 1975.

Innis, Mary Quayle, ed. The Clear Spirit–Twenty Canadian Women and Their Times. Toronto: University of Toronto Press, 1966.

Seventy-Five Years of CFUW/Soixante–quinze ans de FCFDU, 1919–1994. Ottawa: CFUW, 1994.

Government Publications

Alberta. Annual Reports to Minister of Education from Deputy Minister of Education (1921–1931). Incorporated in Annual Reports of Minister of Education to the Lieutenant–Governor of Province of Alberta (1921–1931).

Better Pensions for Canadians–Green Paper. Includes "Focus on Women" supplement. Ottawa: Government of Canada Department of Health and Welfare, Finance, 1982.

Periodicals and Pamphlets

"History of Accomplishments." Consumers' Association of Canada Newsletter, (December, 1975).

University of Alberta Hospital Newsletter, "The Twelfth Street Beat," Vol. IV, No. 2 (February, 1965). [Includes write–up on University Women's Club's Hospital Library.]

"Task Force on Women at University." St. John's Edmonton Report, Vol. I, No. 8 (January 11, 1974).

Pearson, Mary. The Second Time Around: A Study of Women Returning to the Work Force. Canadian Advisory Council on the Status of Women, 1979.

Summary of Proceedings and Recommendations–Pension Reform for Women. Edmonton: Women's Program, Faculty of Extension, University of Alberta, June 12, 1982.

"Women at University–The Early Years." Alberta History, Vol. 44, No. 1 (Winter, 1996) pp. 8–13.

Unpublished Theses

MacKinnon, Christy. "The Social Construction of Rutherford House." Honours History thesis 344895, University of Alberta, 1998.

Puffer, Frances A. "Friendship and Commitment in a Voluntary Association (The University Women's Club of Edmonton)." M.A. thesis, University of Alberta, 1966.

Newspapers

Edmonton Bulletin
Edmonton Journal
Strathcona Chronicle

Biographical Material on Members

From the Past to the Future–A Guide to the Holdings of the University of Alberta Archives. Edmonton: University of Alberta, 1992.

"Interview with Mrs. D. J. (Agnes Wilson) Teviotdale." Bowen Papers. University of Alberta Archives, Accession No. 79–112, Item 15, 1969.

Dawber, Michael. "MP Cora Casselman: One of the Self–Made Kind." The Whig–Standard Companion, Kingston, Ontario, October 16,

1993. Cora Taylor Casselman Papers. Provincial Archives of Alberta, Accession No. 70.154.

Misener, Dr. Geneva. University of Alberta Archives, Accession Nos. 77–179-1, 85–91–355 (picture 2315-2).

Montgomery, Jessie. University of Alberta Archives 81–117–1. Includes article on her, "First Librarian to the Hinterland," New Trail, 1945.

Photographs

University of Alberta Archives Gateway, 1919: Mrs. Eleanor Broadus, Mrs. Evelyn Muir Edwards, Mrs. H. M. Tory, Mrs. Kathleen Morrison, Mamie Simpson

Evergreen & Gold, 1922/23: Mrs. C. E. Race, Mrs. Lucile Kane, Grace Studholme, 1926: Mrs. Inez Calhoun

U of A Biography File: Mabel Patrick

Provincial Archives of Alberta
Mrs. Thryza Bishop, PAA BP-1-3095

CFUW Edmonton Records

Canadian Federation of University Women Edmonton records are kept at the Provincial Archives of Alberta (PAA). The material deals directly with the activities and concerns of the Edmonton Club, although some CFUW and IFUW material is included. The Accession file at the Provincial Archives totals 26 pages; only records that were most often consulted or are rather difficult to find, are listed here. Records since 1988 are held by the Executive Committee of CFUW Edmonton awaiting deposit in the Provincial Archives.

Academic Awards

76.41/17 (1973–74); 80.340/1–4 (1976–79); 87.204/3 (1973–84)

Day Care

69.22/12–including Resolution on Day Care to Government, pp.496–7 (1943)

69.22/85–including Report regarding Day Care and Kindergartens (1961)

69.22/52–Brief to Child Welfare Committee (June, 1959)

78.476–Day Care Briefs to University of Alberta, Alberta Government, and City of Edmonton (1966)

Education

69.22/112–(1937–40, 1951, 1963, 1967)

69.22/50–Adult Education, Continuing Education for Women

69.22/51–Annual Reports, including Vocations Committee (1931,1932)

69.22/52–Annual Reports including comparative surveys of 1922, 1923

69.22/54–includes Summary Report of EPSB (1961)

69.22/43–44; 69.22/51–58

77.323/13; 82.324/6; 82.394

Environmental Concerns

76.41/19–Brief on Pollution taken to CFUW and IFUW (1970, 1971)

77.323/13–Ecology Caravan (1973–74); Environmental Concerns Study Group (1970s)

Libraries

69.22/64–Briefs of 1959, 1961–63

69.22/65,66–Reports

69.22/67–1928, 1944, 1956–65, including University Hospital Library

69.22/67/43e–"What's Wrong with Comic Books;" Government of Alberta Advisory Board on Objectionable Literature (1954)

69.22/68, 69–Proctor Centennial Library correspondence (1964–66)

Meetings

69.22/1–24–Minutes (1909–1967)

76.41/1–5–Minutes (1967–1974)

79.325–Minutes (1975–1979)

92/275–Minutes (1983–1988)

69.22.60–Records of Golden Jubilee Celebration (January 1960), including Kathleen Teskey's talk on IFUW meeting of 1922 and Mabel Patrick's account of her first involvement with the Club

Miscellaneous

69.22/29–letter of Mrs. Broadus concerning pictures for Women's Lounge (1911)

77.323/2,3–Drama Group

69.22/63–International Affairs–UN Association, League of Nations, Dr. Julia Fluger, Club refugee protegé (1943–1965)

69.22/75–79 (1919–1965) Scrapbooks with newspaper clippings, photos, and publicity

Penal Reform

69.22/71, 69.22/119

69.22/106, 107–CFUW Chronicle regarding Penal Reform Committee (1949–1958)

Rutherford House

78.176/3–9

Status of Women

69.22/86–Women's rights 1943–65, including Continuing Education for Women Report (1964/65)

69.22/50–Brief to Royal Commission on Status of Women (1968)

69.128–Briefs to federal government 1953, 1958, 1960, and 1963

69.22/106, 107–Succession Duties, Taxation (1949–1958)

85.203/6–New Approach to Taxation of Women (1968–1969)

85.203/7–Implementation of Royal Commission on Status of Women, Foster the Roster, International Women's Year (1975)

85.203/8–Family Law Reform (1979–1982)